Prophet, Pastor, and Patriarch

Prophet, Pastor, and Patriarch
The Rhetorical Leadership
of Alexander Campbell

PETER A. VERKRUYSE

The University of Alabama Press
Tuscaloosa

2003

Copyright © 2005
The University of Alabama Press
Tuscaloosa, Alabama 35487–0380
All rights reserved
Manufactured in the United States of America

Typeface: ACaslon

∞
The paper on which this book is printed meets the minimum requirements of
American National Standard for Information Sciences—Permanence of Paper for
Printed Library Materials, ANSI Z39.48-1984.

Library of Congress Cataloging-in-Publication Data

Verkruyse, Peter, 1959–
    Prophet, pastor, and patriarch : the rhetorical leadership of Alexander Campbell /
Peter A. Verkruyse.
        p. cm.
    Includes bibliographical references and index.
    ISBN-13: 978-0-8173-1477-4 (cloth : alk. paper)
    ISBN-10: 0-8173-1477-6
    1. Campbell, Alexander, 1788-1866—Language. 2. Rhetoric—Religious aspects—
Christianity—History—19th century. I. Title.
    BX7343.C2V47 2005
    286.6′ 092—dc22
                                                                    2005008010

To my children
Joye Louise
Peter James
Amy Beth
Cassandra Lee

Contents

Acknowledgments

Although this project has evolved significantly over the past several years, my greatest debt is still to Tom Conley of the University of Illinois at Urbana-Champaign who first encouraged me to consider Alexander Campbell's rhetoric as a dissertation topic and without whose guidance this work could never have been completed. I am also grateful to Joe Wenzel and James Jasinski for their helpful contributions to this process as well as to Celeste Condit for her encouragement when I wrote my very first critical essay on Campbell's "Sermon on the Law." I am also indebted to my former seminary professors Wayne Shaw, James Strauss, Enos Dowling, Lynn Hieronymus and Robert Rea in the areas of homiletics, church history, theology, and hermeneutics.

I also owe thanks to several colleagues for their support. Chief among these is Neil LeRoux whose scholarly assistance and personal encouragement have often kept this project alive. Several others, through their response to conference presentations or by some other means, have been sources of help and support: Michael Casey, Ken Chase, Tom Duncanson, Carol Jablonksi, Tom Lawson, Beth Innocenti Manolescu, Gary Selby, and Lee Snyder. A special thanks is due my colleague at Illinois College, Adrienne Hacker Daniels, for her encouragement.

I am also grateful to the International Society for the History of Rhetoric, the Religious Communication Association, and the National Communication Association for opportunities to present early stages of this work; to the Department of Speech Communication at UIUC, the Appalachian College Association and Illinois College's Malcolm F. Stewart Award fund for financial assistance; and to Sara Harwell of the Disciples of Christ Historical Society and the library staffs of Illinois College and Lincoln Christian College for research assistance. Most recently, I am indebted to the review board of the University of Alabama Press for considering this manuscript worthy of publication and suggesting several helpful revisions.

More than anyone, I thank my family—Debby, Joye, P.J., Amy, and Cassie—who made many sacrifices so that I could complete this project.

Introduction

Alexander Campbell—farmer, teacher, preacher, statesman, postmaster, author, editor, debater . . . So great was his influence and fame that those who disagreed with and opposed him gave the name "Campbellism" to the system of doctrine that he and others taught, and they dubbed his associates "Campbellites."[1]

A thorough consideration of the rhetoric of Alexander Campbell remains one of the great unwritten chapters in the annals of American Christianity. A charismatic leader and gifted communicator, Campbell (1788–1866) exerted unparalleled influence within what is today commonly designated the "Stone-Campbell Movement"—one of the most significant mass movements within that wave of religious populism which did much to Christianize American society during the first half of the nineteenth century.

Possessed of similar sentiments about grassroots church reform, both Alexander Campbell (who immigrated to America in 1809 following after a term of study at Glasgow University) and Barton Stone (who had participated in Kentucky's famous Cane Ridge Revival of 1801) eventually found themselves leading loosely organized fellowships of independent Christian churches. An informal union between many of these churches was announced in 1832 and by the end of the century cumulative membership grew to exceed one million. Collectively one of the largest religious sects in nineteenth-century America, its impressive increase was also unique in that it was strictly an American movement, with little if any of its growth a result of immigration.[2] Today, the Stone-Campbell Movement represents the common heritage of three major contemporary denominations: the Christian Church (Disciples of Christ), the Churches of Christ (non-instrumental), and the independent Christian Churches and Churches of Christ.

The leadership provided by Alexander Campbell during this movement's first generation was unique in at least two important ways. First, Campbell remained the dominant voice within the movement for more than four decades—from its inception, through its separation and crystallization as a body of independent churches, into its full maturity as a self-sufficient sect with its own heritage. His was not the only important voice, however, especially within the early years of the movement.

Barton W. Stone was fifteen years older than Campbell, he began his labors for church reform several years before the Campbells arrived in America, and the scope of his influence in the West was remarkable.[3] In November of 1826, Stone inaugurated an influential monthly journal, *The Christian Messenger,* which contributed significantly to the cohesion of the growing movement. With brief interruptions, it was published until Stone's death in 1844.[4] However, Stone himself would eventually acknowledge Campbell as "the greatest promoter of this reformation of any living man"[5] and Lester McAllister and William Tucker have noted that, "Alexander Campbell was the acknowledged leader of the movement. After Barton W. Stone moved to Jacksonville, Illinois, in 1834 there was no doubt of that."[6]

Walter Scott (1796–1861), educated at the University of Edinburgh prior to immigrating to America in 1818, was a younger associate of Campbell whom he met in 1821.[7] His preaching as an evangelist for the Mahoning Association (Ohio) netted over 3,000 converts on the Western Reserve within a three year period (1828–30). His popularity grew enormously after his 1828 report to the association and it has been estimated that he baptized as many as one thousand persons per year for the next thirty years. He published both an influential monthly journal (*The Evangelist,* 1832–44) and the movement's first weekly journal (*The Protestant Unionist,* 1844–47). And for one year, he served as the inaugural president of the movement's first college (Bacon College, 1836).[8] Campbell, however, was instrumental in creating important opportunities for Scott. Campbell's influence within the Mahoning Association and his "sponsorship" of Scott contributed greatly to his appointment as its evangelist, Scott first published in and later used Campbell's *Millennial Harbinger* to launch *The Evangelist,* and Scott undoubtedly benefited from the Campbells' endorsement of the "ancient gospel" he preached.[9]

Campbell's leadership was also unique in another important way. Because of Campbell's (and concomitantly the movement's) commitment to the autonomy of the local congregation, his leadership was not exercised via the authority of office or from any position within a denominational hierarchy. No such form of government existed for these churches and thus no such offices were available for Campbell. His ordination to the ministry of the Brush Run Church in 1812 invested him with no official authority beyond the opportunity to preach to this one small congregation.[10]

By the 1840s, the continued growth of the movement would prompt *voluntary* cooperative efforts beyond the level of the local congregation. The first was the American Christian Bible Society organized by four churches in Cincinnati in 1845. Though Campbell was chosen as one of nine vice presidents, he took a dim view of the organization and declined to attend its inaugural meeting. The American Christian Missionary Society was formed in 1849 and Campbell, though not present, was elected president. By the 1840s, however, this was much more a case of the societies (the creation of which generated a storm of controversy) drawing credibility from their association with Campbell than Campbell enhancing his credibility from their offices. Throughout these years, then, Campbell first gained and then maintained his remarkable influence and reputation (both national and international in scope) exclusively through discursive means—sermons, debates, lectures, books, and journals. It thus seems most appropriate to refer to his influence as a "rhetorical leadership."

Interest in the relationship between rhetoric and leadership is as old as the rhetorical tradition itself. Isocrates' ideal citizen was the "statesman-orator" who was able to wed wisdom and eloquence in the interests of civic service. Even many of the speeches in Homer arguably reflect a keen interest in this matter. Thus, recent interest in the study of leadership from a rhetorical perspective[11] is but a variation of this timeless inquiry.[12] Differences in perspective not withstanding,[13] what distinguishes such inquiries is a common interest in the dynamic interaction between the practice of rhetoric and the exercise of leadership.[14] The discourse of Alexander Campbell represents a unique opportunity to analyze this constitutive dialectic between rhetorical activity and the ability of a leader to gain and maintain influence within a community of faith.[15]

Surprisingly, although a reasonable body of literature pertaining to Alexander Campbell has been published over the years, little of it has examined his rhetoric.[16] In particular, a sustained analysis, fully dedicated to an extensive and thorough examination of Campbell's rhetoric, applying contemporary methods of rhetorical criticism in the close reading of specific rhetorical acts, has yet to be written. This volume attempts to fill that void.

The fact that Campbell exercised his enduring influence through discursive channels rather than via the authority inherent within a denominational office suggests an appropriate orientation for a *diachronic* perspective on his rhetorical leadership (i.e., one concerned with how rhetorical patterns emerge and evolve over time). Aristotle long ago affirmed the central role of source credibility in rhetoric when he included *ethos* among the three *pisteis* (artistic proofs) of rhetoric. His specific understanding of *ethos* as credibility constructed *through the speech* is particularly apt for describing Campbell's credibility and influence. In Book I, chapter 2 of his *Rhetoric,* Aristotle points out that persuasion is "through character [*ethos*] whenever the *speech* is spoken in such a way as to make the speaker worthy of credence" and that "this should result from the *speech,* not from previous opinion" (1356a, emphasis added). In the commentary that accompanies his recent translation of Aristotle's *Rhetoric,* George Kennedy thus distinguishes between *ethos* and *authority:* "Aristotle thus does *not* include in rhetorical ethos the *authority* that a speaker may possess due to his position in a government or society, previous actions, reputation for wisdom, or *anything* except what is actually contained in the speech and the character *it* reveals" (emphasis added).[17]

The thesis of this book builds upon this distinction, arguing that one significant reason why Campbell was able to successfully lead his movement from birth to maturity was because his rhetoric generated for him a leadership *ethos* that was progressively adapted to the shifting needs of the movement—first as prophet, then as pastor, and finally as patriarch. In support of this thesis, I offer close readings of four key rhetorical episodes that transpired at critical junctions within the movement's first generation, describing the discursive strategies featured therein and the *ethos* that emerges from within their rhetorical action. These rhetorical acts range from 1816–60 and the analyses ground the book's diachronic perspective in a series of *synchronic* criticisms (i.e., those which privilege discrete rhetorical acts as relatively finished responses to particular, immediate situations).

The pervasive methodological commitment within this volume is to the "textual criticism" or "close readings" criticism so well described by Stephen Lucas, Michael Leff, and others. What each of the analyses attempts is to explain how the rhetorical elements of the text function individually and how they interact to "shape the text as a strategic, artistic response to the exigencies of a particular situation." To accomplish this, such criticism will "slow down" the "action within the text so as to keep its evolving internal context in sharp focus and to allow more precise explication of its rhetorical artistry." Social contexts, linguistic contexts, and internal textual context coalesce in assessments chiefly characterized by a "radical attention to the internal dynamics of the text itself."[18]

As Lucas points out, however, "beyond the fact it will foreground the text, the final shape of this study is unpredictable" and "this kind of study will seldom be achieved by adhering to any single method of criticism."[19] And so, with the goal of understanding each text on its own terms, the analyses in this book will also reflect the commitment to methodological pluralism inherent in Kenneth Burke's dictum that the critic should "use all there is to use."[20] Beyond the commitment to featuring the action of the texts, then, no single method is sustained throughout. Instead, a diversity of methods is employed in order to best illuminate the most significant dimensions of the artistry in each text. In each analysis, the predominant critical method is chosen for its ability to explicate the peculiar dynamics of its object. Over the course of the various analyses, then, the reader will encounter methodological categories and taxonomies drawn, at different times, from traditional Aristotelian categories; from Maurice Charland's work on constitutive rhetoric; from the prose analysis of Richard Lanham; from Chaim Perelman's concepts of liaison and dissociation; from Kenneth Burke's pentadic ratios and notions of hierarchy, transcendence and identification; and from Ernest Bormann's fantasy theme analysis.

The first two chapters of this book will place Campbell's rhetoric in historical and theoretical perspective. Chapter one provides a brief overview of the conditions prevailing in early nineteenth-century American religion, a concise account of the rise of the Stone-Campbell movement, and a summary of Campbell's restoration plea. Chapter two explores the affective tradition of rhetoric to which Campbell was introduced at the University of Glasgow and the general features of Campbell's rhetoric following his immigration to America. Specifically, the latter part of chapter two considers the impact of Baconian induction and Scottish common sense realism upon his rhetorical proofs, his shift from a classical Ciceronian five-part arrangement to a "natural" pattern of discourse that corresponded to the principles of faculty psychology, the significance of his concern for perspicuity and vivacity in style, and his preference for an extemporaneous delivery.

No diachronic treatment of Campbell's rhetoric could be complete without an analysis of his famous "Sermon on the Law,"[21] delivered at the annual meeting of the Redstone Baptist Association in Cross Creek, Virginia, on September 1, 1816. Church historians generally regard this sermon as the inaugural event in Campbell's "restoration" movement, echoing sentiments expressed by Campbell himself years later.

Chapter three argues for the constitutive significance of this sermon by measuring it against the qualities of consitutive rhetoric identified by Maurice Charland in his classic essay, "The Case of the Peuple Quebecois."[22] Specifically, this chapter analyzes how this sermon not only calls its own audience (the movement) into being but also does so in a way uniquely appropriate for the faith community to whom the sermon is addressed. The constitutive significance of this sermon, this chapter suggests, consists not only in the nature of the audience it calls into being but also in the leadership *ethos* that it begins to generate for Campbell—as a divinely authorized prophet-reformer in the "true" Protestant tradition.

Campbell himself admitted that his "Sermon on the Law" resulted in seven-year "war" to oust him from membership in the Redstone Baptist Association, and the publication of his journal the *Christian Baptist*[23] (1823–30) parallels a subsequent seven-year period during which "Campbellite" churches were purged from various Baptist associations. Campbell himself would later describe its first volume as "the most uncharitable . . . most severe, sarcastic and ironic" material that he had ever written, noting, "it was an experiment to ascertain whether society could be moved by fear or rage."[24] In chapter four, selections from the *Christian Baptist* (including the "Third Epistle of Peter" and excerpts from his series "A Restoration of the Ancient Order of Things") are examined to illustrate the emergence of a more extreme prophetic *ethos* for Campbell.

In 1830, Campbell launched a new journal, *The Millennial Harbinger* (1830–66).[25] As the emergent leader of a now independent fellowship of autonomous Christian Churches/Churches of Christ, Campbell found himself addressing the tensions that accompanied the ideological differences within his movement. His responses to the "Lunenburg Letter" in 1837 were an attempt to manage controversies over the practice of baptism, in particular, and, more significantly, the question of what was "essential" to being a Christian. His rejoinders to correspondence from readers, also penned for the multiple audiences who overheard this dialogue, represent a significant *pastoral* moment for Campbell as he discursively fills the dual roles of "peacemaker" within his movement and "ambassador" to the Protestant community at large.

The analysis of this rhetorical act in chapter five draws upon the taxonomy of both Kenneth Burke and Chaim Perelman to describe how, through a series of dissociations, Campbell constructs a hierarchy of spiritual classes that serve as a basis for transcending levels of conflict, constructing diverse grounds of identification, and ultimately transforming the rhetorical situation. Consequently, a more pastoral *ethos* emerges for Campbell who is able to construct a persona of "prudence" and occupy rhetorical middle ground—not only between two extreme positions on baptism (one making it a "savior," the other ignoring its import altogether) but between two more extreme rhetorics (avoiding both a rhetoric of essentiality and a rhetoric of triviality).

By 1860, the movement had grown to a membership of almost a quarter of a million. Growth brought both a need and desire for cooperation beyond the local level. Campbell was the driving force behind the creation of the American Christian Missionary Society in 1849 and continued to serve as its chief advocate. When Campbell addressed the national convention of the ACMS in 1860, he was seventy-two years old and in declining health. The only national assembly of these churches, it was the last such meeting prior to the Civil War, after which it would be national in name only. This would be Campbell's last public address to a national audience of his churches.

Delivered in the midst of controversies over the right of the society to exist and dwindling financial support, the address's instrumental purposes serve these ends. These purposes notwithstanding, the address incorporates significant narrative and visionary elements that impart an epideictic quality to the discourse (i.e., as in a speech of praise) and construct a *patriarchal* ethos for Campbell. The final chapter offers a fantasy theme analysis of this address to demonstrate how it offers Campbell's movement a coherent rhetorical vision that simultaneously interprets its past, defines its present, and directs its future. Campbell emerges as the great "father" of the movement, its inaugural missionary, and its preeminent storyteller who functions both as steward of its now crystallized heritage and as its chief visionary who speaks not only to his own generation but to the next as well.[25]

In closing, the major observations offered in the individual analyses are drawn together to suggest that Campbell possessed a keen sense of what the ancients called *kairos*—the "timeliness" of having the word appropriate for the moment. In this regard, his rhetorical leadership was above all marked by that quality which every effective rhetor needs in some measure—an ability to adapt, to devise discursive strategies that continue to evolve an *ethos* appropriate for the hour. To this, possibly more than anything else, we can attribute an influence in nineteenth-century American religion matched by few and exceeded, perhaps, by none.

Prophet, Pastor, and Patriarch

I

Alexander Campbell's Restoration Movement

The nineteenth century will always be known in American history as the century of the great immigration . . . Many of these first-generation Americans would leave an indelible mark in shaping the new national culture. In religion, few would have greater impact than an Irishman of Scotch ancestry who came to the new world in the first decade of the nineteenth century.[1]

What Henry Webb writes above about Thomas Campbell even more aptly describes Campbell's eldest child—Alexander. A New Light Anti-Burgher Seceder Presbyterian minister[2] and a graduate of the University of Glasgow, Thomas was teaching school in southern Ireland and completing seminary when, on September 12, 1788, his wife Jane gave birth to their first child. Serving small churches, Thomas continued to teach to supplement his income and personally supervised his son's education. Under his father's tutelage, Alexander became extensively well read in literature, philosophy, and religion; instructed in both Latin and Greek; and especially familiar with the works of John Locke.[3]

A harsh climate and the cumulative demands of ministering to rural churches and conducting schools took their toll on the health of the elder Campbell. When Thomas's physician recommended a long rest and perhaps a sea voyage, eighteen-year-old Alexander disclosed his intention to migrate to America when he became of age. It was decided that Thomas would make an initial trip to America and that his family would later join him if he so approved. He arrived in Philadelphia in the spring of 1807.[4]

Alexander oversaw his father's academy for the following school year. Having received word from Thomas in March of 1808, the family sailed to join him on October 1.[5] A week later, their ship was blown into a reef near the Isle of Islay off the coast of Scotland. Although no lives were lost, the Campbells decided to spend the winter in Glasgow and continue their journey the following spring. Alexander took advantage of the opportunity to enroll at the university—a decision of no small consequence, as we shall see. The family eventually arrived in New York on September 29, 1809 and was reunited with Thomas ten days later.[6] The New World as the Campbells found it, as well as the impact they would have on it, are described in the pages of this chapter.

The Rise of Religious Populism

The early decades of the nineteenth century have been referred to as "the time of greatest religious chaos and originality in American history" and "the most important single generation in the modern history not merely of English religion but of the whole Christian world."[7] The Campbells soon found themselves enmeshed in controversy and at the forefront of developments that, according to Nathan Hatch, "left as indelible an imprint upon the structures of American Christianity as . . . [the Revolution] did upon those of American political life."[8]

Hatch's careful and thorough analysis of religious movements during the early republic has presented a strong case that traditional accounts of the "Second Great Awakening" have, in fact, "obscured the egalitarianism powerfully at work in the new nation." Whereas church historians have typically characterized the Second Great Awakening as a conservative force through which traditional religious elites rescued the young nation from the brink of disaster by imposing social and moral order upon a secularized society, Hatch concludes that such interpretations have "ignored the most dynamic and characteristic elements of Christianity during this time: the displacement from power of the religious people of ideas by those who leaned toward popular culture." Far from being a "unified, cohesive movement," the Second Great Awakening actually (1) sprung from a "populist upsurge" and a communications revolution that sparked several mass popular movements, (2) debated and redefined matters of religious authority along social and class lines as much as or more than intellectual or theological ones, and (3) "splintered American Christianity and magnified the diversity of institutions claiming to be the church." It was, Hatch argues, the "entrepreneurial energy" produced by the "conjunction of evangelical fervor and popular sovereignty" that "accelerated the process of Christianization within American popular culture, allowing for indigenous expressions of faith."[9]

It was no mere coincidence that the popular religious movements of these years rallied around charismatic leaders who were highly skilled communicators. By 1830, what Ernest Bormann refers to as "the rhetorical tradition of romantic pragmatism" had become "a widespread and influential persuasive style in the religious and cultural life of the United States."[10] Further, as diverse as their theologies may have been, all of these movements took root in a common soil—a milieu that favored certain leadership styles. The reforming work of the Campbells would both aid in the construction of and eventually thrive within a religious environment largely characterized by a democratization of the church, a demonization of the clergy, an interest in restoring the patterns of primitive Christianity, an expectation of millennial harmony, and the use of innovative communication strategies.

Democratization of the Church

When the separation of church and state was written into the Bill of Rights, religious freedom was legally established as a corollary to the nation's new political freedom.[11] The availability of large areas of sparsely inhabited land also presented Americans with a new opportunity to establish religious diversity and experimentation as a part of their daily experience. The American Revolution, however, did more than alter the legal and geographical landscape of religious freedom. It provided leaven for a passionate cultural debate over the very meaning of freedom itself. Vehement controversies arose over the fundamental nature of authority and leadership. A confidence in the ability and right of individuals to think for themselves, born of the ideology and vocabulary of revolutionary rhetoric, fed a general erosion of respect for authority, tradition, social station, and higher education, as the significance of such matters as equality, sovereignty, and representation was hotly contested.

Church polity in the early republic was profoundly altered by this process of radical democratization. Religious reformers drank deeply from the well of democratic vocabularies and revolutionary rhetoric; no section of the country was left unaffected by this democratic upsurge.[12] Movements led by James O'Kelly and Rice Haggard in the southeast and by Abner Jones and Elias Smith in the northeast both sought increased independence at the level of the local congregation. Alarmed by the demands and growing power of the bishopric, O'Kelly and other Methodist ministers withdrew from the general conference of the Methodist Episcopal Church in America in 1792 and organized the Republican Methodist Church in Maryland in 1793. In an "open door" conference a year later,

Haggard was responsible for renaming the body "Christians."[13] Baptist ministers Jones and Smith became advocates of religious freedom in New England. Jones established autonomous "Christian Churches" in Vermont, New Hampshire, and Massachusetts between 1801 and 1804. Smith launched the first religious newspaper in America—*The Herald of Gospel Liberty* (1808–17)—and through this medium the movements became aware of each other.[14]

More specifically, Hatch identifies three respects in which "the popular religious movements of the early republic articulated a profoundly democratic spirit": (1) an association of virtue with ordinary people rather than an elite and a concomitant rejection of the clergy-laity hierarchy, (2) a willingness to take the spiritual experiences of ordinary people (including religious "enthusiasts") at face value rather than subject them to the scrutiny of doctrinal orthodoxy, and (3) a confidence that the overthrow of oppressive church structures would naturally give birth to religious and social harmony.[15] These trends will figure prominently into the subsequent discussion.

Demonization of the Clergy

Arguably, the contributions of such churchmen as Timothy Dwight (1752–1817) and Lyman Beecher (1775–1863) to the Second Great Awakening were largely prompted by the rise of a threat to their notion of a respectable, Christian minister. As Hatch states,

> The fundamental religious quarrel of the late eighteenth century was not between Calvinist and Arminian, orthodox and Unitarian, evangelical and free thinker but between radically different conceptions of the Christian ministry. As respectable clergymen in these turbulent years reiterated their confidence in learning and civility, potent strains of anti-clericalism swelled up within the bounds of the church, challenging the right of any special order to mediate the gospel . . . Sustained volleys of criticism about pride, spiritual apathy, and love of station and wealth continued to discomfit clergymen.[16]

While anticlericalism had long been a staple of Protestant dissent, Hatch suggests two reasons why it became increasingly virulent and popular in America near the end of the eighteenth century: (1) it portrayed society as "horizontally polarized" and (2) it was accompanied by an "intensely egalitarian" reading of the New Testament. As Kenneth Cmiel has observed in his analysis of the controversies surrounding popular speech in nineteenth-century America: "Sloughing off the hereditary aristocracy was supposed to inaugurate a rule of the wise and the virtuous, but republican hostility to titles had led to a demeaning of all distinctions of talent and breeding. Academic education was attacked because 'plain, unlettered' men could best communicate with the people . . . Talent was equated with mustering votes or amassing fortunes."[17] As this horizontal polarization reflected a fundamental conflict over whether a natural aristocracy had a right to speak for all people, so new readings of the New Testament produced by obscure Christians lacking formal education generated a popular theology opposed to the traditional assumption that the higher social classes of society were a more likely repository of wisdom.[18]

Attacks upon the clergy in these years thus fed and were fed by the broader crisis of authority that dominated popular culture. Benjamin Austin's *Independent Chronicle* and William Duane's *Aurora,* for example, "tarred and feathered Yankee clergymen" as "an intolerant clerical-political aristocracy." Lorenzo Dow, the militant Methodist itinerant preacher, took much delight in "exposing the pretensions of genteel clergymen" as well as in railing against the legal profession and orthodox medicine. Ridicule became a common tactic among "ungenteel" speakers whose ambivalent attitude toward education was reflected in their derision of the style of educated orators. William Henry Milburn, whose works, according to Bormann, typify the theory of the period's ungenteel rhetoric, cited an oft repeated story about a "windy" gentlemen who, interrupted by someone calling out that "his breeches was torn out behind," then "clapped a hand to the part indicated, and was destroyed—overwhelmed in inextinguishable laughter."[19] And Elias Smith, who shared both Austin's radical Jeffersonianism and Dow's opposition to the established medical profession, filled both his paper and his preaching with invectives against "priestcraft" and "religious manufactories." One of his early pamphlets, *The Clergyman's Looking Glass,* merits further consideration in chapter four.[20]

Restoration of Primitive Patterns

The history of the church has been punctuated with "back to the Bible" movements and America's restoration perspective, central to its life and thought since the earliest settlements of New England's Puritan founders, was a legacy of the Protestant Reformation.[21] According to Richard T. Hughes and C. Leonard Allen, American "primitivism" descends from "a sixteenth century tradition that viewed antiquity, and especially the primitive Christian church, as the standard for all subsequent faith and practice." This tradition of "primordial reform," in which "*chronos* is reversed until profane history is transcended and the believer stands squarely in the first age," dominated "the world view and the theological method of Christian Humanism, the Reformed tradition, and the Puritans." However, what was once the basis for dissent in England became the basis for established churches in America.[22]

According to Bormann, a recurring use of "the restoration drama" ("purification through rebirth and restoration") was central to the rhetorical vision of the romantic pragmatism that was so popular in the nineteenth century.[23] Indeed, during the years of the early American republic, the radical rejection of traditional sources of orthodoxy and the intense religious pluralism which ensued nourished an extraordinary zeal for religious reconstruction. Many within the popular religious movements saw their task as completing what the American Revolution had only begun. Hughes and Allen observe, "Indeed, from their perspective the American Revolution was only half won. Despotic political powers had been silenced, but religious despots continued to coerce the consciences of the faithful."[24]

Many of the leading personalities among these movements, as Hatch observes, shared the common sentiment that "since the age of the apostles, a great falling away had severed the relationship between God and man, leaving the visible church virtually extinct during the Dark Ages. They also agreed that, whatever good the Protestant Reformation had done, it had not reopened the heavens or restored authentic Christanity."[25]

Significant features of this Christian primitivism included a polarization of primordial (sacred) and profane (secular) time and, in some quarters, a radical rejection of creedal authorities. "Sacred" time, in these cases, consisted of pure, primordial beginnings (a first age whose perfections have been lost, i.e., the primitive Christianity described in the New Testament) and the restoration of those pure, primal norms in the millennial age (expected to arrive imminently). All intervening history was considered profane, the aftermath of a fall from primal purity. Hughes and Allen compare this to Fred Somkin's "image of America straddling the stream of history, with one foot planted squarely in the primordium and the other in the millennial dawn." Barton Stone's "Christian" movement, in particular, considered "the traditions of Christian history embodied in creeds, synodical decisions and clerical decrees" responsible for the fall from purity and the chief impediment to religious liberty. Accordingly, "they routinely conceived of their restoration task as one of pruning and negation . . . not as one of positive construction, but rather as one of elimination. They would prune the traditions of history and remove the encrustations of time until the primitive church in all of its effulgent purity emerged once more."[26]

A preoccupation with restoring primitive patterns became so pervasive that, by 1849, John W. Nevin, based on his survey of fifty-three American Protestant denominations, would declare that "no creed but the Bible" had become "the distinctive feature of American religion."[27]

The theological journeys of Smith and Jones are again illustrative. After rejecting traditional theological systems as untenable, both experienced an intense intellectual and spiritual turmoil that was eventually resolved by a commitment to the "Bible alone" and their own (as they perceived it) unmediated encounters with the ancient order of the New Testament.[28] Many others shared similar experiences as they searched for some new ground of certainty amidst the chaos generated by a proliferation of religious dissent.[29]

The quests of these movements and their leaders to restore the primitive church had several specific effects. In the context of religious pluralism and dissent, it provided a standard of legitimization, as some denominations claimed to duplicate primitive Christianity more closely than others. Ironically, as Hughes and Allen point out, it enabled "Christian soldiers" to simultaneously "proclaim freedom from the housetops" and "de-Christianize their neighbors and consign them to the wrath of God."[30] Their sects also appeared "self-spring from the Bible" and their efforts were shifted, in Hatch's words, "to the center stage of the cosmic drama. Restoring the apostolic order—and thus heralding the millennial Kingdom—could only be done by the recreative power of the handfuls of faithful believers intent on following the New Testament pattern. Saints on that mission had no reason to bow to the well-placed graduates of colleges and seminaries. . . ."[31]

Ultimately, much of the popularity of these movements may well be due to the fact that, in the words of Hughes and Allen, "each reflected primordial concerns to a primordial people." As the quest for a primordium within the Jeffersonian American Enlightenment turned increasingly to the Book and God of Nature (sharing the method if not the theology of the Puritans), a new civil religion had emerged as well. Its elements were rooted in the common conviction that, because the new republic had transcended history and recovered the ancient primordium, with its liberties for all people, the United States constituted a uniquely Christian nation. As a result,

> the popular religions of the early nineteenth century reflected in powerful ways a revolutionary identity already in place. Mormons, Baptists, and "Christians" were no mere cults, destined to strut upon the American stage and then to die. In fact, one of the principal reasons for their immense, collective appeal to so many thousands of Americans at the time was their uncanny accuracy in reflecting the myth of the first times so central to the American ethos. One might even argue that the Mormons and the "Christians" were, in fundamental ways, creations of that ethos. . . . [32]

Expectation of Millennial Harmony

Taken from the Latin word for "thousand," *millennialism* refers to various doctrines taken from the reference to a thousand-year reign of Christ in Revelation 20:1–10. Various forms of millennialism expect this thousand-year period to be a "final, golden age of human history . . . characterized by peace, justice, and righteousness."[33]

Millennial expectations had been intensifying in America since the First Great Awakening of the 1730s and 1740s. However, whereas discussions of millennialism during most of the eighteenth century remained largely limited to the polite speculation of genteel theologians, the success of the revolution ushered in a widespread sense that developments of apocalyptic significance had suddenly been made possible. Many Americans were convinced that the millennium was dawning.[34]

Bormann describes the millennial vision shared by many:

> The adherents of the ungenteel style dramatized the subsequent developments such as the Revolutionary War, the drafting and adoption of the Constitution, and the opening of the valley of the Ohio river for settlement as further evidence that man and

society were to be perfected in the New World. The ground was sacred; . . . the Old World was corrupted and would not be suitable as the setting of the millennium but the new pristine lands of the West were ideal for the Second Coming. The new lands were vital battlegrounds between the hosts of the devil and the hosts of God.[35]

The front page of the first edition of Smith's *Herald of Gospel Liberty*, for example, declared that "the foundations of Christ's millennial Kingdom were laid in the American and French Revolutions."[36] In *The Declaration and Address of the Christian Association of Washington* (1809), Thomas Campbell also discerned the "signs of the times" in these same revolutions, which he described in apocalyptic terms.[37] Hatch observes that even the Mormons developed an eschatology that was distinctly American in the sense that it attributed "a special character to the land and its people that would allow the kingdom of heaven to be restored despite the corruption of the current generation." Thus, these movements were "empowered by an incomparable ideology: their innovations were the handiwork of God and the meaning of America."[38]

The most popular eschatology of the century's opening decades was postmillennialism. According to Bormann, this variation of the vision " . . . saw the world hastening to get better, more and more souls being saved for the true religion, less sinfulness, less suffering, great opportunity, greater progress in all departments of life, the formation of a grand new system of government that would encourage freedom and liberty and the steady march of progress until the world was perfect enough; this state would last a millennium, after which Christ would come for a second time."[39] Anticipation of an imminent millennium lent urgency and power to the evangelistic efforts of the populist movements. In Bormann's words, "since the West was rapidly filling up with settlers, the time was short and the crisis upon the adherents of the ungenteel vision."[40]

As late as 1835, even when millennial thought was shifting from postmillennialism to premillennialism,[41] millennial fervor remained undiminished. In that same year, the revivalist Charles Finney was moved to write, "If the church will do her duty the Millennium may come in this country in three years" and William Miller published a series of influential lectures predicting that the second advent of Christ would transpire in 1843. The new opportunities afforded by the surge of populist movements for the restoration of apostolic Christianity and for mass religious revival were viewed as providential developments and their growth soon came to be seen as evidence of the success of their efforts to usher in the millennium.[42]

The perceived potential for restoring the primitive church and the proliferation of millennial expectations were not merely coincidental. Although, according to Ruth Bloch, both secular and sacred versions of millennialism coexisted in late eighteenth-century America, the boundaries were vague and it was widely held among the popular religious movements of the nineteenth century that the American experiment by itself would be insufficient to usher in the millennium apart from the restoration of the primitive church.[43] Hughes and Allen capture the symbiotic relationship between restorationism, ecumenism, and millennialism within Stone's "Christian" movement:

> After all, a united church capable of inaugurating the millennium would not be built on historic creeds and traditions, but rather on the platform of the apostolic age—a platform that all Christians shared. The themes of restoration and unity were so intertwined in the thinking of the "Christians" that insistence on the one almost always involved insistence upon the other. The dynamic that gave urgency to both was the eager expectation of the millennium, though the millennium itself was contingent on the restoration of the apostolic church and the realization of Christian unity. Clearly, restoration, unity and millennialism were interrelated and mutually reinforced themes . . . The intimate connection of millennial, ecumenical and primitivist views in "Christian" thought appears in literally hundreds of their assertions.[44]

Together, then, the democratization of the church, the rejection of a genteel clergy, the restoration quest, and millennial expectation formed a unified, coherent, and grand vision for life in the new republic. It was empowered by the innovative communication strategies adopted by its adherents.

Innovative Communication Strategies

In the introductory essay to his anthology *Communication and Change in American Religious History*, Leonard Sweet has observed that "those religious leaders who have made the biggest advances have been those who worked out of their tradition to express their faith through innovative ways and means, idioms and technologies accessible and adapted to the times in which they lived."[45] The populist religious movements of the nineteenth century were no exception to this generalization.

Common to the rhetoric of these movements was a keen sensitivity to its audience. Hatch observes that, in one sense, the breadth of dissenting views collectively represented in these movements constituted a pluralism "capable of Christianizing a people in all of its social, geographic and ethnic diversity." Nonetheless, as Bormann observes, the strongest appeal of Baptists, Methodists, and "Christians" was to "the common people." Whereas their rhetoric was generally unattractive to "the learned and influential clergymen in the older settled portions of the colonies" who "abhorred the denigration of learning" and "saw those who shared the new consciousness as crude, unlearned and repulsive," it found a sympathetic audience among those who were not a part of the new elite and especially among people "living in frontier conditions without the benefit of education and some of the other niceties of manners and culture which were common" among the "new nobility."[46]

For preachers, authors, and editors this generally meant appealing to the "common sense" of the individual, trusting in public opinion as an arbiter of truth, and measuring theology by its acceptance in the marketplace. The power of this spiritually egalitarian rhetoric in the context of nineteenth-century democracy, as Cmiel suggests, was derived in large proportion from its "willingness to take the audience seriously." To its audiences, this rhetoric imparted a sense of purpose, empowered by visions of self-confidence and self-respect.[47] As Hatch notes,

> All of these movements challenged common people to take religious destiny into their own hands, to think for themselves, to oppose centralized authority and the elevation of the clergy as a separate order of men. These religious communities could embrace the forlorn and the uprooted far more intensely than any political movement and offer them powerful bonds of acceptance and hope . . . These new movements could also impart to ordinary people, particularly those battered by poverty or infirmity, what Martin Luther King called "a sense of somebodiness". . . . [48]

This popular audience orientation was also a wellspring for several kindred innovations in communication.

For example, the channels through which these movements made their appeals were subversive in relation to the communication decorum of the day. The expanded role of the press in spreading revolutionary dissent had made newspaper reading a way of life for many—between 1790 and 1810, the number of papers in the nation increased from 90 to 370. America's network of print culture continued to flourish well after 1815. From 1810 through 1828, newspaper circulation increased twice as rapidly as the population and, whereas fewer than one hundred magazines were published in the early 1820s, by 1850 that total grew to exceed six hundred. Now a much less expensive endeavor due to new technologies such as stereotyping, steam-powered printing, and machine papermaking, printing was transformed from a specialized medium catering to genteel tastes into a truly mass medium.[49]

Populist religious movements were on the cutting edge of this new age of mass communication, producing millions of tracts, pamphlets, hymn-books, devotional books, journals, magazines, and newspapers of every sort. Hatch observes that "religious periodicals had, by 1830, become the grand engine of a burgeoning religious culture, the primary means of promotion for, and bond of union within, competing religious groups." Gaylord Albaugh has estimated that by 1830 the fourteen religious journals in existence prior to 1790 had grown to more than six hundred and that between 1800 and 1830 the number of subscribers grew from around five hundred to approximately five hundred thousand.[50]

Many of these authors and editors, like Elias Smith, considered it their democratic duty to short-circuit a hierarchical flow of information. Also, considering their preference for vernacular expression and their fondness for using sharp ridicule, bitter sarcasm, and profane humor to topple clergy and other elites from their positions of social authority, it is, as Hatch notes, "little wonder that gentlemen such as Timothy Dwight came to equate the reading of newspapers with tavern-haunting, drinking and gambling." Nonetheless, through the use of these media, populist religious leaders were able both to significantly extend the reach of their persuasion by gaining large audiences among churches favoring local and democratic control and to impart a sense of coherence and direction to sweeping movements consisting of geographically dispersed congregations.[51]

Though long a staple of religious communication, preaching was also transformed by populist movements into a medium to reach the masses.

The popularity of lay preachers, the development of the colloquial sermon, the rise of itinerant preaching, and the phenomenon of the camp meeting all contributed to a revolution in religious public address.

Bormann notes that "the tendency to sanction the use of lay exhorters that began in the 1740s was institutionalized by many of the revival groups in the years following the revolutionary war." And, consistent with their ambivalence toward education and celebration of values associated with common practical people, Hatch observes that "a firm commitment to lay preaching constituted the foundation of the insurgent religious movements of the early republic." Rejecting the upper-class ideal of the polished, respectable clergyman, these movements invited "even the most unlearned and inexperienced to respond to the call to preach."[52]

A homiletical revolution ensued as traditional, classic sermons (i.e., "stylized texts delivered on a regular occasion by a university trained clergyman in a settled parish," as Hatch describes them[53]) were displaced by those more colloquial.[54] Bormann associates such preaching with "the rhetorical tradition of romantic pragmatism." He describes it as "romantic" because "it subordinated form to content, manners to feeling, and encouraged freedom of invention and delivery" and "emphasized imagination, emotion and introspection as central to the art of communication . . . The natural orator, untrained and therefore unspoiled by formal education, was the exemplar of the good speaker." Participants in the tradition were "pragmatists" in that they "stressed the usefulness of their messages, and the immediate, visible effects of their speeches" as "evidence of success or failure."[55]

In particular, Bormann refers to the left wing of that tradition as the "ungenteel style"[56] because of the way its "rhetoricians butchered the language of educated speakers practicing the genteel style, because of the way they invented their own terms, and because of their crudeness." Narrative preaching, characterized by what Hatch calls "true-to-life passion, simplicity of structure, and dramatic creativity," emerged as an alternative to traditional doctrinal preaching. Such preachers were inveterate users of personal experience and biblical narrative, materials that were readily accessible to the uneducated minister of the frontier. Illustrations from common life, overt humor (including sarcasm and ridicule), homely language, and graphic description were also prominent features of this preaching.[57]

According to Bormann, this rhetoric also applied "a persuasive theory of the psychology of conversion" that moved individuals from a sense of personal guilt over atrocities for which they were morally responsible to the joy of salvation through the drama of a "new birth." Such sermons "developed the Puritan practice of the searching sermon to a high level of vituperative perfection," frequently employing a tactic that became known as "taking the hide off the audience." The loud, vehement, emotional manner in which these sermons were usually delivered (a commonly applied term was "thundered") was consistent with their tone.[58]

Hatch points out that while such preachers "believed in fervent emotion . . . they were also capable of devastating logic to achieve their own purposes." Adherents of the "ungenteel style" shared common assumptions about argument and evidence. A literal interpretation of the Bible was, as Bormann puts it, "the supernaturally sanctioned avenue to knowledge" and experiential-based common sense reasoning served as an important form of proof. The Jeffersonian notion that people should think for themselves was also a forceful theme in this preaching, which was driven by a missionary impulse. Hatch sums up the broader situation well, noting that while "literary preaching retained vitality for citizens of the new republic—at least those in cities and towns, . . . for Americans in the hinterland, away from cosmopolitan centers, the most accessible preaching was increasingly folk- rather than clergy-dominated."[59]

If the popularity of lay preachers and the development of the colloquial sermon dramatically altered the source and substance of preaching for these movements, the rise of itinerant preaching and the phenomenon of the camp meeting significantly expanded its setting. As the nation's population expanded with the frontier during the late eighteenth and early nineteenth centuries, Methodist circuit riders and Baptist farmer-preachers were able to reach dispersed audiences by imitating the itinerant practices of George Whitfield and other early revivalists. Those who responded to a felt "call to preach" were "charged to proclaim the gospel anywhere and every day of the week—even to the limit of their physical endurance." Preaching took on a ubiquitous character as Methodist and Mormon preachers traveled from house to house in search of audiences. In 1804 alone, Lorenzo Dow traversed some ten thousand miles and, in 1805, spoke at between five and eight hundred meetings. Just a year later, Francis Asbury covered more than four thousand miles and fifteen states within an eight-month period.[60]

The camp meeting also proved a haven for populist preaching. A mobile institution that was able to move west with the expanding frontier, it became "a phenomenally successful instrument for popular recruitment."[61] The Cane Ridge Revival of 1801 was typical of such meetings. Between ten and twenty-five thousand people participated in this camp meeting at a time when nearby Lexington, Kentucky's largest city, had a population of approximately two thousand. Sermons were preached by numerous ministers of Presbyterian, Methodist, and Baptist persuasions and their efforts were assisted by a large number of lay exhorters. Paul Conkin describes the preaching and exhorting that took place there: "Although only ministers preached prepared sermons, or had allocated times to perform, literally hundreds of people served as exhorters . . . Here and there almost anyone, including those who rose from the ground as well as child converts, might burst out with exhortation. Women, small children, slaves, shy people, illiterate people, all exhorted with great effect."[62]

Hatch reports that Asbury boldly advocated the camp meeting, once describing the "overwhelming power" of a four-day meeting held twenty miles northeast of New York and attended by three thousand people and later boasting that the annual attendance at such meetings averaged three to four million annually (roughly half of the total population of the United States). A thorough study of revivalism in this era by John Boles has documented how, after Cane Ridge, such meetings proved to be far more than "a mere frontier aberration" and became an essential feature of "Bible Belt religion" that spread from state to state with amazing rapidity.[63]

Considering its popular audience orientation, it is hardly surprising that this populist religious rhetoric also appealed to an alternative leadership *ethos*. This new *ethos* drew its credibility not from literary education, social status, family connections, or even ordination but from individual charisma. And, as Hatch notes, "Authority flowed to those claimants whose person, language and deportment best resonated with the interests of the common people. . . . " Thus, leaders emerged who "were often the inverse of the pulpit's traditional decorum" and whose discourse appealed to popular tastes through vernacular expression, biting sarcasm and "common sense" reasoning.[64] In the words of Walter Brownlow Posey, many churches did not want an educated minister to use "high-falutin' words to render them uncomfortable."[65] Bormann sums the matter up well:

> For the speakers and theorists of the ungenteel style, the claims
> of scholarship and social distance, the use of dignity and apart-
> ness, to establish the authority of a preacher, which had character-

ized the power structure of colonial New England was no longer persuasive. For such claims of speaker credibility, the new rhetoric substituted effectiveness, the ability to talk the language of the common man, unstudied natural eloquence, crudity, and ungrammatical expressions . . . What was not wanted was nonsense, foolishness, airs, pedantry, erudition, dead languages, classical allusions, or studied elocutions. What was wanted was a natural man, deeply feeling the emotion he was trying to communicate to his audience.[66]

The subject of *ethos* need not be further developed here since it will be attended to at length in subsequent chapters.

These, then, were the predominant features of the mass popular movements within early nineteenth-century American religion. Armed with a message that resonated with the masses, energized by a missionary zeal and aided by a communications revolution, this populist upsurge in religion "did more to Christianize American society than anything before or since."[67] None of these movements, however, were more widely received than the Stone-Campbell movement.

The "Restoration" Movement of Stone and Campbell

What has since become known as the "Stone-Campbell Movement" originated as two separate and independent movements under the leadership of Barton W. Stone in Kentucky and Thomas and Alexander Campbell in Virginia. Common elements of their movements included several of the aforementioned themes: a rejection of the authority of denominational creeds, an affirmation of the unique authority of the Bible, a call to reform the present church after the "simpler" pattern of primitive Christianity as found in the New Testament, and the autonomy of local congregations.[68] These provided the foundation for a united movement that placed "American culture and values . . . at center stage."[69]

The Stone-Campbell Movement

Stone's reforms actually predated those of the Campbells. Stone was the host minister of the Cane Ridge Revival that brought the Second Great Awakening to Kentucky in 1801. Along with fellow Presbyterian ministers Robert Marshall, Richard McNemar, John Dunlavy, and John

Thompson, Stone came under the scrutiny of the Kentucky Synod because of the "religious exercises" that had occurred during the revival. When the Synod defrocked McNemar and Thompson for heresy, the five ministers joined in renouncing the jurisdiction of the Synod and formed their own presbytery. In January of 1804, they issued *An Apology for Renouncing the Jurisdiction of the Synod of Kentucky*, authored by Marshall, Stone, and Thompson, rejecting the Westminster Confession as the standard of orthodoxy and professing their belief in the sufficiency of the Bible alone as a rule of faith and practice for all Christians.[70]

Their new presbytery soon grew to include fifteen congregations. However, the position on the authority of denominational creeds expressed in their apology eventually led them to disband the new presbytery itself when they concluded that it had no authorization from the Bible. *The Last Will and Testament of the Springfield Presbytery*, probably authored by McNemar,[71] was published on June 28, 1804, and proclaimed the dissolution of the presbytery. From among this group, Stone eventually emerged as the leader of this new movement of independent congregations. McNemar and Dunlavy converted to Shakerism in 1805. Marshall and Thompson returned to the Presbyterian fold in 1811. However, Stone's periodical, the *Christian Messenger* (1826–45), became a significant force among the independent Christian churches of this area.

While Stone was dissolving his presbytery in America, Thomas Campbell, still in Scotland, had begun to develop a strong opposition to divisions over matters that he believed had lost relevance for the church. Laboring to unite the two branches of the Seceder church, he was sent to Glasgow where he unsuccessfully argued his case before the General Synod of Scotland.[72] Shortly after his immigration, he found himself enmeshed in the religious controversies of the early American republic and the struggle of denominational authorities to exert control over church leaders with populist sentiments.

Upon his arrival, Thomas Campbell, a New Light Anti-Burgher Seceder Presbyterian, was appointed minister of several churches in the Chartiers Presbytery of southwestern Pennsylvania. However, Presbyterians of various sorts were widely scattered throughout this newly settled territory, where the visits of ministers were often separated by periods of months or even years. When asked to visit a few isolated Anti-Burghers at Cannamaugh on the Allegheny River, Campbell officiated at a communion service there. Many of other Presbyterian persuasions were present and desired to partake of the emblems. Rather than "fencing the communion table" (as required by a 1796 act of the Synod prohibiting communion with other bodies of Presbyterians), Campbell suggested that all might partake regardless of their Presbyterian affiliation. Another Seceder minister who accompanied him on the trip reported his actions, and Campbell was suspended by the presbytery in February of 1808. His suspension was eventually revoked by the Synod in May but the presbytery refused to make any preaching appointments for him. In September, he withdrew from the Chartiers Presbytery and the Associate Synod of North America.[73]

Sympathetic friends rallied to support Thomas Campbell, however, and he continued to receive invitations to preach in western Pennsylvania. In August of 1809, a group led by Campbell formed the Christian Association of Washington, a society dedicated to "the promotion of Biblical Christianity and Christian union." On September 7, a mere three weeks before he was reunited with his family, Thomas completed and ordered the printing of a fifty-six page booklet, the *Declaration and Address of the Christian Association of Washington.*[74]

One of the most influential documents in the history of the Stone-Campbell movement, the *Declaration and Address* described the purpose, policy, and program of the Association. The "Declaration" set forth the four main principles underlying the Association: (1) the right of private judgment, (2) the sole authority of the Bible, (3) the evils of sectarianism, and (4) the basis for Christian unity to be found in exact conformity to the Bible. The "Address" contained a discussion of Christian unity expressed in thirteen propositions, which McAllister and Tucker summarize as follows: (1) the essential unity of the Church of Christ, (2) the supreme authority of the Bible, (3) the special authority of the New Testament, (4) the fallacy of human creeds, (5) the essential brotherhood of all who love Christ and try to follow him, and (6) the ability of followers of Christ to unite upon the biblical platform if human innovations can be removed from the church.[75]

Upon their reunion, Thomas informed his family of his decision to part ways with the Presbyterian church. Alexander was, in fact, quite relieved. While at Glasgow, he had become sympathetic to the Scottish movement for a return to the primitive Christianity of the New Testament.[76] He had become so troubled over his allegiance to the Seceder church that, in its semiannual communion service in the spring of 1809,

he deposited his communion token on the plate and left without participating, thereby renouncing his Presbyterian affiliation.[77] When Thomas
disclosed his proofs of the *Declaration and Address,* Alexander enthusiastically joined him in pursuit of the aims of the Christian Association of
Washington.

Alexander, however, would soon surpass his father in influence and
become the chief advocate of the principles set forth in the *Declaration
and Address.* When the Association was refused admission into the area
presbytery, it reorganized as the Brush Run Church, an independent congregation in Washington County. In 1812, Alexander was ordained to the
ministry and licensed by the congregation to preach.

In 1815, the Brush Run Church responded to the overtures of the Redstone Baptist Association and entered into an uneasy affiliation with
them. In spite of the similarities in faith and practice that attracted the
Association to them, including the Campbells' conversion to an immersionist position on baptism, there were also significant differences, particularly in regard to the authority of the official Baptist creed, the Philadelphia Confession of Faith. Many Baptist clergy remained suspicious of
Alexander Campbell's reformatory preaching and his "Sermon on the
Law," preached before the association in 1816, marked the beginning of
an open antagonism that would climax with the purging of Brush Run
from the Redstone Association in 1825 and of other "Campbellite" or "Reforming Baptist" churches from various Baptist associations over the next
several years.[78] During these years, Campbell published the *Christian
Baptist* (1823–30), a periodical dedicated to "the eviction of truth, and the
exposure of error."[79] He also participated in the first of several significant
public debates (with John Walker, 1820; with William Maccalla, 1823; with
Robert Owen, 1829; with John Purcell, 1837; and with Nathan Rice, 1843).

Although significant differences would remain between them, recog-
nitions of common sympathies between the movements of O'Kelly, Haggard, Smith, Jones, Stone, and Campbell resulted in efforts to consoli-
date. An immersionist sect of the O'Kelly movement led by William
Guirey organized the Virginia Conference in 1810 and correspondence
with the Smith-Jones movement in New England led to a union in 1811.
Though there is no record of any personal contact between O'Kelly and
Stone, Haggard was with Stone in 1804 and, much as he had with the
O'Kelly movement, influenced Stone's decision to adopt the name "Christian."[80] The "Christian Connexion" later coalesced around the Smith-

Jones churches, the Guirey sect of the O'Kelly movement, and the Stone churches that did not merge with the Campbell movement.[81]

The most dramatic union, however, was that between the Stone and Campbell movements—the "Christians" and the "Disciples" (the name preferred by Campbell and by which many of his "Reformed Baptist Churches" became known subsequent to their separation from the Baptists). Campbell and Stone met in Georgetown, Kentucky, in 1824 and subsequently corresponded with each other.[82] Late in 1831, they began to exchange opinions on the subject of union. Full coverage was given to the discussion, both in Stone's *Christian Messenger* and Campbell's *Millennial Harbinger* (which succeeded the *Christian Baptist* in 1830). The two men often disagreed and the exchange frequently became heated. Nevertheless, in April of 1831 a union was effected between the Christians and Disciples in Millersburg, Kentucky. A larger meeting in which Stone participated, held in Lexington, on December 31, 1831, and January 1, 1832, is usually regarded as the decisive moment of union between the two movements, although neither group had any representative bodies with authority to pronounce such a union. Stone announced the union in the January issue of the *Christian Messenger* and throughout the winter of 1831–32 unions in several other states followed. Some congregations called themselves "Christian Churches" or "Churches of Christ"; others called themselves "Disciples of Christ." Campbell was not present at the Lexington meeting but supported the union, expressing "guarded hope for the success of the venture."[83]

Alexander Campbell's "Restoration Plea"

Whereas Barton Stone probably played a larger role in bringing the "Stone-Campbell" movement together, it was Campbell who more precisely and systematically articulated the movement's distinct message. However, his "restoration plea" was not entirely without European antecedents. While a student at Glasgow, Campbell would attend a Seceder church on Sunday mornings. On Sunday evenings, however, he would attend the Congregational Church where Greville Ewing preached. In his home, Ewing would hold discussion groups for university students. It was both in Ewing's church and home that Campbell became acquainted with the teachings of Scottish reformers who thought in terms of a restoration of primitive (New Testament) Christianity.

According to Lynn McMillon, the Scotch Baptist Church bore more similarity to the Campbells' restoration movement than did any of the other Scottish churches and Alexander's personal library would eventually include the complete works of Archibald McLean, founder of the Scotch Baptists. As a young man, Alexander heard the preaching of Rowland Hill, an independent religious leader who toured northern Ireland ca.1801, and may well have heard James Haldane who preached that same year at Rich Hill, near Ahorey, where Thomas Campbell settled into a pastorate in 1798. Another early Scottish restorationist, Alexander Carson, also ministered nearby at the time. Prior to Alexander's arrival in Glasgow, Ewing and William Innes had broken from the church of Scotland to form a congregation dedicated to following only the New Testament, and Campbell's close ties with Ewing brought him into contact with the teachings of John Glas, Robert Sandeman, and Robert and James Haldane. Whereas Carson and the Scotch Baptists developed a theology of baptism, the Haldanes stressed the importance of evangelism and Glas and Sandeman the authority and pattern of the New Testament. Though Campbell's own theology would not precisely parallel any of these, their influence is clear. In his "General Observations on Church Government," written into the blank pages in the back of his Glasgow essay book during the latter part of 1811, Campbell employs language and thought about the organization of the New Testament church that are distinctly those of Glas and Sandeman.[84]

Since Campbell's debt to these early Scottish antecedents has been thoroughly documented elsewhere[85] and because his interest in restoring primitive patterns of Christianity, as has been noted, was not unprecedented in American contexts, the subsequent discussion will be restricted to a summation of that program of reform advocated by Campbell himself. Campbell's "plea" may be tentatively summarized in three basic precepts.[86]

The first was his contention that the evangelization of the world by the church would usher in the millennium.[87] Campbell himself was a postmillennialist.[88] He believed that beginning in America, especially in the West, the church would eventually convert the world and that this would usher in a thousand-year period of significant Christian influence that would climax in Christ's return and the restoration of paradise.

In number XXI of a series devoted to "The Coming of the Lord" in the *Millennial Harbinger,* he wrote: "Although we did not expect that our title of *Millennial Harbinger* was to be so literally and exactly coincident with the facts of an immediate Millennium, as some of our brethren, and all of the Millerite school, would have us think; still I expected, as I yet expect, a Millennium—a thousand years of triumphant Christianity, and at no very distant day."[89]

While Campbell may not have expected the inauguration of the *Millennial Harbinger* to "literally and exactly" coincide with an immediate millennium, the purpose that Campbell projected for this journal in its "Prospectus" of January 1830 sums up well the ultimate utopian hope of his movement: "This work shall be devoted to the destruction of Sectarianism, Infidelity, and Antichristian doctrine and practice. It shall have for its object the development, and the introduction of that political and religious order called the MILLENNIUM, which will be the consummation of that ultimate amelioration of society proposed in the Christian Scriptures."[90]

His confident anticipation of the millennium, however, was dependent upon a second precept. Campbell also held that the unity of Christians was prerequisite to evangelizing the world. He based this belief upon his reading of Christ's prayer in John 17:20–21 which he published in 1825:

> With his eyes raised to heaven, he says;—"Holy Father—now, I do not pray for these only (for the unity and success of the apostles) but for those also who shall believe on me through, or by means of their word—that they all may be one,—that the world may believe that you have sent me." Who does not see in this petition, that the words or testimony of the apostles, the unity of the disciples, and the conviction of the world are bound together . . . The words of the apostles are laid as the basis, the unity of the disciples the glorious result, and the only successful means of converting the world to the acknowledgment, that Jesus of Nazareth is the Messiah or the Son of the Blessed, the only Saviour of men.[91]

Similarly, in 1830, he wrote, "We assume it for a principle . . . that the union of christians, and the destruction of the sects, are indispensable prerequisites to the subjection of the world to the government of Jesus, and to the triumphant appearance of Christ's religion in the world."[92]

Campbell did not necessarily equate "christian unity" with "church union," however. Both Stone and Campbell recognized that there were Christians in all Protestant denominations but denied institutional legitimacy to the denominations themselves. Campbell compared his plea to "what the Spirit saith to saints in Babylon—'Come out of her, my people that you partake not of her sins, and that you receive not of her plagues'. . . . "[93] Campbell nonetheless supported efforts toward union—in an 1839 article on the "Union of Christians" he proposed a conference of delegates from all Protestant denominations as well as Greek and Roman Catholic churches with a view to accepting whatever was universally agreed upon as a basis for union. However, as Douglas Foster points out: "He prefaced the entire discussion, however, with the statement that the union of sects would not be the union of Christians, nor would a union of Christians likely be a union of sects, although an effort to unite the sects might tend to unite Christians."[94]

Campbell tended to describe his concept of unity in more generic terms, as "a more intimate, spiritual, celestial sort of thing, into which we can enter only in our individual capacity and upon our own individual responsibility."[95] He did not insist upon a rigid uniformity but sought to distinguish between matters "essential" and "nonessential," proffering liberty on nonessentials. "There is but 'one faith,'" Campbell argued in his 1829 debate with Robert Owen, "but nowhere is it written that there is but *one opinion*." Similarly, a year later he wrote, "We do not ask them [Christians] to give up their opinions—we ask them only not to impose them upon others."[96] In light of the popularity within the movement of an old slogan—"In faith, unity; in opinions and methods, liberty; in all things, charity"[97]—this loosely defined notion of church unity may be seen as a kind of religious pluralism, albeit limited to matters Campbell considered "non-essential" (i.e., pertaining to the realm of "opinions" rather than the realm of "faith").[98]

Campbell actually devoted most of his energies to propagating a third precept, however, for he considered it foundational in relationship to the others. Only a restoration of the simple religion of the New Testament, he believed, could provide an adequate basis for christian unity.[99] In 1830, Campbell wrote:

If, upon any human scheme, creed, or platform the Millennial Church should be built, what would it be? Ask every sect, one by one, this question, and what answer will each present? Everyone saith, "Upon mine; because, forsooth, nighest the scriptures." This answer is proof positive that it can never be accomplished on such grounds . . . We never expect that the sects will have a meeting to agree on principles of union . . . but we will attempt to show that there will be, or that there is now, a scheme of things presented, in what is called the *Ancient Gospel,* which is long enough, broad enough, strong enough for the whole superstructure called the Millennial Church—and that it will alone be the *instrument of converting* the whole human race, and of *uniting* all christians upon one and the same foundation.[100]

Campbell held that the original unity of the primitive church had been destroyed by the development of denominational creeds and their elevation to a position of authority greater than that of the Bible. In advocating the local autonomy of congregations and the recognition of the New Testament as the only rule of faith and practice for those churches, restorationism was his means of eradicating (or perhaps transcending) the denominational structures and the creeds that had divided Christianity. In the first of his articles devoted to "A Restoration of the Ancient Order of Things," Campbell described the foundational significance of this phase:

A restoration of the ancient order of things is all that is necessary to the happiness and usefulness of christians . . . To bring the societies of christians up to the New Testament, is just to bring the disciples individually and collectively, to walk in the faith, and in the commandments of the Lord and Saviour . . . Celebrated as the era of reformation is, we doubt not but that the era of restoration will as far transcend it in importance and fame, through the long and blissful Millennium, as the New Testament transcends in simplicity, beauty, excellency, and majesty, the dogmas and notions of the creed of Westminster and the canons of the Assembly's Digest. Just in so far as the ancient order of things, or the religion of the New Testament, is restored, just so far has the Millennium commenced, and so far have its blessings been enjoyed.[101]

The relationship between the three fundamental precepts of Campbell's restoration plea, then, was not merely one of chronological progression but one of logical and essential interdependence. As Hughes and Allen note, "in Campbell's thought . . . the primordial age and the millennial age were but opposite and congruent ends of the same historical continuum. What made them congruent was simply that the former gave to the latter its texture and shape. Further, with Campbell, the continuum closed full circle and the congruent ends embraced and interlocked."[102]

Conclusion

In the decades following the union of 1832, the Stone-Campbell movement would experience tremendous growth, both numerically and institutionally. As the influence of the elder Stone began to wane following his move to Jacksonville, Illinois, in 1834, Campbell would exert unparalleled leadership within the movement, ceaselessly devoting his energies and resources to advocating this restoration plea.

His manner of advocacy, however, also reflects the influence of a rhetorical tradition with a long legacy. Before we proceed to close readings of significant rhetorical acts representative of Campbell's rhetorical leadership, we should also consider both the influences within which Campbell formed his philosophy of rhetoric and the more common characteristics of his application of the art.

Alexander Campbell's
Philosophy of Rhetoric

The tongue of the eloquent orator and the pen of the ready writer are
the two most potent instrumentalities of moral good or moral evil in the
world.[1]

The shipwreck that stranded Alexander and his family in Scotland for
the winter of 1808–09 led, by strange coincidence, to the realization of his
father's goal. Robert Richardson, Alexander's son-in-law and biographer,
points out that the intent of Thomas's instruction, clearly based on the
curriculum he experienced at Glasgow, was to prepare his son to someday
study under the professors there.[2] Because Alexander Campbell's experiences at the University of Glasgow would eventually have a profound
effect upon his philosophy of rhetoric, it is essential that we take notice
of this intellectual milieu. Subsequently, this chapter will also identify the
more common characteristics of the discourse through which he became
a significant leader within American Christianity.

Alexander Campbell at the University of Glasgow

Alexander Campbell matriculated at the University of Glasgow on November 8, 1808, and remained there through May of 1809. His last composition was dated June 1 of that year.[3] Richardson describes the nature
of his studies: "The classes he entered were those of Professor Young,
both public and private, in Greek; those of Professor Jardine, public and
private, in Logic and Belles Lettres, and Dr. Ure's class in Experimental
Philosophy . . . In addition to the above regular classes, he resumed the
study of French, and gave considerable time to English reading and composition."[4]

At that time, Winifred Horner points out, "Scottish lower schools
were free and varied in quality and students were not only young but
often ill prepared when they came to the universities," the average age
ranging from fourteen to sixteen years.[5] At the age of twenty, Campbell

was not only more mature than the typical student but better prepared. Richardson's biography indicates that his facility in Latin and Greek, acquired from his father, not only enabled him to read in the advanced classes but also to produce his own translations from Homer and Sophocles.[6]

As Michael Casey observes, Campbell would later reflect that the classical education he received from his father led him "directly or indirectly to the all absorbing subject of oratory or eloquence."[7] At Glasgow, he would have been able to gain experience in public speaking by participating in the university's debating and literary societies, one of which was affiliated with the logic course.[8] A fragment of "AN ORATION to be delivered on Saturday the 4th Feby. in the Society of Logicians—to prove that murder is the only crime to be punished by death," which survives among Campbell's Glasgow essays, suggests that he participated on at least one occasion.[9]

When Thomas Campbell enrolled in the "First Philosophy" class in 1783, George Jardine was in his ninth year of teaching that course which, by then, he had radically reformed after the principles expressed in his *Outlines of Philosophical Education*.[10] In 1808, Alexander enrolled in the same course, still taught by Jardine. The flyleaf on Alexander's class notes reads, "Lectures in Logick Delivered by Professor Jardan in the University of Glasgow, 1808."[11] Also, as Carisse Berryhill notes, his wife Selina, in 1873, donated to Bethany College the "certificates of the different classes in which he graduated at the Glasgow University" and one bears the signature "Geo. Jardine L. D."[12]

It is worth asking, then, how Jardine conceptualized the art of rhetoric and how this might have influenced Campbell. However, because Jardine's own view of rhetoric proves largely derivative,[13] we must begin with sources that exerted a more formative influence upon the "affective" tradition of rhetoric that dominated Scottish universities during the late eighteenth century.

The Intellectual Milieu

The Renaissance of the fourteenth, fifteenth, and sixteenth centuries shook the intellectual foundations of European culture and left in its wake radically new accounts of the world, human nature, and especially the human mind. The paradigmatic shifts that took place in philosophy, science, and psychology during these years had a significant impact upon subsequent views of rhetoric and the context of Alexander Campbell's formal and informal education. More specifically, the art of rhetoric, as it was conceptualized within the Scottish universities of the eighteenth century, was directly influenced by the faculty psychologies[14] of Bacon and Descartes, the associationist psychologies of Locke and Hartley, and the common sense realism of Buffier and Reid.

Francis Bacon characterized the operation of the mind as a chainlike interaction of various "faculties": Understanding (external senses turning objects of expression into objects of thought), Reason (comparing, classifying, generalizing, particularizing and/or judging the materials provided by Understanding), Imagination (retaining impressions made upon the senses as images), Memory (preserving a record of activity), Appetite and Will (sources of action).[15] Accordingly, he adopted an unconventionally restricted notion of the nature and purpose of rhetoric: "Rhetoric is subservient to the imagination as Logic is to the Understanding; and the Duty and Office of Rhetoric . . . is no other than to apply and recommend the dictates of Reason to Imagination, in order to excite the Appetite and Will . . . The end of Rhetoric is to fill the Imagination with manifestations and likenesses that bring aid to Reason."[16]

John Locke[17] identified two means by which the "simple" ideas generated by "sensation" and "reflection" could be connected to generate "complex" ideas: "reason" and "association." "Reason" could either *combine* several simple ideas into a compound idea, *compare* any two ideas (simple or complex) to observe the relations between them, or *abstract* a general idea out of a number of other ideas. "Association," however, refers to an arbitrary union, "wholly owing to *chance* or *custom,*" produced by a process of conditioning. He thus considered it a kind of "madness" that stood in "opposition to reason."[18] David Hartley adopted the principle of association as a comprehensive explanatory principle, reducing the operation of all mental faculties to a cause-effect relationship between neural vibration and association.[19] As to the effect of language upon the mind, Hartley held that "Words and Phrases must excite ideas in us by Association, and they excite Ideas in us by no other means."[20]

Collectively, these "modern" philosophers took a dim view of the conventional rhetoric of their day. For the faculty psychologists, rhetoric's ability to affect the imagination was fraught with the danger of hindering reason's ability to engage in logical inference. Locke held that rhetoric was "for nothing else but to insinuate wrong ideas, move the passions and thereby mislead the judgment," and so a "perfect cheat."[21] Alternatively, they advocated an art of rhetoric devoted to a type of "expository fidelity,"[22] a plain style that would ensure that the words used by speakers would invoke the same ideas in the minds of others that existed in their own.

In response to the problems he perceived in these psychological models,[23] Claude Buffier sought a first principle of knowledge that was neither solely in consciousness (i.e., "inside" the mind) nor sensation (i.e., "outside" the mind). He defined "common sense" as "the disposition which nature has put in all men, or clearly in the greatest number of men, to form . . . a common and uniform judgment concerning objects different from the objects of one's own consciousness." Thomas Conley points out that this ability to allow "the experience of objects, the probable, and matters of sound opinion" as legitimate, self-evident starting points of knowledge enabled Buffier to "rescue rhetoric from the oblivion to which both Descartes and Locke had sought to consign it."[24] Transmitted by Thomas Reid to his colleagues at Marischal College in Aberdeen, common sense realism would have a significant impact upon how rhetoric was taught there as well as at other Scottish universities (e.g., Edinburgh and Glasgow).

Though not identical in every respect, the notions of rhetoric that emerged within this intellectual milieu possessed a singularity of spirit.[25] As James Berlin has noted, common sense realism's affirmation of the mind's ability to directly know the external material world discouraged the use of "proofs" or argumentative commonplaces traditionally associated with the part of rhetoric known as "invention." Alternatively, the sum total of what was considered necessary to persuade was an ability to manage "facts," i.e., phenomena apparent to all, and an ability to "affect" the mind by appropriately engaging its faculties.[26] Thus, Conley's description of what Bacon meant by rhetoric aptly sums up these Scottish rhetorics as well: "Rhetoric is the means by which knowledge may be made 'present' to the imagination; and the proper study of rhetoric is the systematic examination of the affective possibilities of language, which is used by reason to affect the imagination 'to excite the appetite or will'."[27]

The influence of faculty psychologies and common sense realism are manifest in several common features of these Scottish rhetorics: a separation of "persuasion" (the realm of rhetoric) from "conviction" (the realm of logic) with each assigned to a different faculty of the mind, a severe attenuation of interest in classical modes of argument, and a privileging of the affective powers of style. Although the work of Hugh Blair (University of Edinburgh) also illustrates this Scottish "affective" tradition of rhetoric in important ways,[28] we shall restrict our current discussion to those individuals who most directly influenced Alexander Campbell: George Campbell (Marischal College in Aberdeen) and George Jardine (University of Glasgow).

George Campbell and the "Affective" Tradition of Rhetoric

George Campbell (1719–1796) was appointed principal at Marischal College in Aberdeen in 1759 and, in 1771, professor of divinity. His *Philosophy of Rhetoric* (1776) would become his most influential work.[29] Although the influence of Reid, Buffier, Bacon, and others on George Campbell's *Philosophy of Rhetoric* has been thoroughly documented elsewhere,[30] a brief overview is warranted here. Specifically, his understanding of the nature and ends of the art, his views about the use of evidence, his recommendations for the arrangement of discourse, and the powers he attributed to style are worthy of note.

Acknowledging from the outset his intention to ground rhetoric in the "science" of his day and his debt to Bacon in particular, George Campbell defined oratory as "that art, whose object it is, by the use of language, to operate on the soul of the hearer in the way of informing, convincing, pleasing, moving or persuading." Similarly, he classified speeches according to the end sought and the faculty addressed: "Eloquence denotes that art or talent by which the discourse is adapted to its end" and "all ends of speaking are reducible to four; every speech being intended to enlighten the understanding, to please the imagination, to move the passions, or to influence the will."[31]

As to achieving these ends, George Campbell had little use for the classical syllogism. "The method of proving by syllogism" appeared to him "both unnatural and prolix" and bore to him "the manifest indications of an artificial and ostentatious parade of learning, calculated for giving the appearance of great profundity to what in fact is very shallow."[32] His chapter on evidence and reasoning (chapter five, book one) advocates, instead, a "logic of facts" grounded in the new empiricism.[33] Herein, evidence is divided into two categories: "intuitive" and "deductive."[34] The former provides the latter with data; the latter reasons from this data to conclusions.

Sources of intuitive evidence include "intellection" or "perception" (i.e., mathematical axioms that are self-evident), "consciousness" (one's "absolute certainty in regard to the reality of his sensations," i.e., the impressions made on our minds by the shape, size, color, etc. of external objects), and "common sense," the principles for which he credits Buffier and Reid.[35]

"Demonstration" and "moral reasoning" are the two processes by which conclusions are drawn from intuitive data. The former draws upon "intellection" to construct series or chains of axioms to draw out conclusions. The latter draws upon consciousness and common sense to infer facts from experience, analogy, testimony, and mathematical calculations. Rhetoric has little to do with demonstration; moral reasoning is its "proper province."[36]

According to Campbell, however, it is also necessary for the speaker to manage those principles properly in our nature that aid reason in promoting belief. After (and only after) addressing the understanding "to evince the truth" (conviction), the speaker then appeals to "the imagination, memory and the passion" and "ushers truth to the heart" (persuasion).[37] Hence, in his treatment of the various ends of eloquence, Campbell suggests that the "natural" order of the operation of the mind's faculties (understanding, imagination, passions, will) be followed when arranging or ordering the parts of a discourse: "In general, it may be asserted, that each preceding species [of discourse], in the order above exhibited, is preparatory to the subsequent; that each subsequent species is founded on the preceding; and that thus they ascend in a regular progression. Knowledge, the object of the intellect, furnisheth materials for the fancy; the fancy culls, compounds, and by her mimic art, disposes these materials so as to affect the passions; and the passions are the natural spurs to volition and action, and so need only to be rightly directed."[38] Though each of the species of rhetoric has its own qualities, that species "the most complex of all, which is calculated to influence the will, and persuade us to a certain conduct, is in reality an artful mixture of that which proposes to convince the judgment, and that which interests the passions" and "its distinguished excellency results from these two, the argumentative and the pathetic incorporated together."[39]

This need to supplement the appeal to "judgment" with an appeal to the "passions" explains why roughly two-thirds of *The Philosophy of Rhetoric* (all of books II and III) is devoted to Campbell's chief concern: the powers of style and their role in persuasion. Since persuasion can never, in his estimate, be accomplished by the eviction of truth alone but, rather, must always speak to the passions,[40] it is not enough that a discourse be true—even if it is true both in its "sentiment" and its "expression" (or style).[41] The "sense" and the "expression," according to book one, chapter four, are the "two essential parts of a speech" which constitute "the thought and the symbol" or "the soul and the body of the oration."[42] The circumstances under which the "sense" of a discourse both addresses the understanding and operates on the passions already having been considered (book one, chapter seven, section five), most of books two and three are devoted to those qualities of "expression" which not only "inform the understanding" but "please the imagination" and "work upon the passions" so that "language and thought, like body and soul, are made to correspond." These qualities are, primarily, "perspicuity" and "vivacity."[43]

"Perspicuity" is that quality of style "by which the discourse is fitted to inform the understanding."[44] Transparency is its ideal: "Perspicuity originally and properly implies *transparency*, such as may be ascribed to air, glass, water, or any other medium through which material objects are viewed. From this original and proper sense it hath been metaphorically applied to language, this being, as it were, the medium through which we perceive the notions and sentiments of a speaker."[45] Conversely, perspicuity is violated when one speaks "obscurely," "ambiguously," or "unintelligibly." Thus, like the grammatical purity described in the first four chapters of book II, perspicuity is essential for observing the expository fidelity between words and things necessitated by Campbell's associationism.[46]

"Vivacity," the focus of book III, is among "those qualities of style by which it [discourse] is adapted to please the imagination" and depends on "the choice of words, their number, and their arrangement." Specifically, figures and devices identified as contributing to vivacity include "specialty" —a preference for words as particular and determinant in their signification as possible. "The more general the term," Campbell observes, "the picture is the fainter; the more special they are, it is the brighter" and more likely to "fix the attention, or to impress the memory."[47]

What is important in all of this for our purposes, as we shall eventually see, is that the rhetoric of Alexander Campbell bears strong resemblances to the doctrines advocated by George Campbell in *The Philosophy of Rhetoric:* the use of common sense reasoning, the arrangement of discourse according to the "natural" progression from understanding to passions, and a style devoted, as his end deems appropriate, to the qualities of perspicuity and vivacity. However, Alexander Campbell's first acquaintance with this tradition of rhetoric came through another source—his own professor of rhetoric, George Jardine.

George Jardine: Alexander Campbell's Rhetoric Professor

Better known for his contributions to educational reform and his defense of the pedagogical philosophy and strategies which then distinguished the Scottish universities from those in England,[48] George Jardine's notion of rhetoric was largely derivative. Nonetheless, his work is important for our present purposes because, as Professor of Logic and Rhetoric at the University of Glasgow from 1774–1827, his students included both Thomas (1783–86) and Alexander (1808–09) Campbell.

His teachings on rhetoric were primarily indebted to George Campbell, as Berryhill notes: "Jardine promulgated the understanding of language and communication that George Campbell had formulated in *The Philosophy of Rhetoric* by applying the inductive method to speech and writing. This state of the art communication psychology, then, formed the base of all Alexander Campbell's linguistic, literary and rhetorical skills."[49] Thomas Reid was also Jardine's friend and mentor,[50] and once described his approach, which followed the familiar path of departing from the classical syllogism to embrace the new psychology.[51] Although Jardine's debts to Bacon, Campbell, and Reid can be amply illustrated from his *Synopsis of Lectures on Logic and Belles Lettres* (1804) as well as his *Outlines of Philosophical Education* (1818), a brief overview, drawn primarily from the synopsis of his lectures, will suffice here.

The object of Jardine's *Lectures on Logic and Belles Lettres* (one of the courses in which Alexander Campbell would enroll) was "to explain the methods of improving the powers or faculties of knowledge, of taste, and of communication by speaking or writing." Like George Campbell, his goal was to ground the principles of taste and communication in an understanding of the mind's "natural" operations: "The original constitution, the growth, progress and decline of the Human faculties form an important branch of the phenomena of nature. Distinct knowledge of Mind cannot be obtained in any other manner, than by directing and fixing the attention of the mind upon its own operations."[52]

He divided his synopsis into two parts, the first of which he devoted to the "powers or faculties of knowledge." Confident that "the analysis of the faculties of the mind may be successfully conducted according to the principles of the Baconian process of investigation," his "general division of the powers of the mind into those of the Understanding and the Will" reflects the same Baconian division of the faculties upon which George Campbell had based his argumentative (addressed to reason) and pathetic (addressed to passions) species of discourse.[53] Although his *Outlines of Philosophical Education* contains a more elaborate description of the familiar chainlike interaction of each of the mind's faculties,[54] a brief description was included at this point in the synopsis of his lectures as well.

Jardine introduced his analysis of "the powers of judging and reasoning" with a brief history of logic. Aristotle's invention of the syllogism as a model of reasoning, according to Jardine, introduced a "clearness and certainty of inference" previously lacking. However, in a manner again similar to that of George Campbell, he argued that subsequent developments in the history of logic began to reveal the "radical defects of that mode of reasoning and investigation" and that both Ramus and Descartes encountered difficulties in their attempts "to reform the ancient method of reasoning."[55]

Eventually, Jardine continued, "the art of reasoning received its greatest reform from the comprehensive mind of Lord Bacon" whose "object was not to reform the ancient system but to overthrow it, and to establish a better mode of reasoning in its place," i.e., "the mode of investigation delineated in his works, *De Augmentis Scientarium,* and his *Novum Organum.*" Thus, he concluded that "the experience of near two centuries has convinced the learned, that in Natural Philosophy, experiment and just induction alone are to be trusted" and that "the principle of the ancient mode of reasoning is radically defective." "Locke, Hume, Reid, Condillac, etc." would improve Bacon's method with even "more clear and distinct notions of the powers of knowledge."[56]

In the second division of his lectures, Jardine turned from the powers of knowledge to the powers of taste. Herein, his treatment of the qualities of style and the ends of discourse are both strikingly similar to George Campbell's. Qualities of style are either "essential" or "ornamental." He identified the "essential" qualities as perspicuity, propriety, purity, simplicity, and energy. The want of these essential qualities, he suggested, would render style defective in that it becomes obscure, affected, and feeble. Compositions may be categorized in the manner of Bacon, "according to the faculties of the mind employed in them, viz. Memory,

Imagination, and Reason." Or, they may be classified according to the end the composer has in view, either:

1. To prove some proposition, or to convince the judgment.
2. To narrate facts—for information, or instruction.
3. To excite emotions and passion—to persuade.

According to the latter scheme, he classified compositions as "Philosophical, Historical, or Rhetorical," respectively.[57]

Alexander Campbell's Glasgow Essays

Throughout his life, Alexander never failed to appreciate the significance of his brief tenure as a student at Glasgow.[58] In 1847, he returned to Scotland for a brief tour and visited the burial site of George Campbell "for whose memory he entertained the highest regard."[59] That he became, at some point in time, well acquainted with the works of George Campbell has been conclusively demonstrated by Berryhill's survey of the volumes in his library, the contents of his notebooks, and his published references to George Campbell's works, including two passing references and one extended reference to *The Philosophy of Rhetoric*.[60]

His tour also included a visit to his old university in Glasgow, an experience that, he later remarked, evoked "many a grateful reminiscence and pleasing association of ideas." In particular, he would recall Jardine as among "my special friends and favorites in the University" and his discussion of the faculty of attention as "the most useful series of college lectures, of which I have any recollection."[61]

His high regard for Jardine is further evidenced by the fact that, as Berryhill points out, "all of his life he kept the textbook he had used in Jardine's class and copies of the compositions written for him."[62] The survival of those notes and essays from Glasgow was discovered at least as early as 1952, when Bethany College received from Australia a handwritten manuscript entitled "Juvenile Essays written at University of Glasgow 1808–1809." What is significant for our purposes is that, as McAllister notes in his introduction to the essays published in 1971, "the essays in Alexander's notebook follow Jardine's method precisely."[63]

The first essay, "On Genius," illustrates Jardine's view of the nature and operation of the faculties of the mind: "Genius when applied to the understanding of men implies a superior degree of excellence in all the faculties of the mind, a Readiness and clearness of Reflection, a hardiness and proneness of attention, a facility of abstraction and Generalization, tenacity of memory but above all a strength and warmth of Imagination, with a soundness of Judgement and depth of Reason."[64] Specific descriptions by Campbell of the operations of the various faculties can be found later in the first essay and in the eighteenth essay, "On the Aristotelian method of Dispute." The roles of sensation, impression, and association in producing knowledge are included in his essay "On the Improvement of the Memory."[65]

Campbell's history of the art of logic in his eighth essay ("On the Socratic Dialogue") parallels that of Jardine from the first attempts of the Greeks to develop such an art and its degeneration into sophistry until "Socrates . . . arose and stemed [sic] the torrent,"[66] at which point he inserts an example of the Socratic dialogue. He does not resume the narrative but a later essay, "Of the Syllogism," provides an extended account of the nature, axioms, and rules of the Aristotelian syllogism. There is no indication of Jardine's rejection of the syllogism in the essays transcribed by McAllister but Berryhill points out that the companion manuscript of Campbell's class notes at Bethany College reveals that Baconian induction was preferred.[67]

However, even the essay transcribed by McAllister suggests that Campbell progressed from the syllogism to the method of reasoning preferred by both Jardine and George Campbell. Upon a referral to "pages of the Latin compend" which ends his account of the syllogism, Campbell initiates a brief discussion "On the Evidence of the Senses" in which such evidence is divided into "3 sorts—Inductive, Deductive and Testimony." Forms of inductive evidence are briefly described before we are referred to his notes.[68]

His sixth essay, "On the Construction of Sentences," illustrates the importance of the "essential" qualities of style since the arrangement of sentences should be "best calculated to express our thoughts and convey our Ideas in a clear perspicuous energetick [sic] manner." Toward this general end, sentences must "be arranged in a certain order and connection in such a manner as sense and Reason requires."[69]

His differentiation between "Philosophical Construction" and "Artificial, oratorical, or Poetical construction" parallels Jardine's classes of composition as well as the natural progression from species of discourse designed for the faculty of reason (i.e., argumentative) to those designed for an appeal to the passions (i.e., pathetic). "Philosophical" construction is that "dictated by Reason and in which the Words follow the connections of the matter." The "oratorical" or "poetical" construction, however, "has more in view than simply stating the fact or expressing the want . . . but also has for its end to instruct, persuade and phrase, in short, to command the passions." This construction is illustrated from Milton and the orations of Demosthenes and Cicero who "address the passion from the same motives and the Imagination."[70]

Alexander Campbell's own essays, then, attest to his grasp of that "affective" tradition of rhetoric that was so prominent within the Scottish universities of the late eighteenth century. However, the most significant evidence of the lasting influence of these Scottish educators lies in the rhetorical philosophy both expressed and practiced by Alexander Campbell on the soil of the early American republic.[71]

Alexander Campbell in America

One might easily assume that Campbell came to America and, fresh from his studies at Glasgow, immediately put his new philosophy of rhetoric to work in the service of his restoration plea. Such was not the case, however. Campbell's respect for his educators and their philosophies duly noted, the single most important influence upon Alexander was nonetheless his father, Thomas.[72]

Thomas Campbell had been trained in the Seceder Presbyterian Seminary to use the Ciceronian sermon arrangement that had dominated European preaching since the Middle Ages. He not only taught this method of sermonizing to his son but modeled it for him as well.[73] Casey observes that, when Alexander came to America, he "at first . . . naively assumed that the cultural and rhetorical context for America was the same as Ireland and Scotland" and prepared his early sermons after this aristocratic, Ciceronian form. But then, "slowly but surely, the American sociocultural context screened the classical and aristocratic rhetorical practices out of Alexander Campbell's preaching" and he "turned to the new modern Baconian Common Sense rhetorical views."[74] To do justice to these aspects of Campbell's rhetoric, we will briefly consider its more common and prevalent features.

"Common Sense" Reasoning

Common sense realism and Baconian method influenced the rhetoric of Alexander Campbell in fundamental ways. His commitment to a "logic of facts" is perhaps best illustrated by the views he held about the relationship between faith, fact, and testimony. In his discourse, it is manifest both in his approach to the Bible and his preference for historical and inductive proofs.

As Granville Walker once wrote, "Axiomatic with Campbell was the proposition that faith was essential to salvation, that testimony was essential to faith, and that facts were essential to testimony." Campbell accepted Francis Bacon's definition of a "fact": "*Fact* means something done . . . by *facts*, we always mean something said or done." The factual grounding of faith was the heart of his apologetic and his starting point for evangelical persuasion, for he considered Christianity "a religion founded upon the action of God within the scene of human events."[75] For Campbell, "All revealed religion is based upon facts . . . The works of God and the words of God, or the things done or spoken by God, are those facts which are laid down and exhibited in the Bible as the foundation of all faith, hope, love, piety, and humanity."[76] However, he recognized some facts as possessing a greater theological significance than others: "To enumerate the gospel facts, would be to narrate all that is recorded of the sayings and doings of Jesus Christ, from his birth to his coronation in the heavens. They are, however, concentrated in a few prominent ones, . . . " specifically his atoning death, burial, resurrection, and ascension.[77]

"Testimony," which in George Campbell's *Philosophy of Rhetoric* played a significant role in the evidences provided by common sense realism, was viewed by Alexander Campbell as the means by which "facts are understood or brought into immediate contact with the mind of man" and thus as the "channel through which these facts, or the hand of God, draws his image on the heart and character of man."[78] Testimony, in his view, provided the mind with a "report" of facts analogous to that provided by the senses in reference to material reality:

> In reference to the material system around us, to all objects and matters of sense, the eye, the ear, the smell, the taste, the feeling, are the five witnesses. What we call the evidence of the sense, is, therefore, the testimony of these witnesses, which constitute the

five avenues to the human mind from the kingdom of nature. They are figuratively called witnesses, and their evidence, testimony. But the report or declaration of intelligent beings, such as God, angels, and men, constitute what is properly and literally called *testimony*.

As light reflected from any material object upon the eye, brings that object into contact with the eye, or enables the object to make its images on the eye, so testimony concerning any fact, brings that fact into contact with the mind, and enables it to impress itself, or to form its image, upon the intellect, or mind of man. Now, be it observed, that as by our five external senses we acquire all information of the objects of sense around us, so by testimony, human or divine, we receive all our information upon all facts which are not the objects of the immediate exercise of our five senses upon the things around us.[79]

If facts are to "operate at all," then, "Testimony is ... necessary of the fact of which it speaks" for it provides the essential link between facts and faith: "*No testimony, no faith* ... To believe without testimony, is just as impossible as to see without light. The measure, quality, and power of faith are always found in the testimony believed. Where testimony begins, faith begins, and where testimony ends, faith ends."[80]

Faith, for Campbell, was thus "only the belief of testimony, or confidence in testimony as true" and was to be distinguished from both "knowledge" (consciousness and personal experience) and "opinion" (inferential or probable reason). In its relation to testimony and fact, it was thus also the end result of a natural process: "Hence, in the order of nature, there is first the fact, then the testimony, and then the belief ... This is the unchangeable and universal order of things as respects belief."[81]

That he considered faith not only a natural but almost inevitable response to the report of facts by testimony is evidenced in his discussion of the process of spiritual regeneration, the end of which extends from faith to feeling:

There is no connexion of cause and effect more intimate; there is no system of dependencies more closely linked; there is no arrangement of things more natural or necessary, than the ideas represented by the terms *fact, testimony, faith,* and *feeling*. The first is for the last, and the two intermediates are made necessary by the force of circumstances, as the means for the end. The fact, or the thing said or done, produces the change in the frame of mind. The testimony, or the report of the thing said or done, is essential to belief; and belief of it, is necessary to bring the thing said or done to the heart. The change of heart, is the end proposed in this part of the process of regeneration; and we may see that the process on the part of Heaven is, thus far, natural and rational: or in other words, consistent with the constitution of our nature.[82]

Because of Campbell's view of the relationship between fact, testimony, and faith and his concomitant distinction between faith, knowledge, and opinion, his rhetoric was capable, as we shall see, of an interesting juxtaposition of absolutism and tolerance. On one hand, his confidence in the evidentiary function of testimony to resolve issues of "fact" frequently manifested itself in an inflexible dogmatism. On the other hand, he consistently refused to impose upon others what he considered to be the personal "opinions" that he inferentially derived from these facts.

Campbell's "logic of facts" also significantly influenced his use of the Bible and his approach to reasoning. The Bible served as his most important source of facts and the repository of divine testimony: "God's own book is a book of facts."[83] He thus considered it both more authoritative and a more suitable foundation for Christian union than denominational creeds: "With us, revelation has nothing to do with opinions, or abstract reasonings; for it is founded wholly and entirely upon *facts*. There is not one abstract opinion, not one speculative view, asserted or communicated in Old Testament or New . . . Facts, then, are the *alpha* and *omega* of both Jewish and Christian revelations."[84] Campbell was especially fond of the book of Acts. One reason for this, as Lee Snyder has pointed out, was his subscription to the Baconian definition of fact—and Acts proved an ample storehouse of facts upon which his program of restoration could be modeled.[85]

However, Campbell approached all scripture as a source of empirical facts that could be studied "scientifically" and the impact of Baconian induction upon his hermeneutic is clear. Casey observes that a significant aspect of Campbell's turn to the common sense tradition was his effort to "understand the Bible afresh by 'natural' methods," i.e., using the methods of George Campbell "who applied the principles of Common

Sense philosophy to biblical criticism and rhetoric." Thus, he typically developed biblical doctrines by studying inductively all the passages on a topic and generalizing to a conclusion based on the contents of the particular passages. Similarly, his word studies demonstrated his belief that "language can be studied scientifically" by collecting "secular examples of the use of that ancient word" and then "comparing other biblical contexts in which it occurs" to determine its meaning.[86]

Not only did Campbell clarify the meaning of biblical testimony through inductive reasoning, he also employed proofs appropriate for defending the credibility of other historical testimony. According to Berryhill, George Campbell considered testimony (a report of an observed fact, such as a miracle) more credible than experience (a generalization from previous facts), provided that the witnesses met appropriate criteria. For Alexander, similarly, the credibility of testimony did not depend upon whether one's previous experience had judged it probable but whether those events had been accurately reported. Consequently, Campbell's reasoning in defense of testimony dealt primarily with rules of observation and qualifications of witnesses and the most common proofs in Campbell's debates were appeals to historical testimony, inductive word studies, and the presentation of inferences from observation, consciousness, and common sense.[87] In sum, Campbell's strict adherence to Baconian induction and common sense principles of testimony are amply evident in his rhetoric.

"Natural" Arrangement

In his early preaching, Alexander Campbell followed his father's pattern and instruction, employing a classical Ciceronian arrangement typical of medieval European sermons.[88] Casey summarizes Robert Richardson's account of Campbell's first sermon:

> Presuming that he would preach among fellow Scottish and Irish immigrants, he wrote out his first sermon while crossing the Atlantic . . . and delivered it memorized on July 15, 1810 on a farm near Washington, Pennsylvania . . . The sermon on Matthew 7:23–27, the story of the wise man and the foolish man from the Sermon on the Mount, followed the Ciceronian form closely. The exordium had six parts, ranging from the importance of Christ's sayings, to comments about the Sermon on the Mount in general.

The division or method of the sermon listed the doctrines of the text. Here he compared and contrasted the wise man and the foolish man. The subdivisions compared their similar privileges, employment and trials, and contrasted their character, manner of employment, and their end . . . [He] explained the metaphorical words: house, rock, sand, wind, and rain . . . [and] following Blair's suggestion for a peroration in a sermon, Campbell's conclusion made applications by drawing two inferences from his sermon theme. . . . [89]

This medieval Ciceronian arrangement can be found in Campbell's preaching as late as his "Sermon on the Law" of 1816,[90] which we will examine thoroughly in the next chapter.

Over time, however, both the content and form of Campbell's sermons began to shift in response to the expectations of western audiences and by 1823 he had rejected this classical approach to arrangement.[91] In "The Missionary Cause," his 1860 address to the American Christian Missionary Society (the subject of chapter five), Campbell noted that he spent the seven years after his "Sermon on the Law" reviewing his past studies.[92] It was presumably during this period that Campbell rejected the medieval Ciceronian method as incompatible with George Campbell's scientific approach to interpreting texts and his common sense, "natural" philosophy of rhetoric.

Berryhill has described how he subsequently "adapted George Campbell's hierarchical series of purposes into a single evangelistic sequence."[93] Just as George Campbell's *Philosophy of Rhetoric* arranged the purposes of informing, delighting, moving, and persuading according to the order in which the relevant mental faculties were be addressed (understanding, imagination, passions, will), so Alexander Campbell recommended that preachers

first address themselves to the understanding, by a declaration or narrative of the wonderful works of God. They state, illustrate, and prove the great facts of the gospel; they lay the whole record before their hearers; and when they have testified what God has done, what he has promised, and threatened, they exhort their hearers on these premises, and persuade them to obey the gospel, to surrender themselves to the guidance and direction of the Son of God. They address themselves to the whole man, his understanding, will and affections, and approach the heart by taking the citadel of the understanding.[94]

Reason, Campbell insisted, must function as a guide for the passions. In one of his "Sermons to Young Preachers," he observed,

All evidences are addressed to the higher and more noble faculties of man. The understanding, and not the passions, is addressed; and therefore an appeal to the latter, before the former is enlightened, is as unphilosophic as it is unscriptural. As the helm guides the ship, and the bridle the horse, so reason is the governing principle of man. Now in preaching Jesus, arguments are to be used— and these are found in the testimony of God. To declare that testimony, and to adduce the evidences which support it, is to proclaim the gospel.[95]

Campbell considered this process not only scientific but biblical as well, once referring to Jesus and his apostles as preachers who "first addressed the understanding of men" and "sought not to move their passions until proper subjects were presented to them."[96] Interpreted in this context, Campbell's criticisms of emotionalism are probably best understood not as a denial that rhetoric should appeal to *pathos* but, as we shall soon see, as a recognition that the "enthusiasts" failed to ground their emotional appeals in historical testimony—i.e., that they failed to address the reason before addressing the passions.

Casey has illustrated Campbell's use of this "natural" method of arrangement in two of his published sermons. In "On the Justification and Coronation of the Messiah" (1850), based on 1 Timothy 3:16, Campbell first engages in a textual criticism of his main passage, next explores the meaning of "justify," then narrates the death and coronation of Christ and concludes with a brief exhortation. In "The Riches of Christ" (1836), Campbell introduces and illustrates his theme, derives from the theme four conclusions as to its obligations upon the audience, and exhorts his audience to act.[97]

"Pure" Language and "Affective" Style

George Campbell's concern for the qualities of purity, perspicuity, and vivacity in style reflected not only his associationist demand for linguistic fidelity but his division of the mind's faculties into specialized functions, each with its own distinct verbal mode of expression.[98] Similarly, Alexander Campbell's rhetoric vigorously espoused and applied his own restorationist version of linguistic purity while observing the respective roles of perspicuity and vivacity in "affecting" the faculties of the understanding (in addressing reason) and imagination (in arousing the passions).

From 1825–1829 Campbell published a series of thirty articles devoted to the "Restoration of the Ancient Order of Things" (*The Christian Baptist*). Immediately following his arguments favoring "restoration" over "reformation" (number one) and an abandonment of creeds (as human inferences that divide the church) in favor of the sufficiency of holy scripture as a comprehensible confession of faith (numbers two and three), his article on "Nomenclature" contended that "another important preliminary to the restoration of the ancient order of things" was "an abandonment of the new and corrupt nomenclature, and a restoration of the inspired one."[99] A pure, biblical speech respected not only the wisdom of God but also a natural relationship between words, ideas, and human understanding:

> This is a matter of greater importance than may, at first sight, appear to all. Words and names long consecrated, and sanctified by long prescription, have a very imposing influence upon the human understanding. We think as well as speak by words . . . Now as all correct ideas of God and things invisible are supernatural ideas, no other terms can so suitably express them as the terms adopted by the Holy Spirit, in adapting those supernatural truths to our apprehension . . . Besides, when men adopt terms to express themselves, it is not the truths themselves, but their ideas of them they communicate. They select such terms as suit their apprehensions of revealed truth, and hence the terms they use are expressive only of their conceptions of divine things, and must just be as imperfect as their conceptions are. It is impossible for any man, unless by accident, to express accurately that which he apprehends imperfectly. From this source spring most of our doctrinal controversies . . . In order, then, to a full restoration of the ancient order of things, there must be a "pure speech" restored. And I think the Lord once said, in order to a restoration, that he would restore to the people a "pure speech."[100]

For Campbell, this pure speech could be violated in either of two ways: "The former dialect rejects the words of the Holy Spirit, and adopts others as more intelligible, less ambiguous, and better adapted to preserve a pure church. The latter dialect takes the terms and sentences of the Spirit, and makes them convey ideas diverse from those communicated by the Spirit."[101] To express his "cure" for these ills, Campbell would eventually coin a phrase that would become a popular slogan within his movement: "*We choose to speak of Bible things by Bible words,* because we are always suspicious that if the word is not in the Bible the idea which it represents is not there; and always confident that the things taught by God are better taught in words, and under the names which the Holy Spirit has chosen and appropriated, than in the words which man's wisdom teaches. There is nothing more essential to the union of the disciples of Christ than purity of speech."[102]

In addition to respecting the need for linguistic fidelity in the pursuit of understanding, Campbell adapted the style of his rhetoric to privilege either perspicuity or vivacity as he appealed, respectively, to either reason or the passions. On several occasions, Alexander Campbell identified "perspicuity" as a quality of style that contributed to the clearness, intelligibility, and precision of expression—not only to that of a speaker but in that of the Bible itself, remarking both about the Greek language of the New Testament as well as its better translations.[103] In practice, he regularly toiled to make precise distinctions between the meanings of different terms, as we shall see on several occasions in subsequent chapters. In another of his "Sermons to Young Preachers," he advised his readers: "In the art of speaking, the great secret is first to form clear conceptions of the subject to be spoken; and then to select such terms as exactly express our conceptions. To do this naturally, is the consummation of the art of speaking."[104]

Alexander Campbell drew directly upon the work of George Campbell to describe the role of "vivacity" in rhetoric. In 1835, he published *Christianity Restored,* a volume designed to "place before the community" a "miniature view" of the restorationist principles that he had "elicited, argued out, developed and sustained" over the past twenty-five years, "a concentrated view of the whole ground we occupy." His position that "the *Bible alone* was . . . the only measure and standard of faith and duty" necessitated that the first of the volume's three parts be devoted to "such cardinal principles as are necessary to the right interpretation of the Holy

Scriptures."[105] At the end of chapter fourteen, as he concludes his discussion of rhetorical tropes, he cites the *Philosophy of Rhetoric:*

> Before dismissing these *seven tropes,* or figures of words, we
> would still more emphatically observe, that as man is always con-
> templated as endowed with imagination, as well as with reason;
> and as his reason can be most agreeably and effectually applied to
> a subject, when his imagination is engaged,—figurative language
> has this advantage over literal,—that it not only affords clearer
> and more impressive views of things, but it also captivates the
> imagination, and thus pleases while it instructs. "The qualities in
> ideas," as Dr. George Campbell well observes, "which gratify the
> fancy, are vivacity, beauty, sublimity, novelty. Nothing contributes
> more to vivacity, than striking resemblances in the imagery, which
> convey besides, an additional pleasure of their own."[106]

Specific devices of vivacity are also abundant in Alexander Campbell's own rhetoric: individuation and tropes—which address the eye—as well as alliteration (repeated letters at the beginning of words), anaphora (repetition in the beginning of sentences) and epistrophe (repetition of sounds at the end of clauses and sentences)—which address the ear. Our analyses of specific cases will, in due course, cite several examples.

"Conversational" Delivery

Because both oral and written discourse played critical roles in Campbell's rhetorical leadership, our subsequent analyses will not be strictly limited to oratory. Given the significance of his oratory, however, some remarks about the character of his delivery are in order.[107]

Alexander would eventually prefer the advice of Jardine over that of George Campbell as to whether a speaker should memorize, read, or present his speech extemporaneously. George Campbell held that either memorization or extemporaneous speaking was more effective than reading a manuscript, although he recommended reading for those of lesser ability. Jardine discouraged memorization and stressed the importance of attaining the more accomplished extemporaneous delivery.[108]

Alexander Campbell's first sermon in America, we noted earlier, was written out and memorized for delivery on July 15, 1810. However, in these first sermons, he later remarked, he "felt as embarrassed as one corseted."

On September 2, just five weeks later, he forsook this practice in favor of speaking extemporaneously from a few notes, including the general divisions of his sermon. Eventually, he gave up the use of notes altogether.[109]

Though he refused the practice of memorization, his abilities as a speaker extempore were clearly aided by an exceptional memory. His sermons on tour averaged between one hour and three and a half hours in length. In his 1829 debate with Robert Owen, Campbell continued to speak extempore for twelve hours (broken into several sessions over two days) after Owen had finished reading a prepared manuscript and surrendered the floor.[110]

Today, we would probably describe Campbell's manner of delivery as "conversational." In keeping with his philosophy of rhetoric, he preferred to describe it as "natural." In one of his "Sermons to Young Preachers," he concluded, "I do think that nature, when followed, is a better teacher of eloquence than Longinus, or all the Grecian and Roman models . . . There is more true grace and dignity in a speech pronounced in the natural tone of our own voice, and in the natural key, than in all the studied mimicry of mere actors, whether stage or pulpit actors. . . . "[111] In another of these sermons, he also advised them, "Nothing is more disgusting to persons of good judgment than affectation. But to affect an awkward and disgusting original or model, makes affectation doubly disgusting. There is nothing more pleasing than the artless simplicity which sincerity produces. We love nature more than art. While we sometimes admire the skill of the artist, we, nevertheless, more admire and are pleased with the work of nature. So the unaffected orator never fails to reach our hearts or to touch our sensibilities sooner, and with more effect, than the imitator."[112]

Campbell also considered this "natural" delivery more consistent with biblical models. He once listened to a description of his delivery by one of his contemporaries, "Raccoon" John Smith: "You leaned upon your cane easily, though somewhat awkwardly, and talked as men commonly talk." Campbell's reply indicated that, though he had studied the "arts of elocution," he purposefully chose a natural style of delivery. He referred Smith to the examples of apostolic preaching in the New Testament: "Suppose that one of them should . . . have plied his arms in gesticulations, stamped his foot in vehemence, and declared his testimony . . . and in a loud stentorian voice?" Instead, Campbell contended that such addresses were characterized by a "composure of manner, natural emphasis, and solemn deliberation."[113] Elsewhere, he would write that there was, in these cases, "no pomp or pageantry of language—no fine lights of fancy —no embellishments of the rhetorical character" and that they made "no effort to soften the heart by melting tones, gentle cadences, or an impassioned mannerism."[114]

None of this should be taken to suggest that Campbell had much patience with lifeless delivery. He once chastised a student for a "dead, cold, monotony" in his reading of a passage.[115] Nor did he consider natural delivery entirely devoid of *pathos*, a quality that he considered extemporaneous speaking best able to impart: "Our words react upon ourselves according to their importance, and hence, we are sometimes wrought up to a pathos, a fervor, an ecstasy, indeed, by the mysterious sound of our own voice upon ourselves, as well as that of others, to which we never could have ascended without it. Hence the superior eloquence of extemporaneous speaking over that of those who read or recite what they have cooly or deliberately thought at some time and in some other place."[116] Campbell's "natural" delivery thus sought what he considered an appropriate balance between reason (*logos*) and passion (*pathos*), seeking to avoid the excesses of enthusiasm on one hand and dull monotony on the other. He believed that the earnestness of a "natural" delivery could attain "an eloquence that would make even an impenitent king tremble before an unjustly arraigned Christian minister"[117] and at the same time achieve a transparency of discourse that would not detract from the ability of its rational dimensions to address the faculty of reason.

Richardson's memoirs include an account of Campbell's speaking[118] based on firsthand experience:

Nothing indeed was more striking than his singular ability to interest his hearers in the subject of which he treated. With this his own mind was preoccupied, and, being free from all thoughts of self, there was in his address an entire absence of egotism, and nothing in his delivery to direct the attention away from the theme on which he discoursed . . . Without any gestures, either empathic or descriptive, the speaker stood in the most natural and easy attitude, resting upon his innate powers of intellect and his complete mastery of the subject, impressing all with the sense of a superior presence and a mighty mind. His enunciation was distinct, his diction chaste and simple, his sentences clear and forcible. The intonations of his clear ringing voice were admirably adapted to the sentiment, while by his strong and bold emphasis upon important words he imparted to what was said a peculiar force and authority.[119]

Summary

When any leader attains, chiefly through discursive means, an influence of such breadth and duration as Campbell's, it is highly unlikely to be the result of any one factor alone. Such a complex phenomenon cannot plausibly be reduced to a single cause. The matters covered in these first two chapters suggest several contributing factors. Clearly, the themes of Campbell's rhetoric were a rich seed that found fertile soil in the utopian optimism, the love of liberty, and the egalitarian ideology that permeated the still young democracy of the Jacksonian era. Schlesinger, Stevenson, Hatch, Hughes and Allen, among others, have covered these matters in more detail. Certainly, Casey has correctly identified a significant factor in Campbell's influence—his shift from an aristocratic Ciceronianism to a natural Baconianism, through which he forged an American democratic form of rhetoric out of a Scottish rhetoric designed for gentlemen. Similarly, Berryhill's analysis of the impact of faculty psychology and George Campbell's *Philosophy of Rhetoric* upon Alexander's "natural" rhetoric indicates some of the advantages inherent in a rhetoric thus well suited for a culture in which the dominant philosophy was common sense realism.

Nor should we underestimate the benefits that accrued to Campbell as a result of certain material advantages. Marrying into wealth alleviated him of the burden to earn a living that weighed so heavily upon his father and secured for him that freedom necessary for extensive research, reflection, writing, and speaking. As the postmaster of his hometown, Bethany, Virginia, Campbell the editor and publisher also enjoyed the perk of free postage for all of his publications.[120]

The present volume seeks neither to reject nor to alter any of these important contributions made by the authors mentioned above. However, it is also important for us to remember that rhetorical acts are both designed for and experienced in the particular. They both shape and are shaped by the exigencies and constraints inherent in the rhetorical situation of the moment. The larger constitutive possibilities of rhetoric notwithstanding, it is precisely rhetoric's radical attention to the particular, the contingent and the local, ephemeral character of its situatedness that distinguishes its essence as an art. Aristotle noted this long ago, when he defined the art of rhetoric as "an ability, in each [particular] case, to see the available means of persuasion."[121]

What the subsequent chapters attempt to illustrate is Alexander Campbell's keen sense of the demands of the specific rhetorical situation. As his restoration movement evolved over time, Campbell faced radically shifting rhetorical situations. His ability to adapt his rhetoric to the exigencies and constraints within those situations generated for him an evolving leadership *ethos* that was progressively adapted to the shifting needs of the movement.

These close readings will describe the discursive strategies featured in four key rhetorical episodes, ranging from 1816 to 1860, which transpired at critical junctions within the movement's first generation—at moments when Campbell's leadership was at a premium. Their aim is to disclose how Campbell's evolving leadership *ethos* emerges from within the rhetorical action of these speeches and texts. This, after all, is how people experienced the rhetorical leadership of Alexander Campbell—first as a prophet, then as a pastor, and finally as a patriarch.

3

The "Sermon on the Law" and
the Art of Constitutive Rhetoric

It is . . . highly probable to my mind, that but for the persecution begun
on the alleged heresy of this sermon, whether the present reformation
had ever been advocated by me.[1]

In the years following his arrival in America (1809), Alexander Campbell
gradually became a well-known preacher among the Baptist churches of
Pennsylvania, West Virginia, and Ohio. He delivered his first public address in the spring of 1810, at the request of his father. Meeting with a
small congregation in the private home of Jacob Donaldson, Thomas delivered a sermon and, following a short intermission, Alexander delivered
a brief exhortation. He was afterwards encouraged to prepare and deliver
his first full sermon, which he did in a grove on a farm eight miles from
Washington on July 15 of that year. His services were soon in great demand; Richardson records that Alexander delivered no less than 106 sermons during his first year of preaching. He was officially ordained to the
ministry of the Brush Run Church on January 1, 1812.[2]

A key development during these early years was a significant shift in
the Campbells' position on the mode and purpose of baptism. As Presbyterians, they had accepted the practice of infant baptism. In response
to the positions published in the *Declaration and Address,* they were challenged to find biblical warrant for that practice.

At first, they passed the matter off as insignificant. Thomas's petition
to the Presbyterian Synod of Pittsburgh on behalf of the Christian Association of Washington declared his view that infant baptism was not authorized by biblical precept or example but also indicated that he considered it a matter of indifference and that he continued to administer it in
spite of his opinion. On February 3 and May 19, 1811, as well as on June 5,
1812, Alexander delivered a sermon which illustrated that he considered
the matter of small importance, stating "As I am sure it is unscriptural to
make this matter a term of communion, I let it *slip.* I wish to think and
let think on these matters."[3]

However, the birth of Alexander's first child and the question of her baptism eventually forced him to a thorough restudy of the matter. His conclusions led him to reject infant sprinkling in favor of the immersion of adult believers. Matthias Luce, a Baptist preacher, agreed to so baptize Alexander, Thomas, and their wives. Soon, the church at Brush Run became a congregation of immersed believers. Whereas this development further fueled the antagonism between Brush Run and Presbyterians in the region, it also resulted in friendly overtures from the Baptists. Members of the Redstone Baptist Association began to urge Brush Run to join them. By the time Brush Run was admitted to the Association in 1815, the pulpits of area Baptist churches had been opened to Alexander and he soon became a popular albeit controversial figure.

Alexander Campbell's "Sermon on the Law" (1816)

Alexander Campbell would preach his most famous sermon on September 1, 1816, at the annual meeting of the Redstone Baptist Association in Cross Creek, Virginia[4]. Although Brush Run would remain a member of the Redstone Baptist Association until 1825 and Alexander would remain a Baptist until at least the late 1820s, church historians generally regard his "Sermon on the Law" as "the point of origin of the separation from the Baptists"[5] and some hail the occasion as the "actual beginning of the Restoration Movement."[6] In 1846, Campbell reflected upon this sermon as a key link in a "chain of providential events" and commented upon its significance for the future of his movement: "This unfortunate sermon afterwards involved me in a seven years' war with some members of the said Association, and became a matter of much debate . . . It is . . . highly probable to my mind, that but for the persecution begun on the alleged heresy of this sermon, whether the present reformation had ever been advocated by me."[7]

The purpose of this chapter is to provide a close reading of this sermon that will explore its constitutive significance both for Campbell's restoration movement and his own rhetorical leadership. A textual analysis of the sermon will illustrate both the Ciceronian dimensions of Campbell's early preaching as well as his common sense approach to language and biblical criticism. This analysis will also provide a basis for identifying the ideological effects through which the sermon called a reforming-restoring community into being and constructed for Campbell a leadership *ethos* that embodied the virtues of a true Protestant reformer. First, however, we should consider the rhetorical situation within which the sermon was delivered.

Situation: A "Seven Years' War"

The relationship between the Brush Run Church and the Redstone Baptist Association had been uneasy and ambivalent from the outset. The initial overtures from the Association were received with little interest. However, a felt need for fellowship with other congregations and a desire to avoid creating another religious sect while pleading for Christian unity eventually brought the question of affiliation before the church for a decision.[8] Brush Run Church eventually decided to apply for admission on its own terms. With their application, they submitted a document specifying the conditions under which they would accept membership. Campbell later described this document as "Some eight or ten pages of larger dimensions, exhibiting our remonstrance against all human creeds as bonds of union or communion among Christian churches, and expressing a willingness, on certain conditions, to co-operate or unite with that Association; provided only, and always, that we should be allowed to preach and teach whatever we learned from the Holy Scriptures, regardless of any creed or formula in Christendom."[9] The Association, on the other hand, still submitted to the authority of the Philadelphia Confession of 1742[10] and there was much debate about whether to admit Brush Run under such conditions. The church was admitted by majority vote in 1815 but a vocal minority remained in objection. A situation ripe for controversy had begun to develop.

It was also true that Brush Run was hardly "Baptist" in either doctrine or practice. In addition to their differences on the authority of creeds and the import of baptism, other significant differences between Brush Run and Redstone included their views on the relationship between the Old and New Testaments, the role of the Holy Spirit in conversion, the frequency of observing the Lord's Supper, the status of the clergy, and the requirement of a religious "experience" as a necessary condition for admission into the church. At the annual meeting of the Association in 1816, Thomas Campbell presented an application for the admission, upon similar conditions, of a small congregation he had organized in Pittsburgh. Its rejection was indicative, not only of the ambivalence toward Brush Run in general, but also of the suspicion with which many Baptist clergy viewed the Campbells in particular.[11]

The aforementioned annual meeting of 1816 was convened on Friday,

August 30, at the Cross Creek Baptist Church in Cross Creek, Virginia —only ten miles from Alexander Campbell's home. By this time he had achieved sufficient popularity to be advocated by many as a keynote speaker for the Lord's Day (Sunday, September 1). However, the host minister, John Pritchard, nursed more than one grudge against Campbell. For one matter, Pritchard had been among the vocal dissenters objecting to the admission of Brush Run into the Redstone Association. For another, toward the end of 1815, Campbell also assisted in the planting of a new church just three miles south of Cross Creek by raising over $1,000 for its new building while traveling to Philadelphia, New York, and Washington. Pritchard was less than pleased with this development.[12]

Privately, Campbell confided to his wife that, in spite of strong popular support, he did not expect to be permitted to speak. To no one's surprise, Pritchard zealously opposed Campbell's nomination. On Saturday, speakers were nominated for Sunday and when Campbell's name was placed in nomination, Pritchard immediately objected, claiming the right, as host minister, to name the speakers. He argued that, because Campbell lived in the vicinity, he could be heard anytime. Appealing to a precedent set by Maryland Baptists of selecting preachers from distance, Pritchard called upon Elijah Stone of Ohio to speak the next day. So many people were disappointed at the turn of events that they sent a delegate, David Phillips, to urge Campbell to address the Association anyway. Campbell, however, refused to violate the decision of the Association.[13]

Phillips, though, would soon return with the news that Stone had suddenly become ill. Campbell would later look back upon this event and consider it an act of divine providence: "He providentially was suddenly seized by sickness and I was unexpectedly called upon in the morning. . . . "[14] At this point, Campbell consented to speak—upon the condition that Pritchard himself extend the invitation. This he did, meeting Campbell as he drove up to the bridge at Cross Creek,[15] no more than two hours before Campbell actually delivered the sermon—the second of three speakers that day. Thus Campbell would later describe it as "a rather extemporaneous address." It was not completely impromptu, however— as evidenced by another extant outline dated June 6, 1813, which adopted the same biblical text and employed the same headings as the "Sermon on the Law" of 1816.[16]

Because the size of the church building was inadequate for the large crowd, Campbell spoke outdoors. At one point, Pritchard seized upon an occasion to interrupt the sermon. When a woman in the congregation fainted, he rushed up to the stand and created a great disturbance. After the commotion, Campbell had to regain his audience's attention to continue his address.[17]

During the intermission following the sermon, Pritchard quickly organized a meeting of the Baptist preachers, urging them to call for a public condemnation of the sermon as heresy before the meeting was dismissed. Cooler heads prevailed for the moment and at least one preacher requested time to examine the matter. Thus Campbell felt "obliged to gather it [his sermon] up from a few notes and commit it to writing."[18] He had it printed that same year in Steubenville, Ohio, and distributed it in pamphlet form to protect himself from false charges and misrepresentations.[19]

However, the "seven years' war," as Campbell described it, had commenced. Charges of heresy were circulated and Baptist pulpits began to close to Campbell. At the next annual meeting (1817), several charges were brought against Campbell and his "Sermon on the Law" but the Association was not yet willing to take a position against him. Efforts to discredit Campbell among the Baptist churches continued and, by 1823, his antagonists felt confident of sufficient support to have Campbell dismissed from the Association at that year's annual meeting. Campbell, though, learned of their plans and transferred his church membership to a congregation in Wellsburg, Ohio, that belonged to the Mahoning Association. When he attended the 1823 meeting of the Redstone Association, as an observer but not as a member, he was beyond its jurisdiction and the plot to defrock him was foiled.[20]

Campbell's personal war with his Redstone detractors thus ended with a whimper. However, by 1825 the Brush Run Church would be excluded from the Redstone Association and a general purging of "Campbellite" churches from Baptist associations in Kentucky, Pennsylvania, and Virginia would begin.[21] Campbell's "Sermon on the Law," then, was a significant turning point both in his own life and in the history of his movement.

Analysis: A Sermon Both Classical and Modern

The more obvious features of the "Sermon on the Law" illustrate both the medieval Ciceronianism of Campbell's early preaching and the extent to which his approach to language and biblical criticism had already been influenced by Baconianism and common sense realism. He used Romans 8:3 as a text for his sermon: "For what the law could not do, in that it was weak through the flesh, God, sending his own son in the likeness of sinful flesh, and for sin, condemnèd sin in the flesh." In a brief "exordium" (i.e., introductory remarks), he called attention to the term "law" as "one of the most important words in our text" and proposed the need "precisely to ascertain what ideas should be attached to it . . . by a close investigation of the context, and a general knowledge of the scriptures."[22] He then "partitioned" his oration into those divisions to be explicated and proven:

> In order to elucidate and enforce the doctrine contained in this verse, we shall scrupulously observe the following
>
> ### Method
> 1. We shall endeavor to ascertain what ideas we are to attach to the phrase, *"the law,"* in this, and similar portions of the sacred scriptures.
> 2. Point out those things which *the law* could not accomplish.
> 3. Demonstrate the reason why *the law* failed to accomplish those objects.
> 4. Illustrate how God has remedied those relative defects of *the law.*
> 5. In the last place, deduce such conclusions from these premises, as must obviously and necessarily present themselves to every unbiassed, and reflecting mind.[23]

As Stevenson points out, the first four headings constitute the "divisions of the text" and the fifth the "applications" (or "uses") of the text, both customary in the simplified adaptation of medieval Ciceronian arrangement common to Puritan sermon structure.[24] The proportion of "divisions" to "uses" (which consist of five separate conclusions) is roughly symmetrical.

Years later, Campbell would offer his own description of the "text preaching" that grew out of medieval homiletics:

> When the text is once or twice read, the preacher proceeds to his introduction, which resembles the exordium of a pagan oration, then comes to his method or distribution, in which he cuts to pieces the text, and after having considered its metaphysical, lit-

eral, anagogical, spiritual, and practical import, and having cautioned his hearers on the great danger of resting on the literal meaning of the text, and of the great necessity of looking through the letter (which is sometimes called dead) to the spirit of the text, which gives life, he proceeds to the improvement of the subject, and having deduced the necessary inferences, he concludes with a fervid and pathetic exhortation.[25]

Although his "Sermon on the Law" clearly rejected the Augustinian allegorical (four-sense) hermeneutic in favor of the more scientific criticism of George Campbell, it otherwise followed this form precisely.

Although Romans 8:3 served as the sermon "text," its function, as customary within this homiletical tradition, was merely to provide a theme that would be amplified through the use of a number of biblical passages. Campbell later observed, "When I commenced preaching it was usual to quote, in a single sermon almost a hundred texts of Scripture. Each head of discourse had its own list of authorities. . . . " Of his own early preaching, he admitted that he was then a "more systematic preacher and text expositor . . . and more accustomed to strew my sermons with scores of texts in proof of every point."[26] In the "Sermon on the Law," Campbell cited more than fifty distinct biblical passages to elucidate his doctrine of the law—as we shall see, a feature not insignificant, however customary.

While the "Sermon on the Law" may illustrate Campbell's early use of medieval Ciceronian arrangement, its approach to language and biblical criticism nonetheless reflects more modern influences. The same linguistic philosophy found in book two, chapter seven of George Campbell's *Philosophy of Rhetoric* is summarily expressed in the sermon's first three sentences: "Words are signs of ideas or thoughts. Without words are understood, ideas or sentiments can neither be communicated nor received. Words, that in themselves are quite intelligible, may become difficult to understand in different connexions and circumstances."[27] According to George Campbell, "absolute perfection" in language would be achieved "if words and things could be rendered exact counterparts to each other; if every different thing in nature had a different symbol by which it were expressed; and every difference in the relations of things had a corresponding difference in the combination of words." Admitting that language is not capable of such ideal grammatical purity, he stressed the need for the communicator to attend to the quality of perspicuity and the ways it can be violated. Because using the same word as a "sign" of different "ideas or thoughts" in "different connexions and circumstances" destabilizes the relationship between sign and referent, it is a violation of perspicuity, a source of confusion and a threat to the intelligibility of language.[28]

Similarly, Alexander argued under the first heading of his sermon, it was precisely because "modern teachers" had violated his restorationist version of the "pure speech" ideal that they had created confusion as to the nature of the law and its place in the life of the church. In particular, he singled out their division and classification of the law of Moses under the headings "moral," "ceremonial" and "judicial" as the source of much "perplexion": "This division of the law being unknown in the apostolic age, and of course never used by the Apostles, can serve no valuable purpose, in obtaining a correct knowledge of the doctrine delivered by the Apostles respecting the law . . . [Its] origin is not divine. If this distinction were harmless, if it did not perplex, bias, and confound, rather than assist the judgment, in determining the sense of the apostolic writings, we should let it pass unnoticed. . . . "[29]

Campbell's objections to applying the phrase "the moral law" to the Ten Commandments illustrated the confusion generated by the distinction. First, he demonstrated that only six of the Ten Commandments met the definition of the term "*moral,* according to the most approved Lexicographers" of his day. Second, he argued that, though the phrase implies that "all morality is contained in them; or, what is the same in effect, that all immorality is prohibited in them," examples to the contrary prove this not to be the case. His third objection was that "this division of the law . . . sets itself in opposition to the skill of an Apostle, and ultimately deters us from speaking of the ten precepts as he did."[30] Noting that Paul, in 2 Corinthians 3:7, 14, referred to the Ten Commandments as the "ministration of condemnation and of death" and affirmed that they were "done away," Campbell illustrated the problem:

> Now calling the ten precepts "the moral law," is not only a violation of the use of words; is not only inconsistent in itself and contradictory to truth; but greatly obscures the doctrine taught by the Apostle in the 3d chap. 2d Cor. and in similar passages, so as to render it almost, if not altogether, unintelligible to us . . . When we say the Moral law is done away, the religious world is alarmed;

but when we declare, the ministration of condemnation is done away, they hear us patiently, not knowing what we mean! To give new names to ancient things, and speak of them according to their ancient names is perplexing indeed . . . Hence it is, that modern teachers by their innovations concerning law, have perplexed the student of the Bible, and caused many a fruitless controversy. . . .[31]

His fourth and final objection added: "any person who wishes to understand the Epistle to the Romans, Galatians and Hebrews" with "this distinction in mind . . . is continually at a loss to know, whether the moral, ceremonial, or judicial law is intended."[32]

Campbell's purpose, then, in this first division of the sermon, was to remedy this confusion and "to ascertain what ideas we are to attach to the phrase '*the law*,' in this, and similar portions of the sacred scriptures."[33] In the last chapter, we observed that a significant aspect of Campbell's turn to the common sense tradition was his use of George Campbell's "natural" methods of biblical criticism—in particular his "scientific" approach to word studies that collected examples of a word's usage and compared the contexts in which it occurs to determine its meaning.[34] In his exordium, Alexander promised to use this very method: "One of the most important words in our text is of easy signification, and yet, in consequence of its diverse usages and epithets, it is sometimes difficult precisely to ascertain what ideas should be attached to . . . the term *law*. But by a close investigation of the context, and a general knowledge of the scriptures, every difficulty of this kind, may be easily surmounted."[35]

The explication of his first division, accordingly, begins with the "common usage" of the term "law" to denote "a rule of action" and then proceeds to illustrate, through several instances of usage, the chronological evolution of its significance in both the Old and New Testaments. It was first "used by the Jews, until the time of our Savior, to distinguish the whole revelation made to the Patriarchs and the Prophets, from the traditions and commandments of the Rabbis." However, "when the Old Testament Scriptures were finished and divided according to their contents for the use of synagogues, the Jews styled them, the law, the prophets, and the psalms."[36]

In this last instance, according to Campbell, the addition of the definite article without some restrictive phrase "alters the signification" so that it denotes "the whole legal dispensation by Moses"—appearing, in this manner, "about 30 times in the Old Testament." After observing that "in this acceptation it occurs about 150 times in the New Testament" as well, he concludes: "To make myself more intelligible, I would observe that when the terms *'the law,'* have such distinguishing properties or restrictive definitions as 'the royal law,' 'the law of faith,' . . . &c. it is most obvious the whole Mosaic law or dispensation is not intended. But when we find the phrase 'the law,' without any such limitations or epithets . . . we must perceive the whole law of Moses, or legal dispensation, is intended."[37] To protect the intelligibility of connection between word and idea, Campbell also identifies two "exclusions"—first the "modern division of the law" discussed above and then "two principles, commandments, or laws, that are never included in our observations respecting the law of Moses": "Thou shalt love the Lord thy God with all thy heart, soul, mind, and strength; and thy neighbor as thyself." These he considered "engraven with more or less clearness on every human heart" as "the basis of all law and prophecy."[38]

A second aspect of Campbell's "natural" approach to biblical criticism, as noted in chapter two, was his method of developing biblical doctrines by studying inductively all the passages on a topic and generalizing to conclusions based on the contents of particular passages.[39] This method is evident in his use of scripture within the next three divisions of the sermon (premises two through four), although they are developed, just as the first four headings develop the sermon theme, through the use of those means of amplification commonly employed in the medieval Ciceronian sermon.[40]

These means include the use of a concordance of authorities (e.g., biblical), "questioning and discussion of words and terms," "division," "discussion of the property of things," "analogies and natural truths," the use of "examples" or "opposites," "cause and effect," and "observation of the end or purpose of a thing."[41] Whereas the first division of the sermon may be said to amplify the sermon theme through the use of "questioning and discussion of words and terms" ("what ideas we are to attach to the phrase, *'the law'*"), divisions two through four ("things which *the law* could not accomplish," "the reason why *the law* failed to accomplish those objects," "how God has remedied those relative defects of *the law*,") employ "the end or purpose of a thing" and "cause and effect."

The headings themselves are also developed using various combinations of these means of amplification. Having discussed the first division of the sermon thoroughly, it will suffice here simply to note that the second is subdivided into "three things which the law could not accomplish" (give righteousness and life, exhibit the malignity or demerit of sin, be a suitable rule of life to mankind in its imperfect state), which are developed through biblical authorities, discussion of the property of the thing, and analogy. The third appeals to the sermon text ("In that it was weak through the flesh") to account for the "reason *the law* could not accomplish those objects" and is amplified through additional biblical authorities and "cause and effect" discussion. The fourth, also drawing upon the sermon text ("by sending his own Son in the likeness of sinful flesh, and for sin, condemns sin in the flesh") to explain "the means by which God has remedied the relative defects of *the law*," is nonetheless subdivided so as to parallel God's remedy with the law's defects (described under the second heading) and amplified through biblical authorities, cause and effect discussion, and analogy.[42]

The use of these various means of amplification notwithstanding, it is nonetheless clear that, throughout these divisions of the sermon, Campbell's appeal depended heavily upon inductive generalizations from scripture and that he conceived of the rhetorical function of biblical authority as a common sense appeal to divine testimony. For, when explaining how righteousness and eternal life are obtained through faith in Christ, he observes: "This righteousness, and its concomitant, eternal life, are revealed from faith to faith—the information or report of it comes in the Divine word to our ears, and receiving the report of it, or believing the Divine testimony concerning it, brings us into the enjoyment of its blessings."[43]

The fifth and final heading encompasses the second half of the sermon in both proportion and purpose, indicating the "uses" or "applications" to be made of the "divisions" of the text—or, in this case, serving "to deduce such conclusions from the above premises, as must obviously and necessarily present themselves to every candid and reflecting mind."[44] Campbell's application of Baconian induction to the study of scripture notwithstanding, the parallels between his description of medieval "text preaching" cited earlier and his phraseology in this heading of the sermon clearly suggest that he viewed these conclusions as "necessary inferences" produced by deductive reasoning. Stevenson acknowledges the influence of Aristotelian logic upon the essentially Ciceronian medieval sermon form[45] as does Casey when he cites Caplan's description:

It comprised a theme from Holy Writ; a protheme, also from the
Bible, which should lead to prayer involving God's aid, and yet
recall the theme; and divisions and subdivisions of the theme,
by means of authoritative passages, from the Bible, the Church
Fathers, and the philosophers, arranged largely in artistic syllogistic order. This scheme was of course not inherited from classical
rhetoric, which could not have such special needs in view. The
Middle Ages are to be credited with inventing it. But the contribution of the principles of Aristotelian logic is evident in its
form. . . .[46]

To some extent, then, the popular form of the medieval sermon represents a synthesis of Ciceronian and Aristotelian traditions.

This is not to suggest that the "Sermon on the Law" employed the
art of syllogizing so fervently criticized by George Campbell, since its
method clearly lacks the number and order of elements requisite for the
classical syllogism (i.e., major premise, minor premise, conclusion). Nor
does it precisely follow either the pattern of the more complex "sorites"
(a progressive chain of inferences involving any number of intermediary
ideas) discussed in Jardine's lectures[47] or George Campbell's descriptions
of "deductive evidence."[48] Generally speaking, however, it resembles both
of the latter in that it depends upon the mediation of related ideas through
which new knowledge is "inferred" or "drawn" from former knowledge
and attributes an obvious necessity and certainty to the conclusions deduced.[49] Beyond this, however, we can only be sure that Alexander was
deducing "the necessary inferences" as typical in that manner of sermonizing to which he had been accustomed.

Specifically, from his four premises, Campbell drew five separate conclusions:

1. "From what has been said, it follows that there is an essential
   difference betwixt law and gospel."
2. "In the second place, we learn from what has been said, that
   'there is no condemnation to them which are in Christ Jesus.'"
3. "In the third place, we conclude from the above premises, that
   there is no necessity for preaching the law in order to prepare
   men for receiving the Gospel."
4. "A fourth conclusion which is deducible from the above prem-

ises is, that all arguments and motives, drawn from the law or
Old Testament . . . to excite the disciples of Christ to a compliance with, or imitation of Jewish customs, are inconclusive. . . . "
5. "In the last place we are taught from all that has been said, to
venerate in the highest degree the Lord Jesus Christ. . . . "[50]

These conclusions were sufficient to have Campbell and his sermon
brought before the Association to face the charge of heresy. Yet, when
Campbell recognized the thirtieth anniversary of his "Sermon on the
Law" by reprinting it in the *Millennial Harbinger* (1846), he remarked in
a preface, "I do not think that there is a Baptist Association on the continent that would now treat me as did the Redstone Association of that
day."[51] Why did this sermon create such a furor when it was preached in
1816? How was it able to call into being a reform-minded community so
radically different from the status quo that it could not be assimilated
within the existing ecclesiastical order? To these and other matters we
will now turn our attention.

Effects: A Constitutive Perspective

The Campbells had clearly begun to articulate their restoration agenda as
early as 1809 when Thomas published the *Declaration and Address*. Nonetheless, because of its inaugural force in that chain of events out of which
their independent Christian churches emerged, the "Sermon on the Law"
may be viewed as a case of "constitutive rhetoric."

All rhetoric is, arguably, constitutive in some sense or another. To the
extent that it hides, reveals, and/or creates reality, rhetoric is always po-
tentially constitutive in its effects. Typically, though, rhetorical criticism
posits, as the subject of rhetoric, the existence of an audience with an
already constituted identity. "Audience," however, is a very complex con-
figuration, and Maurice Charland has argued for "the possibility that the
very existence of social subjects (who would become audience members)
is already a rhetorical effect." Adopting Kenneth Burke's notion of rhetorical identification (i.e., "identifications of social identity . . . are discursive effects that induce human cooperation"), Charland's analysis of the
rhetoric of the *Peuple Quebecois* seeks to illuminate the process by which
a rhetorical act itself constitutes the identity of its "subject-as-audience"
and thus "calls its audience into being."[52]

Specifically, Charland identifies three ideological effects as characteristic of such "constitutive rhetoric," as well as the means by which they are generated. The first is "the constituting of a collective subject." That is, such rhetoric offers what is "in Burke's language, an 'ultimate' identification permitting an overcoming or going beyond of divisive individual or class interests and concerns" in the interests of "a transcendental collective interest that negates individual interest." The instrument for constituting this collective subject is some narrative history. The second ideological effect of constitutive rhetoric is the "positing of a transhistorical subject." A "time collapse" takes place as the subject identifies with the narrative history. The past has thus become an extension of the present— "our" past. This shared past, in turn, identifies and positions the audience in relation to the future. The third effect is an "illusion of freedom." The narrative serves as "a structure of understanding that produces totalizing interpretations" and thus constrains the subject to "follow through" on the narrative and act in a manner that maintains its consistency.[53]

Although Campbell's "Sermon on the Law" does not possess the overt features of historical narrative, close attention to the rhetorical action within the text reveals an implicit narrative that serves all three of these constitutive functions. The antagonists in this narrative are not the Baptists, in particular, although many of the Baptist clergy opposed Campbell. For several years Campbell would insist that he desired to remain within the Baptist fold, compliment the Baptists for their willingness to tolerate his vociferous dissent, and eventually lament that his departure from the Baptists had been forced upon him.[54] Rather, the "enemy" in this sermon is located in the tension that his "pure speech" principle (Bible names for Bible things) generates between the human and the divine: the human corruption of divine revelation, personified in certain commentators and embodied in doctrines and institutions of "human origin."

Campbell invokes the apocalyptic imagery of Revelation to characterize the "modern" division of the law as "like many distinctions, handed down to us from Mystical Babylon" which "bear the mark on their forehead that certifies to us, their origin is not divine." He deplores how "modern teachers by their innovations concerning law, have perplexed the student of the Bible, and caused many a fruitless controversy." It is their practice of giving "new names to ancient things" that "is perplexing indeed" and "greatly obscures the doctrine taught" about the law in many of the Pauline epistles "so as to render it almost, if not altogether, unintelligible to us."[55]

He regrets that "our translators, by an injudicious supplement should have made the Apostle apparently contradict himself" in Romans 7:10. Regarding Romans 6–7 he mourns, "What a pity that modern teachers of divinity should have *added to* and *clogged* the words of inspiration" through the addition of "unauthorized sentences."[56] He defends his "abolition of the Jewish law, in respect to Christians" against the objection that it would lead to licentiousness by comparing it to the objection made against Paul's doctrine of the law in Romans 6:15 and opposing the "ancient way" to the "modern way" advocated by modern teachers: "Now whether the ancient way of guarding the New Testament, or the Gospel, against the charges of Antinomianism or a licentious tendency, or the modern way is best, methinks is easily decided amongst true disciples. Not so easy, however, amongst learned Rabbis and Doctors of the Law."[57]

As the last example illustrates, Campbell's sarcastic tone often intensifies the process of demonization. As to whether there is biblical precedent for the modern division of the law, he remarks, "You might as well inquire at the Apostles, or consult their writings, to know who the Supralapsarians or Sublapsarians are, as to inquire at them, what is the moral, ceremonial, or judicial law." Similarly, as to whether one can read even "one word of the 'covenant of works'" in the Bible, or "of the Jewish law being a rule of life to the disciples of Christ," he comments, "Of these you hear no more from the Bible than of the 'Solemn League' or 'St. Giles' Day.'"[58] When he objects to denominating the Ten Commandments "the moral law" because they do not, as the phrase implies, either contain all morality or prohibit all immorality, he adds:

> We are aware that large volumes have been written to shew how much is comprehended in the ten precepts. But, methinks, the voluminous works of some learned men on this subject, too much resemble the writings of Peter D'Alva, who wrote forty-eight huge folio volumes to explain the mysteries of the conception of the Messiah in the womb of the Virgin Mary! And what shall we think of the genius, who discovered that singing hymns and spiritual songs was prohibited, and the office of the Ruling Elder pointed out, in the second commandment? That dancing and

stage plays were prohibited in the seventh; and supporting the clergy enjoined in the eighth!![59]

Those who proposed "the law as a rule of life to Christians" because they considered it a necessary guard against licentiousness become the butt of Campbell's humor:

And, indeed, every attempt to guard the New Testament or the gospel, by extrinsic means, against an immoral or licentious tendency, bears too strong a resemblance to the policy of a certain preacher in Norway or Lapland, who told his hearers that "Hell was a place of infinite and incessant cold. When asked by an acquaintance from the south of Europe why he perverted the scriptures, he replied, if he told his hearers in that cold climate that Hell was a place of excessive heat, he verily thought they would take no pains to avoid going there![60]

Finally, as to "a favorite text of the law preachers" (Galatians 3:24), he considers it "an insult to the understanding of any person skilled in the use of words" to attempt a refutation of their use of that text since "every smatterer in Greek knows" how it ought to be read.[61]

In her analysis of the rhetoric of the women's liberation movement, Brenda Robinson Hancock demonstrates the significance of naming an enemy for an emerging movement.[62] Not only does it serve to isolate the movement as victim, it helps to construct the identity of the movement by negation—as an antithesis of the enemy. In this sense, naming and demonizing an enemy, as Campbell's sermon clearly does, aids in the constitution of a collective subject. His sympathizers become protagonists whose "ultimate" identification is derived from a transcendental collective interest in discovering divinely revealed truth and preserving it against the incursion and corruption of human tradition.

Another element of the "Sermon on the Law" that lends itself to the ideological effects of constitutive rhetoric is its appeal to a transcendent authority to support absolute truth claims. Though Romans 8:3 serves as the sermon text, we recall that Campbell's divisions of the text actually serve as a framework for a thematic exposition. Campbell's word study and inductive development of a doctrine of the law establish a "correct" interpretation of scripture. This, in turn, functions as a theological norm that the final heading applies to protest many of the cherished doctrines and practices of the Baptist community.

Though Campbell divides his sermon into five headings, the proportion of "premises" (first through fourth headings) to "conclusions" (fifth heading) is roughly symmetrical. The progression from premise to premise, as well as the deductive progression from premises to conclusions, suggest a logical demonstration from which Campbell's protests derive a sense of inevitable logical validity which is, in turn, absolutized by the phrasing of the fifth heading (". . . as must obviously and necessarily present themselves to every unbiased and reflecting mind").

Also, the rhetorical function of the Bible as authoritative proof is pervasive in the sermon. As noted, more than fifty distinct passages are cited. However, the transcendent nature of its authority is also a rhetorical effect of the presence Campbell creates for the doctrine of divine inspiration. Prior to the time of Christ, the "law" denoted "the whole revelation made to the Patriarchs and Prophets" as distinguished from "the traditions and commandments of the Rabbis or Doctors of the Law." Similarly, when David extolled God's law, he was referring to "all divine revelation extant in his time." The scriptures represent "the whole scope of Divine truth." They are "the words of the Spirit," "the Divine word," "the Divine testimony," and "the words of inspiration"; in all, the "Gospel dispensation is the most perfect revelation of salvation."[63]

As George Campbell considered testimony (as the report of an observed fact) a more credible form of evidence than experience (a generalization based on previous facts), so Alexander considered the Bible, as divine testimony, a more authoritative test of doctrine than experience: "Some, notwithstanding the scriptural plainness of this doctrine, may urge their own experience as contrary to it. It would however be as safe for Christians, to make Divine truth a test of their experience, and not their experience a test of Divine truth. Some individuals have been awakened by the appearance of the Aurora Borealis—by an earthquake—by a thunderstorm—by a dream; by sickness, &c. How inconsistent for one of these to affirm from his own experience, that others must be awakened in the same way!"[64] Thus, both Campbell's use as well as his characterization of the Bible construct it as a transcendent, divinely inspired authority—a "norm of norms." Though Campbell's premises are established in order to provide a normative basis for the protests embodied in his conclusions, the Bible ultimately serves as the transcendent normative standard by which the premises themselves are judged.

Collectively, the sermon's construction of and appeals to a transcendent authority in support of claims of absolute truth lend themselves to all three of the ideological effects associated with constitutive rhetoric. By positing a source of divinely revealed truth that transcends time, space, and the limits of human wisdom and by constructing a quest for that truth, Campbell's sermon creates a collective interest (discovering and preserving divine truth) which transcends that of the individual. The new collective subject, then, not only experiences identification as an antithesis to its common enemy but is also able, through a mutual submission to the higher authority of divine testimony, to transcend the fruitless controversies generated by human creeds that might otherwise divide them.

The new collective subject also becomes transhistorical. The timeless validity and sufficiency of the ancient and apostolic pattern for the past, the present, and the future of the faith community create a "time collapse" which aids in the construction of that narrative within which the subject acts. What the Israelites once did and what the Apostles began to do, the newly constituted protagonist can continue to do. This new collective subject thus becomes the heir of the apostolic church and its mission, the steward and guardian of the inspired scriptures. Freedom is illusory within the totalizing interpretation produced by the sermon's absolutism. For the sake of argument, Campbell postures to "coolly and dispassionately hear, examine, and weigh all arguments pro and con." However, his refutative arguments ultimately admit of no contrary proofs. Without exception, objections are "rather imaginary than real" or "totally groundless."[65] Thus, it is not possible to act consistently with the identity of this newly constituted collective and transhistorical subject without, of necessity, supporting Campbell's protests. Conversely, it is not possible to resist his protests apart from rejecting the entire framework of understanding within which this new identity is constituted. It is not surprising, then, that responses to Campbell's "Sermon on the Law" were radically polarized. Most who heard and/or read it either embraced him as a hero or branded him a heretic.

Ethos: A Divinely Authorized Reformer

When we view Campbell's "Sermon on the Law" as a strategic response to the exigencies and constraints that defined the rhetorical situation, another of its constitutive dimensions becomes apparent. Not only did this sermon constitute a new social identity for its audience, it also constructed for Campbell a leadership *ethos* fitting for this newly constituted community. Ultimately, it was the sermon's preacher who embodied the divinely authorized voice of protest against the incursion of human tradition upon the truth revealed in scripture.

Campbell's conclusions boldly attacked several doctrines and practices held dear by the Baptist community. His first conclusion was that the law had been abolished by the New Testament in favor of the gospel. Christians, he concluded in the second place, were not under the law, either as a covenant of works or as a rule of life. Third, he concluded that, though customary among Baptist clergy, it was neither necessary nor consistent with the pattern of the apostles to preach the law to convict people about sin and guilt as preparatory to the preaching or reception of the gospel. His fourth conclusion named several common practices, drawn from the law, as "repugnant to Christianity": infant baptism, the paying of tithes to teachers, the observance of holy days or religious feasts as preparatory to the observation of the Lord's Supper, the sanctification of the seventh day of the week, entering into national covenants, and the establishment of any form of religion by civil law. His final conclusion, calling for a veneration "in the highest degree" of the Lord Jesus Christ, would probably have been uncontroversial in most contexts. But when contrasted to a "strange infatuation" with Moses on the part of "all who cleave to him," it served as a sharp rebuke.[66]

However, this profaning of Baptist holy ground notwithstanding, the allegation of "heresy" probably had much more to do with two fundamental issues that provided the theological underpinnings for these diverse doctrines and practices. Campbell faced two significant constraints as he used this sermon to call for reform. One was his desire to remain within the Baptist fold. He held a firm conviction that the unity of the church was essential for carrying out its mission in the world and, consequently, abhorred divisions within the church. Thus, we may recall, he wanted to avoid adding another party or sect to the already long list of Protestant denominations.

The other major constraint was the authority of the Philadelphia Confession that the Baptists had adopted as their standard of orthodoxy and their basis of union and communion. By 1816, both Campbells had long since rejected the authority of all such creeds and we recall here that

Brush Run's application to the Redstone Association had been accompanied by a lengthy document stating the conditions of their membership and specifying their protest against creedal authorities.

However, the authority of the Philadelphia Confession as a community standard could not be blithely dismissed. Campbell preached this sermon as a Baptist (of sorts) among Baptists—there was, as of yet, no independent "restoration movement" as such. We must also keep in mind that the Baptist community, generally speaking, did not view the Philadelphia Confession as *displacing* the authority of scripture but, rather, as *applying* its authority by restating its doctrines in a manner that could guide the faith and practice of the church. In other words, most Baptists believed that the Philadelphia Confession was merely the embodiment of biblical truth.

The manner in which the "Sermon on the Law" addresses these constraints defines both the essence of Campbell's protest and the specific character of his leadership *ethos* as it emerges from the sermon. His sermon responded to these constraints in two ways.

First, Campbell's choice of text and topic (Romans 8:3, "what ideas we are to attach to the phrase, 'the law'") was no coincidence, regardless of how quickly he was forced to gather his thoughts to speak. His largest complaint with the Philadelphia Confession was that it was a creed of human origin and, in his opinion, like all such creeds, responsible for the controversies that had divided Protestantism. This was not his only complaint, however. He understood that the Philadelphia Confession embodied a specific *hermeneutic* and that many of the particular doctrines and practices to which he objected were a product of that hermeneutic.

A distinct aspect of what might be called the confession's "level Bible" hermeneutic was its manner of applying the Old Testament, and the law in particular, to Christians. Since Calvin, Protestant reformed theology had generally divided the law into three categories as stated in chapter XIX of the Philadelphia Confession:

> The same Law that was first written in the heart of man, continued to be a perfect rule of Righteousness after the fall; and was delivered by God upon Mount Sinai, in Ten Commandments. . . .
>
> Besides this law, commonly called moral, God was pleased to give to the people *Israel* Ceremonial Laws . . . all which Ceremo-

nial Laws being appointed only to the time of the reformation, are by Jesus Christ . . . abrogate and taken away.

To them also he gave sundry judicial Laws, which expired together with the state of that people, . . . their general equity only, being of moral use.

The moral Law doth for ever bind all, as well justified persons as others . . . : Neither doth *Christ* in the Gospel any way dissolve but strengthen this obligation.

Although true *Believers* be not under the Law, as a Covenant of *Works*, to be thereby Justified or condemned; yet it is of great use to them as well as to others: in that, as a Rule of *Life*, informing them of the Will of *God*, and their Duty, it directs and binds them, to walk accordingly. . . . [67]

Much of this phraseology, as we have seen, finds its way into the "Sermon on the Law." What is not so obvious from this brief excerpt, however, is how all three categories of the law were, nonetheless, made binding upon Christians as a "rule of life." The "moral" law was still considered binding because it was held to embody moral principles that transcended the Mosaic covenant. Though superseded by the teachings of Christ, the "ceremonial" law was still used to explicate Christian practices because it was considered typical of them. And the "judicial" law, though "expired with the state of that people," could still be used as a guide for civil law in a Christian commonwealth (e.g., Calvin's Geneva).[68]

Arguing that such distinctions were inconsistent with the use of the phrase "the law" in scripture, Campbell concluded that Christians were not under the law as a "rule of life" in any sense: "And all reasons and motives borrowed from the Jewish law, to excite the disciples of Christ to a compliance with or an imitation of Jewish customs, are inconclusive, repugnant to Christianity, and fall ineffectual to the ground; not being enjoined by the authority of Jesus Christ."[69] Campbell was, in effect, challenging the hermeneutic embodied in the Philadelphia Confession. The authoritative status of the Confession was thus separated from, even placed in opposition to, that of the Bible, which it purported to represent. To appropriate that communal space, Campbell's sermon both modeled and advocated an alternative hermeneutic.

The hermeneutic embodied in the Philadelphia Confession reflected the covenant theology expounded by the English Puritan William Ames (d. 1663) and especially developed by the Dutch theologian Johannes Cocceius (d. 1669), which posited a single covenant of grace under three different dispensations (patriarchal, Mosaic, and Christian) as a basis for applying the Old Testament to Christians. Alternatively, Campbell sharply distinguished between the Old and New Testaments ("law" and "gospel") as successive but separate covenants.[70] Within his second premise, Campbell anticipated the biblical authorities he would cite in his first conclusion by using an analogy to illustrate why the law "was given to the Jewish nation, and to none else":

> As the inscription on a letter, identifies to whom it belongs; as the preamble to a proclamation, distinguishes who is addressed; so the preface to the law, points out and determines to whom it was given. It points out a people brought from the land of Egypt, and released from the house of bondage, as the subjects of it. To extend it farther than its own preface, is to violate the rules of criticism and propriety. How unjust and improper would it be, to convey the contents of a letter to a person to whom it was not directed—how inconsistent to enjoin the items of a proclamation made by the President of these United States, on the subjects of the French government. As inconsistent would it be to extend the law of Moses beyond the limits of the Jewish nation.[71]

In the years to come, Campbell would develop this distinction between the covenants into one of his most (if not his most) important exegetical principles,[72] elaborating upon and systematizing the use of covenant contexts as a basic framework for (1) determining the significance of biblical texts for the life of the church and (2) privileging the New Testament over the Old as a rule of faith and practice for the church.

The second sense in which this sermon responded to the constraints within the rhetorical situation was a consequence of the first. By elevating scripture to a unique position of divine authority independent from that of all creedal statements, Campbell was, in effect, appropriating a form of authoritative proof that had been at the heart of the Protestant Reformation—the principle of *sola scriptura*.[73]

It is important to note, however, that Campbell's version of the principle of *sola scriptura,* as exemplified in this sermon, was imbued with the spirit of early republican populism. It was, in this way, markedly different from that of Reformers such as Luther and Calvin or of eighteenth-century American evangelicals such as Wesley, Whitfield, and Edwards, none of whom suggested that people should seek biblical understanding apart from clerical guidance or the mediations of theological tradition. Confident of the right and ability of free individuals to think and decide for themselves, Campbell and other preachers of the Second Great Awakening appropriated the more radical potential inherent within the principle of *sola scriptura,* invoking the unique and transcendent authority of scripture to set the Bible *against* systematic theology, denominational creeds, and clerical authority. Thus on one hand, Campbell's sermon, by appropriating a principle as old and as trusted as *sola scriptura,* remained within the larger, transcendent authoritative tradition of the community's Protestant heritage, calling the Reformation back to its own tradition of reform. At the same time, by a subtle shift in emphasis, it was able to protest cherished Baptist doctrines and practices by rhetorically displacing the Philadelphia Confession and its hermeneutic from their authoritative space within that community.[74]

Throughout the 1820s, Campbell would vehemently denounce Protestant church polity and satirize the Protestant clergy whom he often described as the "little popes" of Protestantism. Nonetheless, when his "Sermon on the Law" applied the Bible alone as a normative standard by which to measure the theological and ecclesiological worth of creedal statements, much as the Reformers had applied the principle of *sola scriptura* in their protests against Roman tradition, Campbell constructed for himself an *ethos* that was, in this sense, clearly "protestant." At the same time that this sermon called its audience into being, then, it also constituted a specific leadership *ethos* for its speaker—as a divinely authorized reformer in the true Protestant tradition.

Summary

The "Sermon on the Law" illustrates both the Ciceronian homiletic that was characteristic of Alexander Campbell's early preaching and his familiarity with Scottish common sense views of language and biblical criticism. More significantly, this sermon became a turning point in the life and leadership of Alexander Campbell and set into motion many of the forces that would eventually evolve his "restoration movement" into an independent faith community with its own distinct identity.

Delivered in the midst of controversy generated by tensions between his emerging popularity as a reformer and the suspicion with which many Baptist clergy viewed his reforming principles, its constitutive significance is seen both in the way it calls an audience into being and in the kind of leadership *ethos* it constructs for its speaker. Its significant rhetorical features lend themselves to the ideological effects characteristic of such "constitutive rhetoric"—the constitution of a new collective, transhistorical subject through an implied narrative that both defines its identity and constrains its actions by producing totalizing interpretations. Campbell himself emerges, through its rhetorical action, as a spokesman whose voice and virtues are well suited for leading the kind of reforming-restoring community that the sermon calls into being.

Subsequently, Campbell would elaborate extensively upon many of the themes and principles articulated in the "Sermon on the Law," which would thus serve a programmatic function for his restoration movement. In his preface to its 1846 reprinting in the *Millennial Harbinger,* Campbell would write, "The intelligent reader will discover in it the elements of things that have characterized our writings on the subject of modern Christianity from that day to the present."[75] The evolution of Campbell's rhetorical leadership would also display significant continuities with the ethical dimensions of this sermon. However, in the years following this sermon, Campbell's protests would intensify and his rhetoric would generate an *ethos* that might be most accurately described not merely as "protestant" but as "prophetic."

4

Ridicule and Residue

The Prophetic Tone of the *Christian Baptist*

... it was an experiment to ascertain whether society could be moved by fear or rage.[1]

The first half of the nineteenth century has been described as "the golden age of regional printing" in America, and Alexander Campbell would eventually take his place at the forefront of an outpouring of religious print. Hatch has suggested that Campbell "sought to transform American religion from the mountains of Western Virginia by two means: an educational institution, Bethany College, and his own printing shop."[2]

Campbell's writing career commenced soon after his arrival in America. His first essays were authored under the pseudonym "Clarinda." Shocked by the behavior of young men and women on the rare social occasions permitted by frontier life (such as husking frolics, quilting parties, and apple-parings), he wrote "to reform the general conduct of our and the opposite sex, in what particularly relates to forming of connections for life." A total of ten essays were published in the May 14 through July 23, 1810, issues of the *Reporter*, a weekly newspaper in Washington, Pennsylvania.[3]

A second series of essays by Campbell, protesting a program sponsored by Washington College, ran in the same paper later that year (October through December) under the name "Bonus Homo." A decade later, between April 7, 1820, and February 25, 1822, Campbell published a series of essays in the *Washington Reporter* under the name "Candidus," protesting the repressive tendencies of the many "moral societies" then popular in the region.[4] These early ventures foreshadowed a prolific writing ministry through which his rhetorical leadership would expand to historic proportions.

As early as 1809, the postscript to Thomas Campbell's *Declaration and Address* had proposed "a periodical publication, for the express purpose of detecting and exposing the various anti-christian enormities, innovations and corruptions, which infect the christian church." This periodical, for which he projected the title "The Christian Monitor," was never published because a sufficient number of subscribers could not be secured at the time.[5] A decade later, however, a significant turn of events would lead Alexander to revive this aspiration.

In 1820, Alexander reluctantly agreed to accept a challenge from Presbyterian minister John Walker to debate the subject of baptism. Prior to this time, Campbell had shared his father's skepticism about the value of using debate to further their cause. His experience with the Walker debate led him to change his mind. Afterwards, he hastened to publish a copy of the debate, reconstructed from his own notes as well as those of his father and a reporter, Salathiel Curtis. The thousand copies printed that fall in Steubenville, Ohio, sold out within months and three thousand copies of a second edition were printed in Pittsburgh in 1822.[6] Now keen to the opportunity of spreading his reforming principles through the print medium, Campbell soon launched a venture that came to be called "a veritable John the Baptist in religious journalism."[7]

The aim of the present chapter is to demonstrate how, during the decade of the 1820s, Campbell shifted toward a rhetoric that was not only thoroughly "natural" but also genuinely *prophetic*.[8] Specifically, critical analyses of representative portions of his journal, the *Christian Baptist*, will illustrate the similarities between Campbell's rhetoric and that of the ancient Hebrew prophets and how Campbell's use of ridicule, residual reasoning, and the "language of the passions" create a prophetic tone for his rhetoric as well as a prophetic *ethos* for his leadership.

The "Christian Baptist" (1823–1830)

Campbell had intended to name his new journal "The Christian." Walter Scott, with whom Campbell had recently formed a close friendship, is often credited with suggesting the title "Christian Baptist," to aid its circulation among the Baptists. However, in 1839, Campbell offered his own account of this decision: "When we drew up our Prospectus for our first publication, we headed it '*The Christian*,' and had it not been that we found ourselves anticipated we should have adhered to that title. I hesitated between the title '*Baptist Christian*' and '*Christian Baptist*,' and on suggesting my embarrassment to a friend, who has since given himself credit for the hint, as an original idea; he thought the latter was a better passport into favor than either of the others. We never fully approved, but from expediency adopted it."[9]

The prospectus was issued on July 4, 1823.[10] Though it elicited little response, Campbell began publication anyway. The first number was issued on August 3, 1823. Thereafter, it appeared on the first Monday of each month, ceasing after the completion of the seventh volume on July 5, 1830. By that time, circulation had reached ten states, Canada, and Ireland, and it was not uncommon for subscriptions in many states to have doubled in any given year.[11]

Campbell set forth the aims of the *Christian Baptist* in his prospectus:

> The "Christian Baptist" shall espouse the cause of no religious sect, excepting that Ancient Sect, called "Christians first at Antioch." Its sole object shall be the eviction of truth, and the exposure of error in doctrine and practice. The Editor acknowledging no standard of religious faith or works, other than the Old and New Testaments, and the latter as the only standard of the religion of Jesus Christ will, intentionally at least, oppose nothing which it contains, and recommend nothing which it does not enjoin. Having no worldly interest at stake from the adoption or reprobation of any article of faith or religious practice—having no gift nor religious office of any worldly emolument to blind his eyes or to pervert his judgment—he hopes to manifest that he is an impartial advocate of truth.[12]

Campbell would later describe the first volume of the *Christian Baptist* as "the most uncharitable . . . most severe, sarcastic, and ironic" material that he had ever written, noting, "it was an experiment to ascertain whether society could be moved by fear or rage."[13] It is thus commonplace for church historians to make much of its "iconoclastic" temper.[14]

The seven years during which Campbell published the *Christian Baptist* witnessed a significant evolution in his movement. As of 1823, the design of Campbell's reformation was clearly for it to be a movement *within* existing churches. The Campbells had established only three congregations (Brush Run, Pittsburgh, and Wellsburg) and each of these either belonged to a denominational association or had attempted to join one.[15] Campbell's success in his debates over baptism with Walker in 1820 and William L. Maccalla, another Presbyterian minister, in 1823 made him a popular hero with many Baptists. However, the opposition that had forced him to transfer his membership from the Brush Run Church and the Redstone Association to the Wellsburg congregation in the Mahoning Association was a harbinger of more trouble to come.

The circulation of the *Christian Baptist* with its scathing denunciation of the pretensions of the clergy, the use of creeds, and the proliferation of (biblically) unauthorized organizations[16] had an "unsettling effect on the Baptist churches."[17] Richardson observed that Campbell deliberately withheld it from circulation in Kentucky prior to his debate with Maccalla (held in Washington, Kentucky) because, believing himself comparatively unknown in the state, "he hoped to obtain a more impartial hearing for the views he wished to present." However, when he told them of his new publication and distributed copies among them, they responded with enthusiasm. The *Christian Baptist* received a vigorous circulation in that state where, during a three-month tour in 1824, Campbell would meet not only Barton W. Stone but several others who would eventually become leading preachers in the churches of his restoration movement, including "Raccoon" John Smith and Jacob Creath, Sr.[18]

As the popularity of Campbell's reforming principles grew, so did tensions with the leading Baptist ministers who opposed his movement. As late as 1827, Campbell wrote, "I do intend to continue with this people so long as they permit me to say what I believe."[19] However, he would later date his "excision and repudiation" by the Baptists to the year 1828.[20] In 1829, the "Beaver Anathema" was adopted by Baptist authorities in Ohio and Kentucky as a basis for excommunicating "reforming" churches. A similar "Dover Anathema" was adopted in Virginia in 1830. In 1831, Campbell wrote, "For our part we cannot fight under Baptist or Paidobaptist colors" and in 1832 his response to the Dover decree was "the Rubicon is passed."[21] The cessation of the *Christian Baptist* upon the completion of its seventh volume in July of 1830 and the inauguration of Campbell's new journal, *The Millennial Harbinger,* in January of that same year suggests that, by then, Campbell saw himself as providing leadership for a movement of independent churches. The publication of the *Christian Baptist,* then, coincided with this period of gradual separation.

A Prophetic *Ethos*

In the preceding chapter, we observed how, in 1816, Campbell's "Sermon on the Law" constituted for him an *ethos* as a divinely authorized reformer in the true Protestant tradition. The *Christian Baptist* illustrates an evolution in Campbell's leadership *ethos.* The intensification of his protests and denunciations, accompanied by other features of these texts, construct an *ethos* that is most accurately described as not merely *protestant* but genuinely *prophetic.*

A Prophetic Dilemma

In fact, Campbell's program for the "eviction of truth and exposure of error," as expressed in the prospectus of the *Christian Baptist,* situated his rhetorical leadership within a dilemma quite similar to that faced by the ancient Hebrew prophets. In his "Sermon on the Law," Campbell had been able to carefully walk a fine line on the edge of his community's boundaries, challenging existing community authorities and practices while remaining within the larger, transcendent authoritative tradition of that community by reappropriating the principle of *sola scriptura.* But to what extent a rhetor can continue to intensify certain rhetorical strategies (e.g., ridicule, satire, condemnation, etc.) without relinquishing his standing as a voice of dissent speaking from *within* the community and removing himself *beyond* the pale of community boundaries is a question that Campbell would soon face.

This same rhetorical dilemma confronted the ancient Hebrew prophets. On one hand, though their message often called for radical and destabilizing change, most of the Old Testament prophets were still integral members of their community, holding positions and occupations within Israelite society. But, on the other hand, even while speaking within the broader context of community sanction and support, they were often driven out of the community by civil and religious authorities when their message became perceived as too rancorous or threatening[22]—as the threats of Jezebel forced Elijah to flee after he confronted the prophets of Baal on Mount Carmel (1 Kings 18–19) and as Herod beheaded John the Baptist though he was popularly regarded as a prophet in the Old Testament tradition (Matthew 14:1–12). Albeit gradually, the "Campbellite" churches suffered their own eviction through the years as Campbell evolved an increasingly prophetic *ethos*—an *ethos* that continued to find a growing audience among churches in Pennsylvania, Ohio, West Virginia, and Kentucky even as it provoked the wrath of Baptist authorities.

The Rhetoric of the Ancient Hebrew Prophets

There are, in fact, many similarities between the rhetoric of the *Christian Baptist* and the prophetic books of the Old Testament that have served, James Darsey argues, as "the primitive source for much of the rhetoric of reform in America." As we shall soon see, all three of the similarities, cited by Darsey, between American rhetorics of radical reform and the discursive tradition of the Old Testament prophets can be amply illustrated from the *Christian Baptist:* "a sense of mission, a desire to bring the practice of the people into accord with sacred principle, and an uncompromising, often excoriating stance toward a reluctant audience."[23] However, before we turn our attention to texts representative of the rhetoric of the *Christian Baptist,* we should first consider some of the particulars of prophetic rhetoric and, especially, the central role of prophetic *ethos* within this discursive tradition.

According to Darsey, the fundamental difference between ancient Jewish prophetic practice and Graeco-Roman rhetorical theory is the separation of *inventio* (the creation of the message) from *actio* (the actions of the speaker). Yahweh is the true agent of the prophetic word; the prophet, an unwilling instrument, is reduced to the status of agency. The *ethos* of the message as the word of God and the role of the prophet as God's spokesperson are both commonly conveyed by the "messenger formula" ("thus saith the Lord").[24]

The prophetic message itself is, at the same time, conservative and radical, rational and yet unreasonable. It is conservative in that its main goal is to reassert the terms of Yahweh's covenant with his people. Central to the common legacy of Israel and Judah, the covenant's terms were accessible to all. The prophetic word is thus a reminder, not a new claim or revelation. To quote Darsey, it "has no power of invention; it can only reveal that which was already there." It is "a rhetoric of showing" (as suggested by its heavy use of metaphor), a rhetoric of self-evidence (i.e., of demonstration). Though conservative, the prophetic message is at the same time radical, engaging society at its very roots. Its condemnation of willing blindness to the values of the covenant threatens the basis of society's self-definition. Its opposition to power structures that disregard covenant standards threatens their legitimacy, which pales beside the supreme power of God.[25]

The rationality of the message is evident in its highly enthymematic[26] character and in the consistent judicial logic in its application of the terms of the covenant. And yet it is "unreasonable" in that it lacks the "bargaining side of intelligence" often associated with "reasonable" persons—its truths are absolute. It is a discourse of separation rather than identification. Its end is qualitative—conformity to God's absolute will as

expressed in his word. As Darsey puts it, "the prophet achieves identification only when the holy remnant has joined him in the purity of the
wilderness; the people must come to God; He cannot come to them."[27]

The *pathos* of prophetic rhetoric is manifest in its expression of God's
wrath. The ideal of justice, prescribed by the covenant, binds Yahweh not
only to bless his people when they are faithful but also to punish them
when they are not. However, God's wrath, as both Darsey and Abraham
Heschel note, is "not the intemperate passion so feared by the Greeks and
their intellectual heirs, but the anger of a loving God upon being made
to punish His people." In Bruce Vawter's words, "this God of pathos, this
God who cares . . . weeps over his own inexorable justice." Relief of the
agony created by the opposition of thesis (God) to antithesis (humankind)
requires a new synthesis—a revival of divine pathos within humanity that
transcends its "a-pathos" or apathy to the covenant demands of justice
and righteousness. This synthesis, however, represents not a compromise
but a purification in which the antithesis is sacrificed and the crisis resolved.[28]

Yet Darsey points out that "at the center of prophetic rhetoric is the
prophetic *ethos*." It is through the *ethos* of the prophet as messenger—as
servant rather than hero—that the identity of prophetic *logos* as the word
of God becomes apparent. His role is submission to God's call and his
message "a performance from script" as he "bear[s] witness" to a message
not his own. Completely subjugated to the will of God, he labors under
a sense of compulsion.[29]

It is also through the prophet's identification with the *ethos* of God, as
he speaks in the voice of divine "I" against "you" the people, that God's
radical confrontation with his people and his compassionate nature are
revealed and within which the message's pathetic agony lies. And yet, the
prophet's own conversion or calling, through which his surrender to
God's will is presented, also serves as a synecdochal realization of the new
synthesis, the complete subordination of the self to the divine will that
resolves the crisis.[30]

Ultimately, the *ethos* of the prophet embodies prophetic rhetoric's response to the community's only option for disputing its message: the
authentication of the prophet's call. The prophet's *ethos* is not derived
hierarchically. As Vawter notes, "The prophets of Israel . . . found their
credentials not in any official position they may have enjoyed, but in their
direct call by God himself." Rather, the source of the prophet's *ethos* is

charismatic—in Max Weber's words, a "certain quality of an individual personality by virtue of which he is set apart from ordinary men." It is on the basis of such qualities, "regarded as of divine origin or as exemplary," Weber suggests, that "the individual is treated as a leader." Validation is thus a social phenomenon. The prophet's "value lies in his reception."[31]

Like these prophets, Alexander Campbell's *ethos* was derived from his rhetorical charisma rather than any hierarchical position. The specific mission of the *Christian Baptist,* as expressed in its prospectus, was to bring the practice of people into accord with sacred principle. Though gracious in person and conversational in speech, with pen in hand, the Campbell of the *Christian Baptist* generally adopted an "excoriating stance" toward an audience he often perceived as reluctant, became the voice of the "divine I" in radical confrontation with what he considered willing blindness, and likened his call to that of a prophet to "saints in Babylon"— "Come out of her, my people, that you partake not of her sins, and that you receive not of her plagues."[32] One reader, R. B. Semple, noting that "Forbearance is certainly a christian grace, strongly recommended by both precept and example, in the word of God," found Campbell "as a man, in private circles, mild, pleasant, and affectionate; as a writer, rigid, satirical, beyond all the bounds of scriptural allowance." Though an opponent of Campbell in future years, the Baptist preacher Jeremiah B. Jeter was not altogether inaccurate when he observed, "The publication of the Christian Baptist was an open, formal declaration of war against all the religious sects and parties in the country."[33]

Campbell's chief weapon in this "war" would be ridicule. Contextualized within residual reasoning and augmented by what George Campbell called "the language of the passions," Alexander Campbell's unremitting and frequently unrestrained use of ridicule functioned rhetorically to construct (by negation) an alternative ecclesiastical identity for his movement as well as a distinctly prophetic *ethos* for his leadership.

A Rhetoric of Ridicule

In *The Philosophy of Rhetoric,* George Campbell's treatment of the rhetorical function of wit, humor, and ridicule (book one, chapters two and three) is preceded only by his introductory chapter on the ends and species of speaking. He divides "eloquence in its largest acceptation" into the "eloquence of conversation" and the "eloquence of declamation." Whereas "that which illuminates the understanding serves as a common founda-tion to both," each addresses the passions in its own way. The "eloquence of declamation" (described in chapter one) is divided into the "species" of "sublimity, pathos, [and] vehemence" and is "an accommodation to affairs of a serious and important nature." The "eloquence of conversation" (de-scribed in chapter two) is similarly divided into three "sorts" ("wit, hu-mour, [and] ridicule") and is "naturally suited to light and trivial matters." However, just as sublimity, pathos, and vehemence "may sometimes enter the precincts of familiar converse," so wit, humor, and ridicule "may often be successfully admitted into public harangues."[34]

In regard to ridicule, in particular, George Campbell observes that whereas the "intention of raising a laugh" may be "merely to divert by that grateful titillation which it excites," it may also be "to influence the opin-ions and purposes of the hearers." When the latter is the case, "there is always an air of reasoning conveyed under that species of imagery, narra-tion, or description, which stimulates laughter" and "these, thus blended, obtain the appellation of *ridicule.* . . . " Ridicule is "confined to questions of less moment" since employing it against such wrongs as "murder, cru-elty, parricide, ingratitude, perfidy, to attempt to raise a laugh, would show an unnatural insensibility in the speaker as would be excessively disgustful to any audience." Hence, "those things which principally come under its lash are awkwardness, rusticity, ignorance, cowardice, levity, fop-pery, pedantry, and affectation of every kind."[35]

Ridicule is also "fitter for refuting error than for supporting truth, for restraining from wrong conduct, than for inciting to the practice of what is right." However, "it is not properly levelled at the false, but at the *absurd* in tenets . . . that which we denominate silly or foolish."[36] In particular, he illustrates in reference to clerical contexts: "With regard to doctrine, it is evident that it is not falsity or mistake, but palpable error or absurdity (a thing hardly confutable by mere argument) which is the object of con-tempt; and consequently those dogmas are beyond the reach of cool rea-soning which are within the rightful confines of ridicule."[37] The logic of ridicule is thus that which suggests: "Such a position is ridiculous—It doth not deserve a serious answer" or "This is such an extravagance as is not so much a subject of argument as of laughter."[38]

Although one cannot be certain that Alexander Campbell intention-ally applied George Campbell's doctrine of ridicule,[39] the rhetorical func-tion assigned to ridicule in *The Philosophy of Rhetoric* would have made it a natural instrument for "the exposure of error in doctrine and practice" to which the *Christian Baptist* had been dedicated.

Ridiculing the Clergy:
The Third Epistle of Peter and a Sermon to Young Preachers

Years before, one of Elias Smith's early pamphlets, "The Clergyman's Looking Glass," satirized clergymen in mock-scriptural style.[40] Strikingly similar, Campbell's "Third Epistle of Peter," which appeared in the *Christian Baptist* (July 4, 1825), illustrates why one church historian has been led to observe that, "The *Christian Baptist* was the lash with which Campbell gave the clergy their 'forty stripes save one.'"[41] Offered as an "epistle overlooked by the early saints of Christendom" but since "found among the ruins of an ancient city by a miserable wandering Monk" and translated "from a French copy presented by the Monk himself," Campbell offers its exact fulfillment as tongue-in-cheek proof that "it was written in the spirit of prophecy."[42]

Addressed "to the Preachers and Rulers of Congregations" as "a Looking Glass for the Clergy," this "epistle" is divided into four chapters which categorize "many outward marks, whereby [those called to preach] shall be known by men." The first category is style and manner of living. Clergy are exhorted to take upon themselves holy titles, to dwell "in houses of splendor and edifices of cost," to minister not in "the garments of men" but "robes of richest silk and robes of fine linen, of curious device and of costly workmanship," to let their "fare be sumptuous, not plain and frugal as the fare of the husbandman who tills the ground," to "drink . . . of the wines of the vintage brought from afar, and wines of great price."[43]

When choosing candidates for the ministry (chapter two), clergymen are exhorted to choose "from among the youth, even those whose judgments are not yet ripe" for the author of the epistle is confident that they shall be able to "make them incline to the good things which the church has in store for them." Among these good things is an *ethos* derived from denominational hierarchy rather than charisma, sanctioned by the approval of the ruling clergy and their bestowal of reverend office, for "if any man believe that he is called by God to speak to his brethren 'without cost and without price,' though his soul be bowed to the will of the Father, and though he work all righteousness and 'speak as with the tongue of an angel'—if he be not made a divine by you rulers and by the hands of a bishop, then he is not a divine, nor shall he preach."[44]

In chapter three, marks pertaining to "the performance of preaching" are described. When going to church to preach, clergy should "go not by the retired way where go those that shun the crowd, but go in the highway, where go the multitude." The sermon itself should be "full of 'the enticing words of man's wisdom'" and "beautiful with just divisions, with tropes and with metaphors, and with hyperbole, and apostrophe, and with interrogation, and with acclamation, and with syllogisms, and with sophisms." As to delivery, they should know "when to bend and when to erect, when to lift [their] right hand and when [their] left." Their voice should be "smooth as the stream of the valley, and soft as the breeze that waves," at times to "swell like the wave of the ocean, or like the whirlwind on the mountaintop" so as to "charm the ears" and soften the hearts of their hearers. Offending people and rebuking sin are to be avoided. Above all they must teach that "the saving mysteries" are for them alone to explain.[45]

"The Clergy's Reward" (chapter four) elaborates upon its opening exhortation, "'In all your gettings,' get money!" The final benediction is biting: "In doing these things you shall never fail. And may abundance of gold and silver and bank notes, and corn, and wool, and flax, and spirits, and wine, and land be multiplied to you, both now and hereafter. Amen."[46]

Though the force of ridicule in these examples speaks for itself, a more subtle strategy intensifies its effect. There are, interwoven into this "epistle," a number of biblical allusions set in opposition to the "exhortations" of the author. The phrase, "speak as with the tongue of an angel," invoked in ridicule of the standards for approving clergy, is an allusion to Paul's first epistle to the Corinthians (13:1). Similarly, the phrase "without cost and without price" may be taken as an allusion to Isaiah 55:1, where the prophet, speaking for Yahweh, so calls upon chastised Israel to "Give ear and come to me; hear me that your soul may live." Adopting the epistolary genre, of course, is itself mimicry of the apostolic epistles of the New Testament. The result, clearly enough, is a most extreme castigation of the entire clerical order.

Other examples of Campbell's unrelenting ridicule of the clergy include his famous "Sermon on the Goats"[47] and a series of "Sermons to Young Preachers." The latter, five in number, were devoted to "young friends" who aspired to preaching in order to "convert" them from "habits and customs" that Campbell considered "injurious."[48] In the first of these sermons, Campbell ridiculed the "pulpit actors" whom he considered "the worst examples for young preachers":

Often have I seen a preacher try to get his mind abroach until he began to snuff the breeze like a whale snorting in the North Atlantic Ocean. It is more easy to bring a seventy-four gun ship into action in a gale of wind, than to get the mind to bear upon the text, until the nostrils catch the corner of a volume of air, and sneeze it out like a leviathan in the deep. I have seen other preachers who can strike fire no other way than by the friction of their hands, and an occasional clap, resembling a peal of distant thunder. In this holy paroxysm of clapping, rubbing, sneezing, and roaring, the mind is fairly on the way, and the tongue in full gallop, which, like a race horse, runs the swifter the less weight it carries. The farther from nature the nearer the skies, some preachers seem to think . . . They can neither speak to God, nor man in the pulpit to purpose, as they think, unless when, like the boiler of a steam boat, they are almost ready to burst. This is one extreme. There are various degrees marked on the scale before we arrive at this dreadful heat. There is a certain pitch of voice which at least is ten degrees above a natural key. To this most preachers have to come before their ideas get adrift. Their inspiration is kindled by some noise they create. I have seen children cry who began quite moderately, but when they heard the melody of their own voice their cries rose in a few seconds to screams . . . Some people have to milk all their sermons from their watch chains—and others from the buttons on their coats.

Now all these habits are no more according to reason, than were the screams and cuts of the prophets of Baal. And as for religion, I hope none of my young friends think there is any of it in a watch chain, or a button, or in mere vociferations.

Some preachers seem to think that suicide is equivalent to martyrdom; in other words that it is a good cause in which they die who burst their lungs in long, and loud, and vehement declamations. I doubt not but that hundreds kill themselves or shorten their days by an unmeaning and unnecessary straining of their lungs.[49]

In the end, Campbell wondered whether such preachers actually outnumbered stage actors. However, he admitted that "which is the more numerous we will not be able to decide until after the census of 1830."[50]

Ridiculing the Creeds: The Parable of the Iron Bedstead

Creeds were another popular object of Campbell's ridicule. For the October 1826 issue of the *Christian Baptist*, Campbell penned his well-known "Parable of the Iron Bedstead" and, in his prefatory remarks under the heading "Ecclesiastical Tyranny," recounted the circumstances that induced him to write it. Both the parable and its prelude are worth considering here.

During the preceding month, Campbell had "the pleasure and the pain" of visiting three Baptist associations: the Stillwater (Ohio) Association, the Mahoning (Ohio) Association, and the Redstone (Pennsylvania) Association (to which he had preached his famous "Sermon on the Law" and from which he had removed his membership in 1823). Of his first visits, he observed, "My visit to the Stillwater and Mahoning associations was altogether agreeable. There was no vain jangling about creeds and forms; no controversy about who should be pope and cardinals . . . nor encroachment upon the liberties of the brethren, considered as individuals or as congregations. All was peace and harmony."[51] He described his approach to Redstone, however, in more sinister terms:

> As I approached its horizon, the sky began to gather blackness,
> the reverberation of distant thunders and the reflected glare of
> forked lightnings from the regions of the Laurel Hill, portended a
> tremendous war of elements, if not a crash of worlds. Three clouds
> of ominous aspect surcharged with wind, one from the east, one
> from the north and one from the south, seemed to concentrate
> not far from the Old Fortification. As they approximated towards
> each other, they rolled out great volumes of hydrogen gas, which
> ignited by some electric sparks, exhibited a frightful aspect, and
> seemed to threaten a fiery desolation, and to hurl ruin far and
> wide. But to our great and agreeable disappointment it eventu-
> ated in a mere explosion of wind, which injured no green nor
> living thing. . . . [52]

The proceedings themselves, according to Campbell, were nothing less than a conspiracy, orchestrated by a minister who " . . . was converted under the ministry of a Methodist, and became all at once a Methodist preacher; and having burned out somewhere near the tropic of Capricorn, the cinder was carried to the arctic circle, and became a Calvinistic Baptist, of the supralapsarian order."[53] This preacher had "bound himself with a sevenfold cord never to have any communion with those who will not say they believe in the whole *Philadelphia Confession of Faith*" and formed a "league" with two others "to carry one point: in plain English, that one of them should be Pope and the other two his cardinals."[54]

The twenty-four churches of the association were each entitled to three voting representatives. In ten of these churches, the "triumvirate" was able to find a majority in favor of their views, but this entitled them to only thirty of the seventy-two votes. Finding themselves in the minority as to their design, they resorted to "manoeuvre and intrigue" and decided that "the good old constitution must be revived, though it has always been a dead letter; for not one association that ever met was ever regulated by it for more than two hours at a time."[55] Because this constitution required churches to refer to the *Philadelphia Confession of Faith* in writing their letters to the association, Campbell is led to remark upon the creed: "This matter has been for years discussed in this association; and the more it has been examined the less it has been relished. The children in many places now see the absurdity of their fathers and mothers declaring their faith to be expressed in the Philadelphia Confession of Faith, which not one in ten of them ever saw, and not one in a hundred of them could understand it if they did see it. . . . "[56] However, by invoking this stipulation, votes were denied to thirteen or fourteen churches and the "triumvirate" was able to "proceed to the greater excommunication, having by a lesser excommunication already dispatched about three-fifths of the whole body."[57]

What was to follow Campbell could only describe in hyperbole: "The only thing to which I could compare it was the tyranny of Robespierre during the reign of terror in the French Revolution."[58] The first of the "non-conforming" churches to be "given over to Satan" was that in Washington: "The guillotine was now erected and the instruments were all prepared for execution. The Pope and his two Cardinals in succession belabored this church for about one hour . . . because they had in their letter refused to call any man Pope or master on earth . . . By a series of what is sometimes called legerdemain, or, in the Welsh dialect, *hocus pocus,* one messenger, perhaps two . . . attempted to call a halt to their procedure, but it was all in vain."[59]

Similar was the fate of the churches in Maple Creek, Pigeon Creek, and Somerset. Upon learning that the expelled churches were planning to meet in November to form a new association, Campbell remarked, "here it may not be amiss to speak in *parables* to the wise. . . ."[60]

The "Parable of the Iron Bedstead" is a satirical[61] narrative of the church's use of creeds. "In the days of the Abecedarian Popes," Campbell wrote, "it was decreed that a good Christian just measured three feet."[62] Hence, an iron bedstead, "just three feet in the casement on the exactest of French scales" and "with a wheel at one end and a knife at the other," was "placed at the threshold of the church." For nearly a thousand years, so the parable continued, every Christian was laid on it to be stretched by the wheel and the rope, if too short, or to have the knife applied, if too long. Thus, "they kept the good christians . . . all of one standard."[63]

However, when Martin Luther "grew to the enormous height of four feet," he proclaimed that the church had been mistaken in fixing three feet as the stature of a good Christian and made proselytes to his opinions among those who, though they had found a way of contracting themselves to the three foot standard, were actually four feet and these soon began "to stretch themselves to their natural stature." Subsequently, "Luther had, in a few years, an iron bedstead *four feet* long, fashioned and fixed in his churches, with the usual appendages."[64]

As men continued to grow "much larger after Luther's time than before," several others ordered their own iron bedsteads. Calvin ordered his six inches longer than Luther's. The "Independents" fixed theirs "at the enormous stature of *five feet*." The Baptists then made theirs "six inches longer than the Congregationalists, and dispensed with the knife, thinking that there was likely to be more need for two wheels." To these were added Campbell's own speculation ("it will be found too short even when extended to *six feet*") and his call to question: "Why not, then, dispense with this piece of popish furniture in the church, and allow christians of every stature to meet at the same table?"[65]

Imitating the parabolic pattern of Christ in the gospels, Campbell followed the parable proper with a straightforward interpretation: "The parable is just, and the interpretation thereof easy and sure."[66] The iron bedstead, of course, is "The Creed," into which the various Protestant parties had reduced the "essentials." Alternatively, Campbell proposed:

What then if an experiment should be made, and a fair trial of the Divine Book should be given; and whenever it fails of the promised end, let any other device be tried . . . I do not think it is likely that it shall ever be proved by actual experiment that the New Testament, without a creed, is insufficient to preserve the unity, peace and purity of any one congregation, or of those of any given district. But above all else, let us have no iron bed-steads, with or without wheels or knives.[67]

As in the case of the "Third Epistle of Peter," not only does Campbell's ridicule serve as a tool to illustrate what he perceived to be the "absurd" in the church's use of creeds, his parody of a biblical genre aligns him with the voice of the "divine-I."[68]

Ridicule is a ubiquitous trait of the *Christian Baptist* rhetoric. Leveled "at the absurd in tenets," George Campbell considered it fitting "for refuting error."[69] To the extent that Alexander Campbell may likewise have considered rhetoric "that art or talent by which discourse is adapted to its end,"[70] one of the stated aims of the *Christian Baptist* ("the exposure of error in doctrine and practice"[71]) may thus have influenced him to methodically choose ridicule from among the means of persuasion available to him. Through its causticity, Campbell adopts an "excoriating stance" toward his audience. When contextualized within parodies of biblical genres, it most clearly positions Campbell as a voice of "divine-I" in radical confrontation with those power structures (clergy, associations) that disregarded covenant standards and ideals (i.e., biblical purity) for the "a-pathos" of human self-definition (creeds). Thus, Campbell's prevalent use of ridicule alone accounts for much of the *Christian Baptist*'s prophetic tone.

Ridicule and Residue

The "exposure of error in doctrine and practice," however, was only one half of the "sole object" of the *Christian Baptist*. Its counterpart was "the eviction of truth."[72] George Campbell considered ridicule alone "fitter for refuting error than for supporting truth."[73] While Alexander Campbell did not completely abandon ridicule toward the latter end, he did contextualize it within another common feature of the *Christian Baptist*'s rhetoric: residual reasoning.

The convergence of ridicule and residue is not altogether foreign to the function of "the derisive" within George Campbell's *Philosophy of*

Rhetoric. Indeed, when discussing the differences between the "contentious" and the "derisive," George Campbell remarks finally upon "the manner of conducting them." Though "in each there is a mixture of argument," the difference is that "the attack of the declaimer is direct and open," whereas "the assault of him who ridicules is, from its very nature, covert and oblique." This is not to say that it seeks to deceive, for that "which distinguishes an ironical expression from a lie" is its transparency: "through the thinness of the veil employed, he takes care that the sneer is discovered."[74] The "reasoning in ridicule," then, while "always conveyed under a species of disguise," nonetheless resembles that species of residual argument characteristic of the rhetoric of Socrates:

> You are quickly made to perceive his aim, by means of the strange arguments he produces, by means of the absurd consequences he draws, the odd embarrassments which in his personated character he is involved in, and still the odder methods he takes to disentangle himself. In this manner doctrines and practices are treated, when exposed by a continued run of irony; a way of refutation which bears a strong analogy to that species of demonstration termed by mathematicians apagogical, as reducing the adversary to what is contradictory or impractical. This method seems to have been first introduced into moral subjects, and employed with success, by the father of ancient wisdom, Socrates.[75]

While this precise pattern can only be observed with varying degrees of exactness in the *Christian Baptist,* a mixture of ridicule and residue, in one fashion or another, is one of Alexander Campbell's more common instruments for both defining and defending an alternative doctrinal and ecclesiastical self-understanding that is wholly other to the existing order.

"The Restoration of the Ancient Order of Things" (1825–1829)

Considered by some historians "the most significant series of articles Campbell wrote in the *Christian Baptist,*"[76] "The Restoration of the Ancient Order of Things" articulated the "pattern" of the New Testament church advocated by Campbell for his restoration movement. It also illustrates his manner of mixing ridicule and residue, as we shall soon see.

In February of 1825, Campbell seized upon the minutes of the September 11, 1824, meeting of the Baptist Missionary Association of Kentucky as an occasion for launching the series. The minutes, from which Campbell printed an extract as a preface to number one in the series, included a call "to bring the Christianity and the church of the present day" up to the state of "the church of the New Testament," promised a conference to discuss the subject, and invited all Baptist ministers to participate. Campbell hailed this as "a most auspicious event" and as one "deeply interested in every effort that is made . . . for the avowed subject of reform"—a subject "familiar to [his] mind, from much reflection and a good deal of reading"—he offered "a few remarks."[77] In fact, he penned no less than thirty-two articles that ran through June of 1829.

Number one in the series laid a foundation for the rest, a foundation grounded in a radical distinction between a *reformation* and a *restoration.* Conceding that previous reformations had produced benefits, the burden of Campbell's argument is to demonstrate that they had all, nonetheless, fallen short of their aims. The spirit and point of the article is captured in this excerpt:

> Human systems, whether of philosophy or of religion, are proper subjects of reformation; but christianity cannot be reformed. Every attempt to reform christianity is like an attempt to create a new sun, or to change the revolutions of the heavenly bodies—unprofitable and vain. In a word, we have had reformations enough. The very name has become as offensive as the term "Revolution" in France.
>
> A restoration of the ancient order of things is all that is necessary to the happiness and the usefulness of Christians. No attempt to "reform the doctrine, discipline, and government of the church" . . . can promise a better result.[78]

As a catalogue of that "ancient order" which Campbell sought to restore, subsequent articles set forth Campbell's positions on matters of practice wherein he clearly differed not only with the Baptists but with most Protestant denominations. Because these articles pertained predominantly to matters of church polity and liturgy,[79] they were not merely rancorous but threatening, at the most practical level, to the status quo. It is little wonder, then, that these articles contributed significantly to the development of tensions between the reforming churches who followed Campbell's principles and the Baptist associations to which they belonged.

Ridicule, Residue, and Radical Reform

The radical implications of Campbell's restorationism, the tenor of its uncompromising absolutism, and Campbell's method of mixing ridicule and residue to articulate its underlying prophetic logic may all be illustrated from the first of four articles on "the breaking of bread" (otherwise known as Communion or the Lord's Supper) which appeared August 1 through November 7, 1825. In and of itself, the matter of communion was of great practical significance for several reasons. Several years prior, it had been the occasion of charges first brought against Thomas Campbell by the Chartiers Presbytery (Pennsylvania). It had since become a point of controversy between the Campbells and the Baptists as well. Finally, Alexander Campbell's strong position favoring weekly observance made it difficult to accommodate differences of opinion in the liturgical matter of planning weekly worship services.

In the concluding paragraph to this first article on "the breaking of bread," Campbell summarizes his argument: "From the nature and design of the breaking of bread, we would argue its necessity and importance as a part of the entertainment of the saints in the social worship of the Lord in their assemblies for his praise and their comfort."[80] Campbell's method, however, is more inductive than this summary might suggest. Constructing a series of dilemmas within which his restorationist pattern is set in opposition to practices he viewed as subsequent corruptions,[81] he proceeds both (1) to offer authoritative (biblical) and empirical (Lockean) proofs in support of his own view and (2) to engage in residual reasoning by employing ridicule to reduce opposing views to the absurd or the impracticable.

In his opening paragraph, Campbell first distinguishes between those who accept the breaking of bread as an act of worship and those who do not. According to Campbell, "Romanists and Protestants of almost every name agree" that the breaking of bread is an act of worship, whereas the "society of Friends form the chief, if not the only exception in Christendom, to this general acknowledgement." Having isolated the Friends through this dilemma, he subjects their position to ridicule. Their spirituality "may be suitable to beings of some higher order than the natural descendants of Adam and Eve" but is "too contemplative, too sublime" for "flesh and blood" human beings who have "tongues and lips . . . bodies, too." After employing ridicule to reduce the opposing position to a state of absurdity, Campbell buttresses the residual position with an enthymeme that draws upon Lockean empiricism for its premise: "And so long as the five senses are the five avenues of human understanding, the medium of all divine communication to the spirit of man, so long will it be necessary to use them in the cultivation of piety and humanity"[82]—i.e., as one does in the breaking of bread by seeing, touching, and tasting the bread and the wine.

Next, Campbell's argument progresses to a second dilemma, constructed by dividing those who accept the breaking of bread as an act of worship according to whether they practice it as a *weekly* observance, on one hand, or as a monthly, quarterly, semiannual or even annual observance, on the other. Campbell first invokes the patternism inherent in his concept of restoration (as defined in the first number of the "Ancient Order" series) to support weekly observance. Since "the primitive disciples did, in all their meetings on the first day of the week, attend on the breaking of bread as an essential part of the worship due their Lord, . . . then it is fairly manifest that the disciples are to break bread in all their meetings for worship."[83] He then opposes human and divine authorities to problematize the alternative positions, "they have custom and tradition to show, but not one argument worthy of a moment's reflection, not even one text to adduce as a confirmation of their practice. Who ever heard of a text adduced to prove a monthly, a quarterly, a semiannual or annual breaking of bread."[84] Argument by direction (i.e., extending the basic logic of the argument) is then coupled with ridicule to suggest impracticable consequences: "their course in regard to this institution, I conjecture, drove the founder of the Quaker system into the practice of *never* breaking bread, just as the views of the clergy make and confirm Deists."[85]

These same alternatives are then opposed based on their manners of observance. The manner of annual, semiannual, and quarterly observers is first subjected to ridicule. Their minds full of "darkness and superstition," they

> generally make a Jewish Passover of it. Some of them, indeed, make a Mount Sinai convocation of it. With all the bitterness of sorrow and gloominess of superstition, they convert it into a religious penance, accompanied with a morose piety and an awful affliction of soul and body, expressed in fastings, long prayers, and sad countenances on sundry days of humiliation, fasting, and

preparation. And the only joy exhibited on the occasion is that it is all over . . . they rejoice that they have approached the very base of Mount Sinai unhurt by stone or dart."[86]

The manner of "intelligent Christians"—the residual—is presented as a stark contrast. To such, the breaking of bread is "joyful to the hope of immortality and eternal life," for "his hope before God, springing from the death of his Son, is gratefully exhibited and expressed by him in the observance of this institution." He observes "with sacred joy and blissful hope" and "the philanthropy of God fills his heart and excites correspondent feelings to those sharing with him the salvation of the Lord." Consequently, one may view the observance as either "a privilege, or a pain" and its frequency as either "a favor or a frown." In the former case, it would be an "inexpressibly greater goodness and grace to allow you the feast in all your meetings . . . but reverse the case . . . and then grace is exhibited in not enforcing it but seldom."[87]

Concluding analogies intensify both the opposition and the ridicule. By "the design of the Savior," the breaking of bread is a "joyful festival." Man is a "social animal" and the "religion of Jesus Christ is a religion for *men*." Thus it "has its feasts, and its joys, and its extacies [sic], too" and "the Lord's house is his banqueting place, and the Lord's day is his weekly festival." Alternatively,

a sacrament, an annual sacrament, or a quarterly sacrament, is like the oath of a Roman soldier, from which it derives its name, often taken with reluctance, and kept with bad faith. It is as sad as a funeral parade. The knell of the parish bell that summonses the mourners to the house of sorrow, and the tocsin that awakes the recollection of a sacramental morn, are heard with equal dismay and aversion. The seldomer they occur, the better. We speak of them as they appear to be; and if they are not what they appear to be, they are mere exhibitions of hypocrisy and deceit, and serve no other purpose than as they create a market for silks and calicoes, and an occasion for the display of beauty and fashion.[88]

In this fashion, then, ridicule also plays an important role in that part of the *Christian Baptist*'s program dedicated to "the eviction of truth." Contextualized within residual reasoning, Campbell's "excoriating stance" toward his audience is combined with that dimension of prophetic rhetoric which, though rational, is yet "unreasonable" in the sense that it sacrifices the "bargaining side of intelligence" in pursuit of its qualitative end of exact conformity to God's absolute will. Dilemmas construct alternatives; ridicule and residue do not permit choices.

There is yet one other feature of the rhetoric of the *Christian Baptist* worth noting here, however, for it both illustrates Campbell's shift toward George Campbell's "natural" philosophy of rhetoric and, by augmenting his prophetic tone, contributes to the construction of his prophetic *ethos.*

A Rhetoric of Affect: The Language of the Passions

It must be kept in mind that while George Campbell held that reason must guide the passions,[89] within his hierarchy of purposes the former cannot *persuade* without the aid of the latter:

> In order to evince the truth considered by itself, conclusive arguments alone are requisite; but in order to convince me by these arguments, it is moreover requisite that they be understood, that they be attended to, that they be remembered by me; and in order to persuade me by them to any particular action or conduct, it is further requisite, that by interesting me in the subject, they may, as it were, be felt. It is not therefore the understanding alone that is here concerned. If the orator would prove successful, it is necessary that he engage in his service all these different powers of the mind, the imagination, the memory, and the passions. These are not the supplanters of reason, or even rivals in her sway; they are her handmaids, by whose ministry she is enabled to usher truth into the heart, and procure it there a favourable reception.[90]

Neither end, attained alone, is sufficient for the purpose of persuasion:

> To say that it is possible to persuade without speaking to the passions, is but at best a kind of specious nonsense. The coolest reasoner always in persuading, addresseth himself to the passions some way or other. This he cannot avoid doing, if he speak to the purpose . . . in order to persuade, there are two things which must be carefully studied by the orator. The first is, to excite some de-

sire or passion in the hearers; the second is to satisfy their judgment that there is a connexion between the action to which he would persuade them, and the gratification of the desire or passion which he excites. This is the analysis of persuasion. The former is effected by communicating lively and glowing ideas of the object; the latter, . . . by presenting the best and most forcible arguments which the nature of the subject admits. In the one lies the pathetic, in the other the argumentative . . . When the first end alone is attained, the pathetic without the rational, the passions are indeed roused from a disagreeable languor by the help of the imagination . . . But, if the hearers are judicious, no practical effect is produced . . . because [they are] not convinced that that action will conduce to the gratifying of the passion raised . . . On the contrary, when the other end alone is attained, the rational without the pathetic, the speaker is as far from his purpose as before. You have proved . . . but I am not affected by it . . . I have no passion for the object.[91]

Persuasion requires, then, that "most complex of all" the species of discourse, "an artful mixture of that which proposes to convince the judgment, and that which interests the passions, . . . the argumentative and the pathetic incorporated together."[92]

On the whole, it is probably fair to say that the pathetic dimensions of Alexander Campbell's rhetoric have been somewhat understated. Perhaps this is because there is abundant evidence of the influence of Baconian and Lockean epistemologies in Campbell's arguments alone or even because the influence of faculty psychology can be found both in the arrangement of his own sermons as well as in his instruction as to how other preachers should arrange their sermons. Or it may well be that the contrast between Campbell's rationalism and the emotionalism of the enthusiasts or revivalists of his day[93] or that descriptions of his conversational speaking style as possessing "no appeal to passion, no effort at pathos"[94] have somehow directed our attention away from such matters.

But herein lies the importance of style, to which, as has been noted, George Campbell devoted roughly two-thirds of *The Philosophy of Rhetoric*. Whereas "perspicuity" is that essential quality of style "by which the discourse is fitted to inform the understanding," "vivacity" is chief among "those qualities of style by which it is adapted to please the imagination"[95] since, as noted above, when the end is "to excite some desire or passion in the hearers," this is "effected by communicating lively and glowing ideas of the object."

Alexander Campbell's style is often characterized by an extraordinary syntactical copiousness. Though this feature of his rhetoric is not confined to the *Christian Baptist,* it is especially prominent there, where this copiousness often follows argumentative passages and its specific features are, by and large, those associated by George Campbell with "the language of the passions":[96] devices of vivacity, associational repetition,[97] and periodic sentence structure. In fact, Alexander Campbell's fondness for long, often complex periodic sentences is probably best understood as an attempt to create vivacity through the arrangement of sentences.

The following passage, from the text analyzed above (the first number on "the breaking of bread"), is illustrative:[98]

[1]The intelligent christian   views   it
                  quite in another light.

[2]It   is
            to him
            as sacred and
              solemn
                 as prayer
                   to God,
        and
        as joyful
               as the hope
                 of immortality and
                 eternal life.

[3]His hope
   before God,
   springing from
   the death
   of his Son,   is gratefully   exhibited and
                                expressed
                                  by him
                                  in the observance
                                     of this institution.

⁴While
he   participates of   the symbolic loaf,
he   shews   his faith in,
                                                  his life upon,
                                                      the Bread
                                                        of life.

⁵While
he   tastes   the emblematic cup
he   remembers   the new covenant
                                                      confirmed
                                                          by the blood
                                                            of the Lord.

With   sacred   joy and
                blissful   hope
he   hears   the Saviour say,
                "This   is   my body broken—
                this   my blood shed
                          for you."

⁷When
he   reaches forth   those lively emblems
                                                      of his Saviour's love
                          to his christian brethren,

the philanthropy
  of God   fills   his heart
                            and
                            excites   correspondent feelings
                                                      to those sharing
                                                          with him
                                                              the salvation
                                                                of the Lord.

⁸Here
he   knows   no man
                          after the flesh.

⁹Ties
  that spring
    from eternal love
      revealed

in blood and
addressed
to the senses
in symbols
adapted
   to the whole man,

                draw forth   all that is within him
                                              of complacent affection and
                                                    feeling
                                                        to those
                                              joint heirs
                                              with him
                                            of the grace
                                            of eternal life.

[10]While
it   represents
                    to him   all the salvation
                                   of the Lord,
it   is   the strength
                                   of his faith,
                                   the joy
                                   of his hope, and
                                   the life
                                   of his love.
[11]It   cherishes   the peace
                                   of God,
                    and
                    inscribes   the image
                                   of God
                      upon his heart,
                    and
                    leaves not
                    out of view   the revival
                                   of his body
                                   from the dust
                                   of death, and
                                   its glorious transformation

to the likeness
of the Son
of God.

[12]It   is   an institution
full
of wisdom and
goodness,
every way adapted
to the Christian mind.

[13]As
the bread and
wine   to the body,
so
it   strengthens   his faith
and
cheers   his heart
with the love
of God.

[14]It   is   a religious feast;
a feast
of joy and
gladness; and
the happiest occasion,
the sweetest antepast
on earth
of the society and
entertainment
of heaven,
that mortals meet with
on their way
to the true Canaan.[99]

Two aspects of this passage are worthy of notice. First, the argument itself is grounded in an appeal to Lockean empiricism and the ability of the emblems to "affect" one's imaginations and passions. One "*tastes* the emblematic cup" and thus "remembers the new covenant confirmed by the blood of the Lord." One "*hears* the Savior say" words that invoke visual images: "my body broken . . . my blood shed for you." When one

"reaches forth those lively emblems" to others, "the philanthropy of God
. . . *excites* correspondent feelings to those sharing with him" and "ties
that spring from eternal love, revealed in blood and *addressed to the senses
in symbols adapted to the whole man,* draw forth all that is within him of
complacent affection and feeling." Thus, the breaking of bread is an "institution full of wisdom and goodness, *every way adapted to the Christian
mind.*"

Further, this passage also illustrates the syntactical copiousness—the
stylistic amplification—by which this discourse "dwells upon its object"
as it does, according to George Campbell, "when the language of the
passions is exhibited."[100] At first, this is somewhat restrained—in sentence two a series of doublets, including an alliterated doublet, in a 2–1,
1–2 arrangement ("as sacred and solemn . . . and as joyful," "as prayer to
God . . . and as the hope of immortality and eternal life") and, in sentence three, one alliterated doublet ("exhibited and expressed"). Sentences
four and five form a doublet of periodic sentences bound together by
anaphora and parallelism, representing the two elements of communion
—bread and cup. Sentence six is introduced with a doublet ("sacred joy
and blissful hope") and the apodosis ("the philanthropy of God . . .") of
sentence seven ends with another doublet ("fills . . . and excites"). Doublets are employed in both the nominative ("revealed . . . and addressed")
and predicate ("affection and feeling") of sentence nine. The apodosis of
sentence ten ("it is . . . ") consists of a triplet of genitive phrases. Sentence
eleven employs three main verbs, the object of the last a doublet. The
predicate of sentence twelve includes a genitive doublet, both the protasis
("As . . . ") and apodosis ("so . . . ") of sentence thirteen employ doublets,
and the predicate of sentence fourteen consists of no less than four elements, two of which are amplified with genitive doublets.

The point here is that, in spite of this syntactical copiousness, there is
very little advancement of thought. There are, however, multiple devices
of vivacity, such as specialty, individuation, and other figures of speech
(e.g., imagery, animation, alliteration, anaphora, etc.), which "subject the
thing spoken of to the notice of our senses" and "greatly enliven the expression," all "in order to more strongly attach the imagination."[101] In this
manner, presumably, the appeal to reason is supplemented with an appeal
to the passions.

The above passage also includes no less than six instances of another
common feature of Campbell's style: the periodic sentence—i.e., one

constructed to suspend the completion of its sense and structure until its close, for example, "If (protasis) . . . , then (apodosis). . . . " What must be kept in mind here is George Campbell's view of the periodic sentence: though simple sentences generally contribute more to vivacity than complex sentences, the periodic, "more adapted to the style of the writer" is "susceptible of vivacity and force" for in it the strength which is "diffused" through the loose sentence is "collected, as it were into a single point. You defer the blow a little, but it is solely that you may bring it down with greater weight."[102] In the style of Alexander Campbell, complex periodic sentences frequently employ an extended protasis, presumably to "strengthen the blow" of that which is deferred.

One example may again be drawn from the first number on "the breaking of bread," a passage that follows Campbell's first residual argument addressed to the society of Friends and much of which, offered in summary, is clearly repetitive:

> For,
>   if there   be   a divinely instituted worship
>   for Christians
>   in their meetings
>   on the first day
>   of the week,
>   as has been proved;
>   if this order
>   or these acts
>   of worship   are   uniformly the same,
>   as has been shown;
>   and
>   if the breaking
>   of bread   be   an act
>   of christian worship,
>   as is admitted
>   by those we address—
>   then
>   it   is   fairly manifest that
>   the disciples   are to break bread
>   in all their meetings
>   for worship.[103]

In this case, parallelism and repetition of forms of the stative verb add a sense of accumulation to the three elements of the protasis ("if" clauses), which form a chain of premises from which the conclusion is drawn. To the extent that force is added to that which is deferred, the "language of the passions," presumably, aids the appeal to reason.

Another example might be drawn from the second article on "the breaking of bread," a passage in which Campbell defends his interpretation of the book of Acts 2:41–42 by explaining his hermeneutical patternism:

> For
> though
> the selling
>   of their possessions   is mentioned
>   as a part
>   of the benevolent influences
>   of the christian religion
>   clearly understood and
>   cordially embraced,
>   as a voluntary act
>   suggested by the circumstances
>   of the times and
>   of their brethren,
>   yet
>   were   a society
>   of christians   absolutely so poor
>   that they could live
>   in no other way
>   than by the selling
>   of the possessions
>   of some
>   of the brethren,
>   it   would be   an indispensable duty
>   to do so
>   in imitation
>   of him
>   who . . .

though

he   was   rich,

made   himself   poor,

that

the poor,

   through his impoverishing himself

        might be made   rich.[104]

This entire sentence is but a complex repetition of the preceding sentence: "And, indeed, their whole example is binding on all Christians placed in circumstances similar to those in which they lived at the time."[105] Yet it enhances the vivacity of the thought, through specialty and individuation, as well as force to the expression through the extended period. The protasis consists of both a countercondition ("though"), the predicate of which is amplified through the use of doublets, and a condition ("yet were"), the predicate of which is amplified through the use of prepositional and genitive phrases. The apodosis itself includes a restrained period ("though"), which forms the first half of a chiasmus (rich, poor, poor, rich).

Campbell's use of the "language of the passions" not only reflects his "natural" philosophy of rhetoric; it also has a more direct bearing upon the prophetic tone of the *Christian Baptist* than one might first suspect. Thomas Conley refers to the eighteenth-century Scottish rhetorics as "operational rhetorics," in which the art is perceived as primarily "affective, a unilateral transaction between an active speaker and a passive listener, between mover and moved" and in which the study of the art consists of "the systematic examination of the affective possibilities of language, which is used by reason to affect the imagination 'to excite the appetite or will.'"[106] The "language of the passions," in this sense, is not altogether unlike the advertisement that, applying behaviorist psychology, flashes the word "S-A-L-E!" in large red letters across a television screen, over and over again. The purpose is to stimulate the imagination and forcefully impress the stimuli upon the senses.

One might plausibly suggest that the purpose of such passages as we have noted is to bombard the senses, if not actually impose the will of the rhetor through the affective powers of style.[107] Combined with the zealousness of Campbell's ridicule and the tenor of absolutism conveyed by his residual reasoning, this "language of the passions" thus aids in constructing the "one sided, unbearable extremism" that Heschel associates with the prophetic *ethos*.[108]

Conclusion

Alexander Campbell's manner of using ridicule, residual reasoning, and the language of the passions all contribute to the prophetic tone of the *Christian Baptist*, the arguments and style of which work together to construct a prophetic *ethos* for his rhetorical leadership during these years. This is not so much an inevitable consequence of practicing what is advocated in George Campbell's *Philosophy of Rhetoric*, to whatever extent Alexander Campbell may have done so, as it is a product of the extremism which distinguishes the use of these same precepts in the *Christian Baptist*. Nonetheless, a close examination of representative texts reveals not only evidence of Alexander Campbell's shift toward a "natural" philosophy of rhetoric but of a genuinely "prophetic" rhetoric—and thus an evolution in his leadership *ethos*.

Alexander Campbell, in the very pages of the *Christian Baptist*, was not averse to drawing parallels between his rhetoric and that of the ancient Hebrew prophets and John the Baptist. In one of his "Sermons to Young Preachers," he wrote:

We must have preachers to introduce a better order of things. Preachers have become as necessary as prophets were in the worst times of the Jewish history. In prosperous times they needed no prophets. Had not Baal had them in hundreds, there would have been no need for Elijah, and Obadiah, and other kindred spirits . . . It is necessary to proclaim *reformation* to such a people who, with all these acknowledgements, are serving diverse lusts and passions, living in malice and envy, hated and hating one another. Indeed, the more I think upon this subject, the more similarity I discover between the circumstances of the people now, as respects Christianity, and the circumstances of those as respects Judaism, in the time of John the harbinger, whom he addressed. I, therefore, think, that there is now more propriety in imitating John, than at first view appears . . . to you, young preachers, I would say, you must, if you would be useful, take John for a model. . . . [109]

As noted earlier, however, the *ethos* of a prophet is charismatic rather than hierarchical and thus his value lies in his reception. The prophetic *ethos* of Campbell's rhetorical leadership, more often than not, polarized his audiences. Nonetheless, it garnered for Campbell's movement a prominence theretofore unattained. And, however readers from that day to this may have responded to the iconoclasm of Campbell's *Christian Baptist,* as a journalistic enterprise it made Campbell a national figure who could no longer be ignored.

5
Managing Ideological Difference
Classification, Transcendence, and
the Letter from Lunenburg

Some of our fellow-laborers seem to forget that *approaches* are more in the spirit and style of the Saviour, than *reproaches*. We have proved to our entire satisfaction, that having obtained a favorable hearing, a conciliatory, meek, and benevolent attitude is not only the most comely and Christian-like, but the most successful.[1]

By the time Alexander Campbell completed the final volume of the *Christian Baptist* in 1830, the challenges confronting his restoration movement had changed dramatically. When he launched this journal (1823), he was an iconoclastic but popular young Baptist preacher who had just successfully championed the immersionist cause in his debate with John Walker. By the close of the decade, "Campbellite" churches were being expelled from Baptist associations as quickly as possible. In the interim, however, the Baptists had contributed thousands of members and whole congregations to Campbell's restoration cause. The challenges of the next decade would result not only from the tremendous growth of the movement but also from the difficulties of managing the tensions between the inclusiveness of a commitment to Christian unity and the exclusiveness of a commitment to biblical authority.

A series of unions between followers of Campbell (who usually called themselves "Disciples of Christ" or "Disciples") and followers of Barton Stone (who usually called themselves "Christians")[2] provided a stimulus for the movement's growth. The most famous of these, which established a pattern for subsequent unions, took place in Lexington, Kentucky, over the weekend of December 31, 1831, and January 1, 1832. "Raccoon" John Smith, an acquaintance of Campbell since 1824,[3] and Barton Stone both participated in these meetings. Campbell himself was not present at the meetings but endorsed the union. Of Smith and John Rogers, who were appointed to travel among churches urging similar unions, Campbell would write: "With these two brethren we are well acquainted. They have both been preaching the ancient institutions for some years, and are very much devoted to the truth. They have both been very successful preachers . . . We most cordially bid them God speed in their conjoint labors under the present arrangement."[4]

This was not the first union, however. The first consolidation of congregations took place on December of 1830 in Beaver Creek, Kentucky, and another in Millersburg, Kentucky, in April of 1831. Congregations in Georgetown united as a result of a four-day meeting on Christmas, just prior to the Lexington meeting. Many others followed the union in Lexington. North remarks, "The union between the followers of Stone and Campbell seemed to represent the best of what the Restoration Movement stood for—the unity of Christians standing solely on the basis of biblical teaching."[5]

Garrison and DeGroot have estimated that, in 1830, membership in the churches of Campbell's movement numbered approximately 12,000–20,000. Hughes has estimated that, by 1823, membership in the churches of Stone's movement similarly numbered approximately 15,000–20,000.[6] The movements combined, then, would have numbered 25,000–40,000. Between 1832 and 1860, membership in Stone-Campbell churches would increase to more than 200,000. According to Alexander Campbell's own figures in 1857, the movement included 225,000 members, 2,700 congregations and 2,225 ministers.[7]

The growth and consolidation of the Stone-Campbell restoration movement was, in many ways, typical of the second-generation experience for most of the populist religious movements born in earlier years of experimentation and novelty. Hatch suggests that "by 1840 populist dissent had diminished in American Christianity" as cultural alienation began to give way to respectability and influence. This quest for respectability, in turn, had powerful effects upon the leadership of these movements, wealth and social standing making it more difficult for them to retain their identities as "alienated, defiant prophets."[8]

This transformation confronted leaders with other new challenges as well. Hatch observes: "This growing civility in popular denominations increased interdenominational cooperation but accentuated internal differentiation . . . [I]ncreased respectability and centralization reinforced tensions between localists and cosmopolitans, primitivists and centralizers, and rural and urban interests." As "powerful, self-made leaders continued to rise within these movements," he adds, established leaders were often confronted with a backlash of controversy.[9] Campbell's movement was no exception to these trends. Concomitant to its numerical growth was a growth in tensions stemming from ideological differences that soon began to emerge within the movement. Managing these differences and tensions would present a significant challenge to Campbell's rhetorical leadership.

This chapter will examine how Campbell adapted his rhetorical leadership to manage an especially prominent controversy that developed over the practice of baptism, in particular, and ultimately, the question of what was "essential" to being a Christian. After a brief consideration of the significance of the medium through which Campbell addressed this controversy (his new journal, the *Millennial Harbinger*), an analysis of his responses to the Lunenburg letter will demonstrate how his rhetoric constructed a hierarchy of spiritual identity that enabled him to transcend and manage differences with diverse audiences and how, consequently, this rhetoric generated for him a leadership *ethos* much more *pastoral* than *prophetic.*

The *Millennial Harbinger* (1830–1866)

In January of 1830, several months before the final issue of the *Christian Baptist* appeared, Campbell launched a new journalistic venture: the *Millennial Harbinger*. It had become sufficiently clear that Campbell was now the leader of a movement consisting of independent churches and could no longer consider himself a Baptist. A new journal, with a new title and a new purpose, was the need of the hour.

On the final page of the last issue of the *Christian Baptist*, the title of which had been chosen to aid circulation among the Baptists, Campbell explained: "I have commenced a new work, and taken a new name for it on various accounts. Hating sects and sectarian names, I resolved to prevent the name of Christian Baptists from being fixed upon us, to do which efforts were making. It is true, men's tongues are their own, and they may use them as they please; but I am resolved to give them no just occasion for nicknaming advocates for the ancient order of things."[10] The title of his new journal reflected his postmillennial eschatology—his belief that the thousand-year reign of Christ mentioned in the book of Revelation (20:4–7) would be fulfilled literally on earth upon Christ's return as the climax to the gradual triumph of the church's evangelistic mission to the world. Because Campbell understood the prayer of Christ in John 17 to imply that the unification and purification of the church was prerequisite to this evangelistic triumph, he saw his restoration movement as a necessary stage in the ultimate millennial triumph of the kingdom of Christ.[11]

Toward this end, he dedicated his new journal. In the opening issue, he wrote: "This work shall be devoted to the destruction of Sectarianism, Infidelity, and Antichristian doctrine and practice. It shall have for its object the development, and introduction of that political and religious order of society called THE MILLENNIUM, which will be the consummation of that ultimate amelioration of society proposed in the Christian Scriptures."[12] Thus, to the extent that it furthered his restorationist cause, Campbell considered his new journal a harbinger of the millennium.

But Campbell also now bore the primary responsibility of providing leadership for the churches of his movement. For more than thirty years, the *Millennial Harbinger* would serve as his chief instrument for leading that movement through its first and into its second generation. Typically twice the size of the *Christian Baptist,* it served not only as a medium for Campbell's rhetorical leadership but also as a repository of news from the churches. It was, without doubt, the Stone-Campbell movement's most significant journal of the century. Campbell would continue to edit and publish the *Millennial Harbinger* until 1863, when declining health and creeping senility forced him to turn editorship over to W. K. Pendleton, who continued the work until 1870 when the journal was discontinued due to decreasing interest.[13]

In many ways, the *Christian Baptist* and the *Millennial Harbinger* are an interesting study in contrasts. North, for example, observes of the *Millennial Harbinger,* "In many ways it was the same Campbell—hard hitting, vitriolic, aggressive. But in other ways it was a milder Campbell."[14] McAllister and Tucker describe the *Millennial Harbinger* as "more constructive and less iconoclastic than the *Christian Baptist.* The responsibility of leading a separate religious movement altered Campbell's point of view more than he was willing to admit. A more positive approach is evident in the second number of the *Millennial Harbinger* . . . The reformer had begun to be tamed."[15]

The contrasts between these two journals have, in fact, led some to perceive in the latter the evolution of a "Campbell Number Two."[16]

In addition to his increased responsibilities to the movement, Campbell's transformation was also influenced by his participation in five highly publicized debates between 1820 and 1843. This volume is not sufficient to tell their story but it is significant to note the diversity of roles Campbell occupied over the course of these debates. In his first two debates, Campbell spoke as a Baptist debating Presbyterians (John Walker, 1820, and William L. Maccalla, 1823). He then represented Christianity against skepticism (Robert Owen, 1829). He eventually represented Protestantism against Roman Catholicism (Bishop John Purcell, 1837). Finally, he debated as the acknowledged leader of the restoration movement (Nathan Rice, 1843).

The debate with Purcell may be singled out since it has been cited as among the key factors in the emergence of a "second" Campbell. According to Hughes, whereas the early Campbell of the *Christian Baptist* characteristically launched scathing attacks upon "the little popes" of American Protestantism, by the 1830s Campbell's concerns were increasingly drawn to what he perceived as a Roman Catholic threat to American liberties. In 1836, Campbell addressed a College of Professional Teachers in Cincinnati, arguing that the Protestant commitment to individuals thinking for themselves was the genius of English-speaking peoples. Bishop Purcell objected and the two met for public discussion (not formal debate) the following week. That same week, Campbell received an invitation, signed by many of Cincinnati's leading citizens, to defend "the cause of Protestantism in the West" and he agreed to meet Purcell in a debate during January of 1837.[17]

The debate marked a turning point in Campbell's thought. Subsequently, he spoke far more as a mainstream Protestant,[18] still refusing to champion the Protestant denominations but gladly championing the Protestant faith.[19] However, 1837 was also an eventful year in other ways, as we are about to see.

The Letter from Lunenburg (1837)

In the June 1837 issue of the *Millennial Harbinger*, Campbell published a letter that he had written to interested parties in England ("Letters to England—No. 1") in which he attempted to describe some of the beliefs of his restoration movement in America. After commenting upon the movement's preference for addressing matters of social justice through "the church in her own proper character" rather than through parachurch organizations (i.e., "Missionary, Education, Tract, Bible, Temperance, Anti-Slavery confederations"), he adds: "We would, indeed, have no objections to co-operate in these matters with all Christians, and raise contributions for all such purposes as, in our judgment, are promotive of the Divine glory and human happiness, whether or not they belong to our churches: for we find in all Protestant parties Christians as exemplary as ourselves according to their and our relative knowledge and opportunities. . . ."[20]

In July, Campbell received a letter from a "conscientious sister" in Lunenburg, Virginia, which he published in the September issue:

Lunenburg, July 8th, 1837,
　　Dear brother Campbell—I was much surprised to-day, while reading the Harbinger, to see that you recognize the Protestant parties as Christian. You say, you "find in all Protestant parties Christians."
　　Dear brother, my surprise and ardent desire to do what is right, prompt me to write to you at this time. I feel well assured, from the estimate you place on the female character, that you will attend to my feeble questions in search of knowledge.
　　Will you be so good as to let me know how any one becomes a Christian? What act of yours gave you the name of Christian? At what time had Paul the name of Christ called on him? At what time did Cornelius have Christ named on him? Is it not through this name we obtain eternal life? Does the name of Christ or Christian belong to any but those who believe the gospel, repent, and are buried by baptism into the death of Christ?[21]

Campbell published his response to the Lunenburg letter in that same issue and his response to subsequent correspondence from other readers in eastern Virginia in the November and December issues.

　　Considering that Hughes views Campbell's responses to the Lunenburg letter as significant evidence of a change in his thought and attitude toward Protestantism and that Tristano sees in these texts a "good means of examining the shift in Alexander's thought,"[22] it is not surprising that they should represent another evolution in the *ethos* of Campbell's rhetorical leadership. Reasons for characterizing these texts as a "rhetoric of transcendence" and Campbell's leadership *ethos* as "pastoral" will be illustrated in the following account of the exigencies and constraints inherent in the rhetorical situation as well as in the subsequent textual analysis.

Over the course of this extended rhetorical intervention, Campbell addressed multiple audiences. The first, and most immediate, was the "conscientious sister" herself. Campbell did not "formally answer all the queries proposed [by her], knowing the one point to which they all aim." On this point, Campbell regarded her as an "essentialist"—one who "may belong to a class who think that we detract from the authority and value of an institution the moment we admit the bare possibility of anyone being saved without it"[23]—and "rather an ultraist on the subject of Christian baptism; so far at least as not to allow that the name Christian is at all applicable to one unimmersed, or even to one immersed, without the true intent and meaning of baptism in his understanding previous to his burial in water."[24] He was suspicious of her motives, for he noted that she supposed her list of questions to involve "either insuperable difficulties or strong objections to that saying" (i.e., the statement which she cited from the June issue) and that "she knew well what answers I would have given to all her queries."[25]

Of course, Campbell was also well aware that "the Protestant sects" (variously, "Protestant parties," "the Protestant public") overheard his entire conversation. While responding to the Lunenburg letter, Campbell desired to maintain his "approach" to the "Protestant teachers and their communities" whom he believed to be "much better disposed to us than formerly."[26]

His November article was addressed to "some two or three intelligent and much esteemed correspondents." "These brethren . . . objected to certain sentences" in Campbell's September article and supposed that he had "conceded a point" (i.e., the essentiality of immersion) on which he had "hitherto been tenacious." At least one of these correspondents—and perhaps not more than one—had also suggested that Campbell had "misapplied certain portions of scripture in supporting said opinion."[27]

The December article was occasioned by the "numerous letters" of a more extended audience. They were "our brethren of Eastern Virginia" whom Campbell considered "too much addicted to denouncing the sects and representing them *en masse* as wholly aliens from the possibility of salvation—as wholly antichristian and corrupt." Though "very zealous brethren," they "gave countenance to the popular clamor" that Campbell's movement did "make baptism a savior." Though "good brethren," their "imprudence and precipitancy" had resulted in loss for the movement's efforts to proselytize. Though "fellow laborers," they had forgotten that "*approaches* are more in the spirit and style of the Savior than *reproaches.*" They had "greatly and unreasonably abused the sects" and "made Christianity to turn more upon immersion than upon universal holiness." "Hasty," "precipitate," and "premature," Campbell suggested that if they had responded as promptly to the sister of Lunenburg as they had to his reply, she would have had no need to write him. Though the September article is directed to this sister, it appears that Campbell had this extended audience in mind even then, for in this December article he remarked, "I felt constrained to rebuke them over the shoulders of this inquisitive lady."[28]

Though not mentioned by name, chief among these eastern Virginian brethren was Dr. John Thomas (1805–71), who later founded a restorationist sect that he named the "Christadelphians."[29] An English physician who had immigrated to the United States in 1832, Thomas soon thereafter met Walter Scott and began to prepare himself to also become an itinerant evangelist in the restoration cause. He visited Campbell at Bethany in 1833, and in 1834 began to edit and publish his own journal, the *Apostolic Advocate.* He eventually settled in Richmond, Virginia, where he agreed to fill the pulpit for a local congregation.[30] Campbell at first expressed praise for Thomas's efforts, referring to him as "our much esteemed brother" (1833) and "our faithful fellow-soldier Dr. John Thomas" (1834).[31] However, when Thomas's journal began to express views that were extremely sectarian and dogmatic, their relationship deteriorated.[32]

One view that Thomas expressed in particularly forceful terms was a doctrine requiring reimmersion for all people who did not understand the precise purpose of baptism at the time of their immersion.[33] Roderick Chestnut summarizes Thomas' position on reimmersion: "Thomas believed that baptism was an expiatory act, that is, baptism, if performed properly, procured salvation. For baptism to be valid the subject, as well as the administrator, had to realize that baptism was for the remission of sins. If that knowledge was lacking, it invalidated the rite, leaving the believer in his sins."[34] Similarly, Hughes describes the sectarian nature of Thomas's dogmatism: "Central to Thomas's sectarianism was his contention that Baptists could not become members of the Church of Christ until they had been reimmersed, since Baptist immersion was nothing more than immersion into Antichrist . . . Thomas relegated the entire

Protestant movement to perdition."[35] In their respective journals, Thomas and Campbell engaged in a heated exchange over this and other issues for a period of more than three years (1835–38).

Thomas's dogmatism and divisiveness finally led Campbell to declare, in the November 1837 issue of the *Millennial Harbinger* (the same issue in which his second response to the Lunenburg letter appeared), "I can no longer regard him as a brother." In the May 1838 issue, Campbell went even further and "resolved that his name shall never again appear on our pages, until he reforms." In December of 1837, Campbell would also devote an entire *Millennial Harbinger* "Extra" to refuting Thomas's views. He also saw Thomas's influence in the Lunenburg letter, observing in the Extra that "the answer I gave to the sister of Lunenburg, I gave with reference to this discussion. I saw the hand of the *Advocate* in those questions and answered them accordingly." Years later, W. K. Pendleton, co-editor of the *Millennial Harbinger*, confirmed that the sister of Lunenburg was, in fact, a disciple of Thomas.[36] As Chestnut argues, the facts that the letter was written at the height of the controversy, from a region favorable to Thomas, and was clearly in sympathy with Thomas's views, strongly suggest that Campbell's articles were "a calculated response to the position taken by Thomas and his followers."[37]

Given this multiplicity of audience, Campbell was faced with significant constraints when penning his responses to the letter from Lunenburg and subsequent correspondents. As—by 1837—an acknowledged leader and the most prominent voice within the restoration movement, he strove, on one hand, to maintain its improved standing within the larger Protestant community, a standing that had been enhanced earlier that year through his debate with Purcell. This entailed rebuking the extreme conservative wing of his own movement, especially Thomas and his followers. On the other hand, to retain credibility as a leader within his movement, he could not afford to be perceived as acting inconsistently with previously stated and published positions on immersion (as would be charged), as embracing the entire Protestant community en masse without qualification, or as abandoning those readers and members of his churches who were "pained" at his initial response.[38]

Campbell thus faced the challenge of choosing rhetorical strategies that would enable him to retain credibility with these diverse audiences while also managing an ideological tension that cut to the heart of a fundamental theological inquiry: "But who is a Christian?"[39] This thus became a significant "pastoral moment" for Campbell as he discursively filled the dual roles of "peacemaker" within his movement and "ambassador" to the Protestant community at large.

A Rhetoric of Transcendence

Though Campbell addresses diverse audiences, what emerges within these texts is a fundamental consistency, a singular dominant strategy that manifests itself in a variety of forms: the use of dissociation and classification to construct a hierarchy of spiritual identity. Within this hierarchy, Campbell is able to position himself at various levels of transcendence and thus retain some degree of identification with these various audiences as the rhetorical act evolves over time. Since the critical taxonomy employed here will be drawn from Chaim Perelman and Kenneth Burke, a brief overview of their understandings of "dissociation" and "identification" will serve as a prolegomenon to the textual analysis.

According to Perelman, arguments are given either in the form of a "liason" or a "dissociation." Whereas a *liason* is a process of association that "allows us to pass from what is accepted to what we wish to have accepted" or "allows for the transference to the conclusion of the adherence accorded to the premises," a *dissociation* "aims at separating elements which language or recognized tradition have previously tied together." Such a form of argument, he notes, is "fundamental for every reflection which, seeking to resolve a difficulty raised by common thought, is required to dissociate the elements of reality from each other and bring about a new organization of data."[40] Dissociation has the potential to resolve difficulties (such as, for example, avoiding contradiction) because this new organization of data actually modifies the concepts themselves: "By process of *dissociation* we mean techniques of separation which have the purpose of dissociating, separating, disuniting elements which are regarded as forming a whole or at least a unified group within some system of thought; dissociation modifies such a system by modifying certain concepts which make up its essential parts."[41]

According to Burke, "identification" is the goal of rhetoric. This does not mean that Burke considered identification a "substitute" for "persuasion" as the key term for rhetoric. Admittedly, since rhetors often persuade by identification and since identification may be the purpose of persuasion, "there is no chance of keeping apart the meanings." However, the term "identification" permits Burke to extend the art of rhetoric as it is traditionally understood. "Identification," for Burke, is a state of "consubstantiality" which is achieved via a type of symbolic transformation. In other words, taking advantage of the "ambiguities of substance" (which he describes in his *Grammar of Motives*), two different entities can become "substantially one"—not "identical" but "identified with"—as they identify with each other in terms of their common relationship to some third entity. Since all identification is thus "in terms of" something else that transcends the level of difference, the negotiation of "hierarchy" becomes the key to rhetorical appeal. The "invitation to rhetoric," then, consists of the ironic implication of division in every instance of identification and the range of rhetoric "deals with the possibilities of classification in its *partisan* aspects; it considers the ways in which individuals are at odds with one another, or become identified with groups more or less at odds with one another."[42]

The argument advanced here is that the invitation to rhetoric inherent in dissociation and the subsequent possibilities for classification, modification, transcendence, and transformation are conspicuously manifest in Campbell's responses to the Lunenburg letter. Close attention to the particulars of these texts illustrates Campbell's use of dissociation and classification, the conceptual hierarchy that emerges from these rhetorical processes, and how Campbell uses this hierarchy to address the challenges posed by his diverse audiences. Subsequently, the "pastoral" *ethos* generated by this "rhetoric of transcendence" will be considered.

Dissociation and Classification

Over the course of these editorials, Campbell divides four distinct groups of people into two classes each. He never actually adopts or defends the position attributed to him in the letter from Lunenburg—"you recognize the Protestant parties *as* Christian" [emphasis added]—but does take up the passage attributed to him—"you find *in* all Protestant parties Christians" [emphasis added]—and defends it through a familiar pattern of argumentation: residual reasoning. Assuming the counter premise—"if there be no Christians in the Protestant parties"—he infers an unacceptable conclusion—that then the Biblical promises (e.g., Matthew 16:18) "concerning the everlasting kingdom of Messiah have failed and the gates of hell have prevailed against his church." The alternative, since "this cannot be," is that "therefore there are Christians among the sects."[43]

The part / whole dissociation sustained throughout this argument, however, divides all Protestants into two classes: (1) the Christians *among* them and (2) those who are otherwise members of the Protestant sects. This metaclassification, established at the outset of Campbell's first (September) article, not only defines the ground to be defended but also initiates his encompassing pattern of argument: dissociation and classification.

Campbell then raises the fundamental question at issue—"But who is a Christian?"—and answers it in a straightforward manner: "I answer, Every one that believes in his heart that Jesus of Nazareth is the Messiah, the Son of God; repents of his sins, and obeys him in all things according to his measure of knowledge of his will."[44] Three subsequent classifications are constructed on the basis of this last phrase ("obeys him in all things according to his measure of knowledge of his will").

First, those who are "in Christ" are divided into classes of (1) the perfect (or *more* perfect) Christians and (2) the imperfect (or *less* perfect) Christians: *"A perfect man in Christ,* or a perfect Christian, is one thing; and 'a babe in Christ,' a stripling in the faith, or an imperfect Christian, is another. The New Testament recognizes both the perfect man and the imperfect man in Christ . . . And hence it is possible for Christians to be imperfect in some respects without an absolute forfeiture of the Christian state and character."[45] The measure of one's perfection, according to Campbell, is not "any one duty . . . not even immersion into the name of the Father, of the Son, and of the Holy Spirit"[46] but one's devotion to and love for the Lord: "Should I find a Pedobaptist more intelligent in the Christian Scriptures, more spiritually-minded and more devoted to the Lord than a Baptist, or one immersed on a profession of the ancient faith, I could not hesitate a moment in giving the preference of my heart to him that loveth the most."[47]

However, love, Campbell argues, is best measured by obedience: "How do I know that any one loves my Master but by his obedience to his commandments? I answer, *In no other way.*" Consequently, another classification emerges: "But mark, I do not substitute obedience to one commandment, for universal or even general obedience." Thus, the obedient have now been divided into two classes: (1) those whose obedience is "universal" or "general" (more) and (2) those whose obedience may be to but "one command" (less). Since "it is the image of Christ the Christian looks for and loves," Campbell argues, "general devotion to the whole truth" is privileged over "being exact in a few items" as a sign of greater love and a more reliable standard of Christian character.[48]

The measure of one's knowledge is an important qualifier for Campbell, since even "general" (or greater) devotion can only be "to the truth *so far as known*" [emphasis added]. This leads to yet another classification, then, as Campbell proceeds to dissociate "mistakes of the understanding" from "errors of the affections": "With me mistakes of the understanding and errors of the affections are not to be confounded. They are as distant as the poles. An angel may mistake the meaning of a commandment, but he will obey it in the sense in which he understands it. John Bunyan and John Newton were very different persons, and had very different views of baptism, and of some other things; yet they were both disposed to obey, and to the extent of their knowledge did obey the Lord in every thing."[49] Thus, for Campbell, "there are mistakes with, and without depravity" and "mistakes are to be regarded as culpable and as declarative of a corrupt heart only when they proceed from a willful neglect of the means of knowing what is commanded." Thus, there are two classes of mistakes: (1) mistakes that stem from an ignorance which is "involuntary" or even "unavoidable" and (2) errors that are "willful" or even "criminal."[50]

These four dissociations and classifications all emerge in Campbell's initial statement of his position in the September article. However, they span the three articles collectively, a dissociation between "inward" and "outward" baptism introduced in the November article as a species of the willful / involuntary mistake dissociation. The progression is as follows:

September
Protestants (Members of Sects/Christians)
Christians (Perfect/Imperfect)
Obedient (General/Exact)
Mistaken (Willful/Involuntary)
November
Baptized (Inward/Outward)
Mistaken (Willful/Involuntary)
Baptized (Inward/Outward)
December
Protestants (Members of Sects/Christians)
Mistaken (Willful/Involuntary)
Obedient (General/Exact)
Christians (Perfect/Imperfect)[51]

In the November article, Campbell introduces a species of his willful / involuntary mistake dissociation with an analogy between his own reasoning on baptism and the apostle Paul's reasoning on circumcision. Just as Paul distinguished between "outward" circumcision ("in the flesh") and "inward" circumcision ("of the heart, in the spirit") in arguing that one could possess the praise of God apart from physical circumcision (cf. Romans 2:28–29), "so is baptism," Campbell contends: "We argue for the outward and the inward—the outward for men, including ourselves—the inward for God; but both the outward and the inward for the praise of both God and men."[52] He then frames this inward / outward dissociation within his classification of mistakes:

> Now the nice point of opinion on which some brethren differ is this: Can a person who simply, not perversely, *mistakes* the outward baptism, have the inward? We all agree that he who willfully or negligently perverts the outward, cannot have the inward. But can he who, through a simple mistake, involving no perversity of mind, has misapprehended the outward baptism, yet submitting to it according to his view of it, have the inward baptism which changes his state and has praise of God, though not of all men? is the precise question. To which I answer, that, in my opinion, *it is possible.*[53]

In his December article, Campbell first defends himself against the "charge of inconsistency." His defense consists of ten representative quotations from previous publications (including passages from the *Christian Baptist*). His classification of Protestants (Members of Sects/Christians Among Them) is a running theme, expressed in various terms: "apostate Christendom" vs. "saints in Babylon," "sects" vs. "disciples dispersed among them," "each party" vs. "Christians" or "disciples," "real [vs. false] members of his body," myriads of Christians *in* all denominations" [emphasis added], and "Christians *among* the sects" [emphasis added].[54] Thus the presence given to this part / whole dissociation is, if anything, more prominent in the last article than in the first.

The second item on Campbell's December agenda is to defend his opinion from "the sectarian application of it" and he divides the unimmersed into two classes: "all the unimmersed are to be ranged in two classes—

those who neither know nor care for the opinion, and those who know it and rejoice in it."[55] As with inward / outward baptism, this dissociation among the unimmersed is also framed within the willful / involuntary mistake classification: "He that rejoices in such an opinion for his own sake, has had the subject under consideration; and it is a thousand chances to one that he is obstinately or willingly in error on the subject; and therefore, in the very terms of this opinion, he is precluded from any interest in it."[56]

The final item on Campbell's agenda is an explanation for "delivering such an opinion at this time."[57] Here, he echoes his classification of the obedient (general or universal / specific or exact), suggesting that "had not a few in some other regions made Christianity to turn more upon immersion than upon universal holiness," he would have given a different answer to the Lunenburg letter. In concluding this article, he invokes the same classification of Christians with which he opened the September article, as if to extend an olive branch to "Our Eastern brethren": "But we are all learning and progressing towards perfection."[58]

A Hierarchy of Spiritual Identity

This set and progression of classifications enables Campbell to achieve two important ends. The first is to create a hierarchy of spiritual identity, as follows:

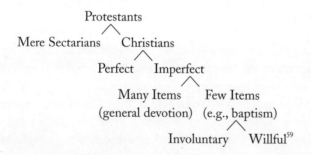

One notices here the same bifurcous manner of division common in the *Christian Baptist*. Now, however, it is employed toward a dramatically different end. Whereas in the *Christian Baptist*, the purpose was most often to isolate, ridicule and "win," here, in the *Millennial Harbinger*, Campbell employs it to construct a hierarchy of spiritual identity within which he is able to transcend a variety of differences and find points of identification with diverse audiences as the rhetorical event evolves over time. This can best be demonstrated by examining, over the course of the three articles, (1) who is included / excluded from the Christian state by these classifications, (2) the degree of probability (or certainty) with which their state is judged, (3) with whom Campbell is aligned and to whom he is opposed, and (4) the basis of his alignment or opposition.

In his September article, Campbell is able to transcend his differences with the Protestant parties over the purpose and necessity of immersion and to identify with the Christians among them on the basis of their common love for the Savior. Since one can be a Christian while less perfect than others, being mistaken does not automatically exclude one from the state of being a Christian. So long as one is disposed to obey and does so to the extent of his knowledge, he who is ignorantly mistaken and not willfully disobedient receives Campbell's "cordial approbation and love as a Christian." Since love of the Savior and general devotion to him are a more reliable standard of the Christian state and character than "being exact in a few items," Campbell offers "the preference of my heart to him that loveth the most." On the other hand, he would choose not to associate with either "the preachers of *'essentials'*" or "the preachers of *'non-essentials,'*" for the former "disparage[s] the heart" while the latter "despises the institution." He especially rebukes the "class who think we detract from the authority and value of an institution the moment we admit the bare possibility of any one being saved without it."[60]

In his November article, Campbell again invokes his willful / involuntary mistake dissociation to position the one who has the "inward baptism" but has "misapprehended the outward baptism" as among those guilty only of "a simple mistake, involving no perversity of mind." Since this is a "point of opinion on which some brethren differ," however, this argument maintains his distance from the one named "an ultraist on the subject of Christian baptism." Yet a significant qualification moves Campbell back toward common ground with his own party. When putting to himself the question as to whether one who "has misapprehended the outward baptism, yet submitting to it according to his view of it" can "have the inward baptism which changes his state and has the praise of God, though not of all men," he responds: *"it is possible*—farther than this I do not affirm." Moreover, he closes this article by privileging the immersed as "certainly safer" by comparison, noting "he only has the praise of God and man, and of himself, as a Christian."[61]

In the December article, even while yet rebuking John Thomas and his disciples, Campbell is able to transcend even these differences to find common ground with the more conservative wing of his movement. The Christian / Sectarian Protestant dissociation is invoked to remind his readers that he views only some (part) not all (whole) Protestants as Christians and has thus not embraced Protestantism en masse. Several species of this dissociation reinforce this shift in focus from the September article (i.e., a shift from who is *included in* to who is *excluded from* the Christian state): apostate Christendom, the sects (rather than the disciples among them), "false" members of Christ's body, etc. Similarly, the willful / involuntary mistake dissociation is again invoked to exclude those who abuse Campbell's opinion as "not justified but self-condemned." His qualifiers intensify as well, as he invokes a dissociation between the "fallible inference of man" and the "sure and unerring promise of our Savior" to support his contention that his own opinion "imparts no certainty of pardon or salvation to any particular unbaptized person whatsoever." Campbell even saves face for "the brethren of eastern Virginia," affirming them as "fast approaching to the habit of calling Bible things by Bible names" and, though opining that they were "hasty and precipitate in expressing themselves," acknowledging, "But we are all progressing towards perfection."[62]

Thus, the same dissociation (perfect vs. imperfect Christians) that, in September, enables Campbell to transcend his differences with Protestants over baptism now enables him to transcend his differences with the conservative extremists within his movement. By carefully constructing and negotiating this hierarchy of spiritual identity to transcend a variety of differences and find points of identification with diverse audiences as this rhetorical act evolves over time, Campbell attempts to walk a fine line between his desire to maintain the improved disposition between his movement and the Protestant communities, on one hand, and his need to manage the differences within his own movement, on the other.

A "Pastoral" *Ethos*

These texts also represent a rhetoric much different from what we found in the *Christian Baptist*. It was observed earlier that the occasion of the Lunenburg letter represented a "pastoral" moment for Campbell—as would many of the rhetorical situations addressed through the *Millennial*

Harbinger. In this particular situation, Campbell discursively filled two leadership roles: that of an ambassador who sought to speak to and for the Protestant parties at large and that of a mediator who sought to manage the differences and controversies that emerged within his own churches. Concomitant to accepting these responsibilities—and the challenges that accompanied them—was Campbell's rhetorical transformation to an *ethos* much more *pastoral* than *prophetic* in nature.

In this case, Campbell's *pastoral ethos* emerges from several of the specific qualities of his "rhetoric of transcendence." First, Campbell emerges as a leader who is able to rise above his own personal opinion to find ground of identification with either side of a controversy—even when he disagrees with each on significant points. The controversy over the mode and purpose of baptism was of no small significance to Campbell. His own immersion as an adult had been a watershed event in his own life. Baptism had been the subject of his debates with John Walker in 1820 and William Maccalla in 1823. Yet in his responses to the Lunenburg letter in 1837, Campbell was able to find transcendent common ground, on one hand, with unimmersed Protestants who love the Savior and, on the other hand, with those whom he considered legalistic "ultraists" as to the essentiality of immersion.

Second, Campbell emerges as a leader who is willing to tolerate the mistakes of others and even seek rapprochement with those who had openly opposed him. While firm with those whom he considered willfully disobedient, he proffers compassion and approbation to those who are simply and sincerely mistaken. One need not be perfect to receive his "love as a christian." Though straightforward in denouncing the positions of his critics, his rhetorical intervention in this controversy ends with a peace offering.

Third, in contrast to the "imprudence"[63] with which he charged "some good brethren," a persona of "prudence" accrues to Campbell over the course of these articles. Campbell's position on baptism does not emerge as rigid and legalistic as that of the more radical voices within his movement. Understood within the theological spectrum of his day, Campbell's own position was unarguably conservative. Yet, when Campbell replies to the query concerning the Christian state of any given unimmersed individual with "it is possible," he rejects an *absolute* reduction of the issue to two exclusive alternatives and reclaims the entire spectrum of varying degrees of probability. His ability to transcend levels of division for levels of identification is itself proof that space for a more prudent perspective, one that avoids polar extremes, both exists and is tenable. He is able to achieve both separation and identification without either dissolving consubstantiality (i.e., not "identical to" but "identified with," as Burke has put it), on one hand, or collapsing the differences necessary to maintain the divisions upon which his classification and hierarchy depend, on the other.

There is, then, a "reasonableness" that accrues to Campbell's benefit as a result of seeking and occupying the rhetorical middle ground—not only between two more extreme positions on baptism (one making baptism a Savior, the other willfully ignoring its import) but also between two more extreme rhetorics (a rhetoric of essentiality and a rhetoric of triviality). Campbell thus represents the perspective of "prudence" and a persona that avoids extremes.

Finally, Campbell emerges as a leader who desires to help all progress toward perfection. To admit that "we are all learning and progressing towards perfection"—employing the inclusive first person plural pronoun —is a gesture of humility that identifies universal common ground for all Christians. Though forbearing mistakes born of ignorance, Campbell's burden for alleviating this ignorance is clearly illustrated in these texts. Similarly, though rebuking the "essentialists," his admittedly "strong" and "pungent" response was ultimately "intended to bring them to the proper medium" and he compliments them on the progress he sees: "I am glad to see our brethren so jealous of a correct style—so discriminating, and so independent . . . I do not indeed blame them for being prompt; for I had rather be an hour too soon as half an hour too late." His final benediction is both transcendent and inclusive: "May the Lord bless *all* the holy brethren, and give them understanding in all things!" [emphasis added].[64]

Conclusion

As one might expect in a situation marked by fundamental theological differences, the web of events and forces surrounding Campbell's responses to the Lunenburg letter are sufficiently complex to preclude any unqualified assessment of this particular rhetorical intervention as either a success or a failure. Dr. John Thomas would prove to be a reluctant and resistant audience. Campbell toured the south in the fall of 1838 and, determined to end the matter, sent word to Thomas that he would stop in

Paineville, Virginia (where Thomas held church membership), and hoped to meet with him, either publicly or privately, to discuss his views. A debate between the two men was arranged but when, after three days, it became evident that they had reached an impasse, a resolution was drafted in which Thomas agreed to discontinue discussion of his divisive views. Campbell recommended that Thomas write a statement of the meeting for publication in the *Millennial Harbinger.* The statement appeared in the February 1839 issue but in it, Thomas, to the contrary, renewed the discussion and defended his views. Campbell finally decided to ignore Thomas and the controversy eventually died out.[65]

When, in its subsequent generations, the Stone-Campbell movement began to splinter into factions, the question of "open membership" (i.e., whether the unimmersed should be accepted into church membership) would be among the many issues (including, among others, the use of instrumental music in public worship, comity agreements on the mission field, etc.) that provided fuel for controversy. Though he passed away in 1866, Campbell's responses to the Lunenburg letter would play a significant role in the open membership debate, often serving as a rhetorical resource for either party. Advocates of open membership would charge their opponents with adopting an inflexible Christian primitivism, with ignoring Campbell's response to the Lunenburg letter, and with distorting Campbell's views. Opponents of open membership would challenge the advocates' reading of Campbell's response to the Lunenburg letter, offering competing readings based on alternative intertextual contexts. Whatever life of its own came to this product of Campbell's rhetorical leadership, it is apparent that this rhetorical intervention did not, in any ultimate sense, *resolve* the tensions it addressed. But we may perhaps conclude that, for a season, it helped to *manage* the deep ideological divisions that existed within his diverse readership.

Such instrumental judgments aside, however, Campbell's responses to the Lunenburg letter offer clear evidence that, as the needs of his movement changed, his rhetorical leadership adapted accordingly. Assuming the responsibilities for a movement that now needed a *pastor* much more than a *prophet,* Campbell's rhetoric evidences a keen sensitivity to the exigencies, constraints, and audiences that define an evolving rhetorical situation. Typically, Campbell exercises his leadership discursively—but now through a rhetoric and an *ethos* that are, fittingly, much more *pastoral* than *prophetic.*[66]

Chapter 6
"The Missionary Cause"
Epideictic Narrative and Rhetorical Vision

. . . it is upon us a paramount duty. We plead for the original gospel and
its positive institutions, however invidious it may seem in some eyes.[1]

The two decades following the controversy surrounding the Lunenburg
letter were eventful in many ways. Barton W. Stone moved to Jacksonville, Illinois, in 1834 and passed away in 1844, after which his own influential journal, the *Christian Messenger*, ceased publication. Thomas
Campbell passed away in 1854.

As noted in the previous chapter, the growth of the movement from
25,000–40,000 members just after 1830 to approximately 225,000 members by 1857[2] was accompanied by significant growing pains. Not all of
these tensions emerged over doctrinal matters, however, as had been the
case with the controversy over baptism raised by the letter from Lunenburg. Many of them had to do with organizational matters—with issues
of church polity and, especially, the manner in which autonomous congregations ought to cooperate beyond the local level. However, in the
minds of many of its leaders, the movement's growth created a need for
more effective organization.

A proliferation of journals aided communication among the churches.
What W. T. Moore said of the movement around the turn of the century
has been regularly quoted since and aptly describes these decades: "the
Disciples of Christ do not have bishops, they have editors."[3] The more
influential journals included the *Gospel Advocate*, launched by Tolbert
Fanning and William Lipscomb in 1855, and the *American Christian Review*, inaugurated by Benjamin Franklin in 1856. Many of the other periodicals, however, represented second-rate efforts by self-appointed editors
and their contributions were often neither constructive nor worthwhile.
Though himself the movement's pioneer editor, Campbell eventually
challenged this "editorial zeal." In 1852, he called for three papers (a
weekly, a monthly, and a quarterly), arguing that this "would save the
community many thousands of dollars per annum for better purposes

than for the reading of diluted ideas in Homeopathic doses, as we now have them dispensed in invisible pills, in the ratio of one to a gallon of water."[4] Though his call did little to stem the growing tide of periodicals, none of these competitors seriously rivaled the *Millennial Harbinger*'s hold on the movement until after 1860.

During the 1830s, Campbell published several articles in the *Millennial Harbinger* about the theory and practice of higher education. Bacon College (named for Francis Bacon), the Stone-Campbell movement's first college, was founded in Georgetown, Kentucky, in 1836. Walter Scott served as president during its inaugural year and was then succeeded by David S. Burnet, who had first met Campbell as a young man.[5] Campbell's own vision for establishing a college was finally realized when Bethany College opened for classes in 1841. Campbell donated the land for the college campus, served as its first president and, when present, delivered morning lectures on the Bible.[6] Other early colleges included Franklin College (near Nashville, Tennessee, in 1845), Hiram College (Hiram, Ohio, in 1849; first named Western Reserve Eclectic Institute), Northwestern Christian University (Indianapolis, Indiana, in 1850; later renamed Butler University), Eureka College (Eureka, Illinois, in 1855), and Christian University (Canton, Missouri, in 1855, later renamed Culver-Stockton College).

The most controversial aspect of intercongregational cooperation proved to be the creation of regional, state, and national organizations. By the 1830s, Campbell saw the advantages of organization beyond the local level. In 1831, he published a series of four articles on "The Co-operation of Churches" in the *Millennial Harbinger* and, in fact, several cooperative agencies and meetings emerged at regional and state levels over the course of this decade. Campbell published another series of articles on church organization in 1841 and an article entitled "Five Arguments for Church Organization"[7] in 1842. In January of 1845, the first national body of the Stone-Campbell movement was organized by four churches in the Cincinnati area: the American Christian Bible Society. David S. Burnet, who had spearheaded the effort, was elected its first president and Campbell, who was not present, was one of nine vice presidents elected.

Campbell initially expressed reservations about the ACBS, for two reasons. First, its purpose overlapped with the work of the (formerly Baptist) American and Foreign Bible Society and he felt that a separate society would neither be a responsible use of financial resources nor consistent with the movement's concern for Christian unity. Second, he questioned the appropriateness of a few individuals in one city unilaterally constituting themselves as a national association. He later removed his objection when the ACBS began to work cooperatively with the AFBS.[8] Opposition to the ACBS was widespread, however, and it never enjoyed much support, folding in 1856. As we shall see, however, the complexities involved in Campbell's ambivalence toward the ACBS are suggestive of the difficulties and tensions that provided fertile soil for future controversy over cooperative agencies.

The Seeds of Division

The final rhetorical event to be analyzed in this volume transpired in the midst of controversies that would contribute significantly to the division of the Stone-Campbell movement. Alexander Campbell's last national public address to the churches of his restoration movement was delivered at the 1860 meeting of the American Christian Missionary Society. The purpose of this chapter is to explore both how this rhetorical intervention addressed the threat these controversies represented to the unity of the movement and how Campbell, after more than forty years of leadership, continued to adapt his rhetorical leadership in an attempt to address not only his own generation but the next.

Because significant narrative and visionary elements impart an epideictic quality to this address, the textual analysis will apply a "fantasy theme" perspective to illustrate how Campbell's rhetoric offered his movement a coherent rhetorical vision that interpreted its past, defined its present, and directed its future. It will also consider how the address evokes a *patriarchal* leadership *ethos* for the elderly Campbell. First, however, a brief account of the controversies that shaped the rhetorical situation is in order.

The Society Controversy

The controversy that most directly shaped the rhetorical situation confronting Campbell was over the legitimacy of regional and national societies as a means of cooperation beyond the level of the local congregation. In February of 1849, as Campbell began to publish another series of articles on church organization, others were calling for a national convention and urging Campbell to set a date for such an event. Campbell published his support for and defense of such a convention and outlined the significance and substance of the meeting in the August issue of the *Millennial Harbinger.* The movement's first national convention was then held in Cincinnati, Ohio, on October 23–29, 1849. The most significant outcome of the first national convention was the creation of the American Christian Missionary Society (ACMS). Though Campbell was unable to attend due to illness, he was far too significant and his support too critical to the success of the venture to be overlooked in the selection of officers. He was elected "permanent president" of the society, an office he filled until his death in 1866.[9]

The most important difference in the fortunes of the ACBS and the ACMS was that the latter enjoyed Campbell's unwavering support. Elected its first president, he was, in many ways, the driving force of the society as well as its leading advocate. The duties of its executive board were to "establish such agencies as the interest of the Society may require, appoint agents and missionaries, fix their compensation, direct and instruct them concerning their particular fields of labors, make all appropriations to be paid out of the Treasury, and present to the Society at each annual meeting a full report of the proceeds during the past year."[10] At this first meeting, resolutions were passed urging Lord's Day observance, the organization of Sunday schools, and the use of care in selecting ministers.[11]

However, according to North, Campbell's support for a national convention and the rise of various societies "created the first, serious widespread area of disagreement within the Restoration Movement."[12] Opposition to such agencies and meetings emerged early and increased in intensity over the years. Tristano explains why such developments were bound to create controversy: "The controversy over organization was rooted in the historical aversion of the Restoration Movement to denominationalism. To recall the genesis of the movement is to recall the rejection of presbyteries, creeds, and schisms, all of which had a nonscriptural and human basis. In the minds of many, to speak of almost any organization was to suggest the abandonment of one of the most cherished principles of restorationism and to become just like the sects."[13] As early as November of 1843, during the Campbell-Rice debate in Lexington, Kentucky, an attempt was made to organize a missionary society but Jacob Creath, Sr., objected strenuously and the plan was abandoned. Eventually, the ACMS, probably because it held the only national meeting that brought the movement's leadership together in one body,[14] became the focus of the hostilities.

From its inception, the ACMS faced two serious challenges: the question of the legitimacy of the society *per se* and practical concerns over ensuring that the integrity of the society as a *missionary* society (i.e., resisting pressure to act on resolutions about matters extraneous to its purpose, as some felt it had at its first meeting). Specifically, both Lewis and Webb summarize the attacks on the ACMS under five headings: (1) the society was without scriptural precedent, (2) it did not represent the churches, (3) membership was based on financial contributions, (4) it "aped the sects," and (5) it was inconsistent with the former view of its president.[15] Soon after the convention, the church in Connellsville, Pennsylvania, adopted and published ten resolutions expressing concerns over the creation of the ACMS. In 1849, Jacob Creath, Sr., in a series of articles, again spoke out strongly, objecting to both the convention and the ACMS, and accusing Campbell of inconsistency. Tolbert Fanning, in particular, became a longtime opponent of the ACMS and crystallized a sizable base of resistance, creating (along with William Lipscomb) the *Gospel Advocate* in part to provide a forum for discussing such organizations.[16]

In truth, there were legitimate reasons for questions about Campbell's consistency. In 1823, Campbell had published the following statement about the apostolic church in the *Christian Baptist:* "They dare not transfer to a missionary society, or Bible society, or education society, *a cent or a prayer,* lest in so doing they should rob the church of its glory and exalt the inventions of men above the wisdom of God. *In their church capacity alone they moved.*"[17] In 1849, he wrote, in the *Millennial Harbinger,* "In all things pertaining to public interest, not of Christian faith, piety or morality, the church of Jesus Christ in its aggregate character, is left free and unshackled by any apostolic authority." He continued, "Frequent conferences or conventions, sometimes called 'associations,' become expedient and necessary to give direction and energy to the instruments and means of social advancement."[18] Specifically, he suggested, "The public press, evangelical missions, domestic and foreign bible translation, religious tracts, and moral agencies of every sort necessary or favorable to the prosperity of the churches of Christ and to the conversion of the world . . . are probably the objects which might advantageously claim a sort of general superintendency."[19]

Campbell denied a contradiction but his replies were neither especially candid nor satisfying to his critics. These apparent inconsistencies merely added fuel to the fires of controversy. So long as he was able, however, Campbell remained the leading advocate of the ACMS.

The Slavery Controversy

The fury among Stone-Campbell churches over the legitimacy of societies was also fed by the consuming national controversy that would threaten not only the unity of every major Protestant denomination but the Union itself—the vehement, and increasingly violent, conflict over slavery. As it became apparent during the 1830s that the antislavery approach was having little impact on the nation's predicament, radical abolitionist sentiment intensified. David E. Harrell summarizes the years leading up to 1860:

> In the decade 1830–40 new and militant leaders assumed direction of the abolitionist movement. The radical abolition impulse which developed after 1830 was dominated in the East by the overwhelming personality of William Lloyd Garrison and in the West by a fervent leadership which included Theodore Weld and James G. Birney . . . The series of crises during the hectic decade that ended with the election of Abraham Lincoln to the presidency in 1860 and included the Compromise of 1850, *Uncle Tom's Cabin*, the Kansas-Nebraska Act, the Dred Scott Decision, and John Brown's Harper's Ferry raid, stirred the slavery issue to increasingly fervent heights.[20]

Both Thomas and Alexander Campbell held ardent antislavery positions.[21] Alexander attacked the injustices of slavery as early as the first regular issue of the *Christian Baptist*[22] but his agenda for this journal precluded much attention to social issues. However, in his prospectus to the *Millennial Harbinger,* he named slavery among the subjects he promised to treat and kept this promise in its very first issue.[23] Elected as a delegate to the Virginia constitutional convention in 1829, Campbell spoke forcefully against slavery, albeit in a lost cause.[24] In 1832, Campbell published what was considered a radical plan for gradual emancipation, urging the U.S. treasury to use part of its $10,000,000 annual surplus to redeem slaves and resettle them in Liberia. Campbell argued that such policy would completely eliminate slavery within twenty years, protect the economic stability of the South, and preserve the unity of the nation while providing an orderly transition to a free labor economy.[25]

By the 1840s, Campbell had witnessed schism among both the Baptists and the Methodists over the slavery issue and had become increasingly concerned about the divisive potential of the radical abolitionist voices within his own movement. In spite of Campbell's personal opposition to slavery, he leaned heavily upon his distinction between "faith" and "opinion" to advocate a policy of tolerance within the movement. In 1845, he published a series of articles entitled "Our Position to American Slavery," the crux of which is reflected in the following excerpt:

> To preserve unity of spirit among the Christians of the South and of the North is my grand object, and for that purpose I am endeavoring to show that the New Testament does not authorize any interference or legislation upon the relation of master and slave, nor does it either in letter or spirit authorize Christians to make it a term of communion. *While it prescribes the duties of both parties, masters and slaves, it sanctions the relation,* and only requires that these duties be faithfully discharged by the parties; making it the duty of all Christian churches to enforce these duties and to exact them under all the pains of Christian discipline, both from the master and from the slave—leaving it to the Lord to judge, correct, and avenge those that are without.[26]

This opened a floodgate of criticism from the radical abolitionists. Campbell, in turn, attempted to avert an open rift in the movement by suppressing further discussion of the matter, banning articles on slavery from the *Millennial Harbinger.*[27]

As extremists chafed under this "ban of silence," centers of belligerent abolitionism in central Indiana and northern Ohio began to launch alternative institutions and publications. By 1850, North-Western Christian University had been founded in Indianapolis, Indiana, with Ovid Butler, a radical abolitionist, as the Chairman of the Board of Directors. In 1854, John Boggs launched the *North-Western Christian Magazine,* which was in turn succeeded by the *Christian Luminary.* Butler's suggestions that "the south claims and receives the principal attention of our leading brethren" and that Bethany College was tainted by the manners of slavery states, along with Campbell's vituperative response, set off a Bethany-

Indianapolis feud that erupted again in 1856 when North-West accepted a number of abolitionist students who had been expelled from Bethany for causing a near riot. And, although there were radical proslavery voices among the southern Stone-Campbell churches,[28] Boggs instead focused his attacks upon Campbell and other leaders who held to a more moderate antislavery position. As Harrell observes: "There was never any real battle between radical abolitionists and proslavery agitators among the Disciples. Geography, utter disgust, and a buffer group of moderates in between them made the radicals in both the North and the South appear almost oblivious to one another. Disciples abolitionists trained their guns almost completely upon their moderate brethren."[29]

By 1860, the controversies over societies and slavery would become intertwined. Abolitionists had criticized the ACMS from its inception in 1849 because it appointed as its first missionary Dr. James T. Barclay who, prior to his appointment, had been a slaveholder. In 1855, Pardee Butler, one of the movement's most aggressive abolitionists, moved from Indiana to Kansas in order to evangelize and resist proslavery forces in the territory. In April of 1858, Butler applied to the ACMS for financial support. Because Butler's political agitations had embroiled him in controversy on more than one occasion following his move to Kansas, the ACMS responded that any support would be contingent upon his agreement to ignore the slavery issue. In 1859, abolitionist leadership in Indianapolis formed the "Christian Missionary Society" to support Pardee and rival the ACMS. Together with at least one college and one significant periodical, the founding of this society solidified a growing faction within the Stone-Campbell movement.[30]

"The Missionary Cause"

Campbell thus delivered his 1860 address—"The Missionary Cause"—to the annual meeting of the ACMS at a significant moment in the history of his movement. Both the movement and the society were embroiled in controversies fueled by the ferment of a national crisis. It would be his last public address to a national audience. The 1860 meeting would be the last national meeting of the movement prior to the beginning of the Civil War. After the outbreak of war and subsequent to its resolution, this meeting would be national in name only as the movement began to divide, primarily over sectional differences.

Campbell was seventy-two years old when he delivered this address and his health was in decline. Though Campbell would attend the annual meeting of the ACMS in 1861, Isaac Errett would preside on his behalf. By 1863, Campbell's keen memory would begin to fail him and his wife would commonly excuse him from speaking situations.[31] For more than four decades now, he had been "the unquestioned leader of the new religious movement that was coalescing in the American West."[32] Yet this address also reflects another evolution in *ethos* for which Campbell's years of rhetorical leadership had paved the way—the *ethos* of a "patriarch."

Campbell's millennial vision had always been predicated upon a global evangelistic effort empowered by Christian unity. Delivered in the face of a significant threat to that vision, Campbell's address adopts a timely theme: "the church . . . of right is, and ought to be, a great missionary society," for "a Christian community without missions and missionaries would, indeed be a solecism in creation, and a gross deviation from the order, economy, and the government of the universe."[33] To prove his assertions, Campbell presents a series of "common sense" evidences— Lockean (empirical) and testimonial (i.e., authoritative) proofs. Woven into the fabric of this address, however, are significant narrative and visionary elements that impart to it an epideictic quality.[34]

The analysis below will first consider the narrative elements of the address, then the vision for the movement manifest in these narratives, and finally how these visionary elements serve to crystallize a heritage for the movement that simultaneously demands and constrains future action. Subsequently, we will consider how this address evokes a "patriarchal" *ethos* for its speaker.

A Rhetoric of Reminiscence

Narrative does not dominate this address in proportion to other genres present within it, but the function of these narrative elements are both strategic and significant in providing fertile "soil" from which the rhetorical vision of the address grows. Two specific narratives constitute this soil.

The address opens with an announcement about the place of the missionary cause in the natural order of creation: "The missionary cause, in its conception and inception, is a rudimental and organic element of the constitution of the Universe."[35] Invoking a reference to "the missionaries of the starry heavens" contained in Jehovah's challenge to Job (Job 38:22) and "the celestial title given to the tenantries of the heaven of heavens" ("what is an angel but a *messenger,* or a *missionary?*"), Campbell's authoritative and empirical proofs immediately coalesce in support of his conclusion: "We have so much data in Biblical statements and in the phenomena of the material universe, as to authorize the assumption that *the missionary idea, in perfect and complete conception, circumscribes and permeates the entire area of all creation.*"

Having placed the physical universe and the angelic order in their natural and divine relation to the missionary idea, Campbell then narrows his focus to humankind and, specifically, his audience: "But we are a missionary society. A society assembled from all points of the compass—assembled, too, we hope, in the missionary spirit, which is the spirit of Christianity in its primordial conception."[36] To elaborate upon the place of the human missionary endeavor within the eternal scheme, Campbell engages in his first narrative—a biblical narrative that encompasses the breadth of the biblical canon.

From Eden to Eschatos: A Biblical Narrative

Moses, we are told, is "the oldest missionary whose name is inscribed on the rolls of time" and Campbell extols his virtues at some length. After a brief allusion to John the Baptist as another member of the missionary "rank," our attention is drawn to "the Lord Messiah himself" who was "the Incarnate Word . . . [God's] only begotten Son[37] . . . superlatively God's own special Ambassador extraordinary" with "all the angels of heaven placed under him as missionaries." "His commission," then, was "given to the Twelve Apostles"[38] and thus "angels, apostles, and evangelists were placed at his command, by him commissioned as ambassadors to the world." An abrupt temporal lurch backward reframes the Moses-John the Baptist-Christ-Apostles-Church progression within an even larger narrative stretching from Eden to the *eschatos*:[39]

> Satan had been expelled from heaven before Adam was created. His assault upon our mother, Eve, by an incarnation in the most subtile animal in the area of Paradise, is positive proof of the intensity of his malignity to God and to man. He, too, has his missionaries in the whole area of humanity. Michael and his angels, or missionaries are, and long have been, in conflict against the Devil and his missionaries. The battle, in this our planet, is yet in progress, and, therefore, missionaries are in perpetual de-

mand. Michael and his angels are still in conflict with the Devil and his angels. Hence the necessity incumbent upon us to carry on this warfare as loyal subjects of the Hero of our redemption.[40]

A brief hortatory section, featuring prominent military and harvest metaphors from the New Testament (specifically, Paul's description of the "armor of God" in Ephesians 6:12ff and Christ's call for harvest "laborers" in Matthew 9:37–38), follows this narrative. Campbell's lament that "schools for the prophets are wanting" and that inadequate salaries force deprivation upon many missionaries subsequently prompts a second, more personal, narrative.

"Days Long Gone By": An Autobiographical Narrative

Campbell's description of the typical missionary's home and lifestyle lead him to reminisce about "days long gone by" when he had witnessed the plights of such missionaries firsthand. An autobiographical narrative[41] begins with his self-appointed role in the missionary cause: "I was then my own missionary, with the consent, however, of one church." His mission was "to mingle with all classes of religious society" that he "might personally and truthfully know, not the theories but the facts and the actualities of the Christian ministry, and the so called Christian public."[42]

Summarizing his travels throughout West Virginia, Pennsylvania, and Ohio between 1812 and 1816, a subsequent period of seven years spent "reviewing . . . past studies, and in actual teaching Languages and Sciences," and an extension of his "evangelical labors into other States and communities," Campbell observes that his baptism and subsequent experiences with the Baptists led him to a conclusion that would become a commonplace in his reformatory rhetoric: "I became, more and more, penetrated with the conviction that theory had usurped the place of faith, and that consequently human institutions had been more or less, substituted for the apostolic and divine."[43]

For Campbell, then, this "period of investigation" ended in a transformation of his mission: "Flattering prospects of usefulness on all sides then, indeed, began to expand before me and to inspire me with the hope of achieving a long cherished object—doing some good in the advocacy of the primitive and apostolic gospel."[44] The narrative draws to a close with references to his 1820 debate with John Walker ("a discussion on the subject of the first positive institution enacted by the Lord Messiah") and his 1823 debate with W. L. Maccalla ("the former more especially on the *subject* and *action* of Christian baptism; the latter more emphatically on the *design* of that institution"). According to Campbell, these debates "embraced the rudimental elements of the whole Christian Institution and gave to the public in general a bold relief outline of the whole genius, spirit, letter, and doctrine of the gospel" and its "missionary spirit, though not formally propounded, was yet impliedly indicated, in these discussions."[45]

Not only do these two narratives, interestingly enough, parallel Campbell's two predominant forms of proof throughout this address—authoritative (biblical) and empirical (natural, experiential)—they also serve to communicate his rhetorical vision. To illustrate how this is the case, the contributions of each narrative will first be considered and, then, the larger crystallizing vision described in the terms of traditional fantasy theme analysis.

A Fantasy Theme Perspective

Sonja Foss observes that fantasy theme criticism, first articulated by Ernest G. Bormann,[46] is "designed to provide insights into the shared world view of a group of rhetors."[47] A fantasy, in this method of criticism, is defined as "the dramatization of a hypothetical or actual situation in the rhetoric generated by the group's participants,"[48] a "creative and imaginative interpretation of events that fulfills a psychological or rhetorical need."[49] A fantasy theme is "the content of the dramatizing message" or "the means through which the interpretation is accomplished in communication."[50] And Bormann refers to the "unified putting together of the various scripts which gives the participants a broader view of things" (i.e., "fantasy dramas" that "chain out in public audiences") as a "rhetorical vision."[51]

Although the fantasy chain process was first observed as a type of communication that emerged in small group settings,[52] Bormann argued that "these moments happen not only in individual reactions to works of art, or in a small group's chaining out of a fantasy theme, but also in larger groups hearing a public speech." Rhetorical visions can be constructed "in face-to-face interacting groups, in speaker-audience transactions, in viewers of television broadcasts, in listeners to radio programs, and in all diverse settings for public and intimate communication in a given society."[53]

Each of Campbell's narratives contribute to the larger rhetorical vision constructed in "The Missionary Cause." The biblical narrative ends by placing its audience within the eternal "battle" between good and evil, Satan and Michael. With the aid of the subsequent metaphors, this narrative is then transformed into a militaristic drama: "Hence the necessity incumbent on us to carry on this warfare. . . . " Campbell proceeds to inventory the "Christian armory . . . well supplied with all the weapons essential to the conflict." These include "the breastplate of righteousness," "the shield of faith," "the helmet of salvation," and "the sword of the Spirit—the word of God." He then surveys the battleground: "the missionary fields . . . numerous and various . . . domestic and foreign."[54]

Though the "armory is well supplied," Campbell must nonetheless lament the lack of missionary warriors: "Bethany College and the Church are annually sending out a few. But the supply is not a tythe of the demand." Hence the drama, as it shifts to harvest metaphors, is able to constrain future action by rebuking the one "who prays for the Lord to send out reapers . . . when he never gives a dollar to a missionary . . . to enable him to go into the field."[55]

Campbell's autobiographical narrative is, quite naturally, extended into a historical drama about the place of the restoration movement in the missionary cause. The "whole Christian Institution," the "rudimental elements" of which were embraced in his debates of the early 1820s, is "the terminus of the missionary work." He mourns that this fact "has been so much lost sight of even by the present living generation." He charges "the great mass of Christendom"—"the Baptists," the "Pedobaptists," and "the respective meridians of Lutheranism, Calvinism, and Arminianism alike" —with responsibility for this error.[56] The "definite commencement of the Christian age or institution," according to Campbell, is Christ's commission to his apostles: "Go you into all the world, proclaim the gospel to the whole creation, assuring them that every one who believes this proclamation and is immersed into the name of the Father, and of the Son, and of the Holy Spirit—shall be saved!"[57]

Therefore, he concludes, "the missionary field is declared to be the *whole world* . . . What an extended and still extending area is the missionary field!" Campbell then divides it into "the four mighty realms of Pagandom, of Papaldom, of Mahometandom, and of ecclesiastic Sectariandom, one and all essentially, and constitutionally, more or less, not of the apostolic Christian-dom."[58] Because the boundaries of the mission field have been drawn to encompass not only the pagan but also the Islamic, the Catholic and the sectarian Protestant, the missionary cause and role fall preeminently and uniquely to the churches of the restoration movement:

> It is, indeed, rather invidious in the esteem of many of our con-temporaries. It is, with some of them at least, a species of arro-gance on our part to assert it; and still more to urge it on their attention. But, nevertheless, it is upon us a paramount duty. We plead for the original apostolic gospel and its positive institutions, however invidious it may seem in some eyes. If the great apostles —Peter and Paul—the former to Jews, and the latter to the Gen-tiles, announced the true gospel of the grace of God, shall we hesi-tate a moment on the propriety and necessity, Divinely imposed upon us, of preaching the same gospel which they preached, and in advocating the same institutions which they established. . . . [59]

What is true for his churches in general is extended to the missionary society in particular, for "in this age of denominationalisms"—the selfish sympathies of which Campbell opposes to the philanthropic motives of the missionary cause—Campbell reminds his listeners: "We meet here, not as the Episcopal, the Presbyterian, the Congregational, the Methodist, or the Baptist Missionary Society, but the *Christian* Missionary Society."[60]

These narratives and the dramas that they yield illustrate the tremen-dous potential of epideictic narrative for not only interpreting the past but also for defining the present and directing the future.[61] Aristotle ob-served that "in epideictic [rhetoric] . . . all speakers praise or blame in regard to existing qualities, but they also make use of other things, both reminding [the audience] of the past and projecting the course of the future." Similarly, Conley reminds us that, historically, a prime function of epideictic address has been not merely to praise or blame individuals but to serve a society's need for "regular reassertions of public values and ideals."[62] In this capacity, it not only reasserts a community's existing standards or virtues, which are invoked in the act of praising or blaming, but also reminds both individuals and the community of the ongoing values or ideals by which the future will be judged.

In the present case, the narrative and dramatistic elements of Camp-bell's address bind past, present, and future together into a unified rhe-torical vision that generates a crystallized heritage for the movement while, at the same time, responding to the exigencies of the immediate rhetorical situation. A description of this rhetorical vision in terms of the traditional elements of a fantasy theme (setting, actors, and actions) should satisfactorily illustrate this process.

Elements of Campbell's Rhetorical Vision

The setting of this divine drama is the missionary field. This field is at once both transcendent and local. In its transcendent state, the missionary field is both universal and eternal. It is universal because even the heavens themselves are missionaries and because "the missionary idea . . . circumscribes and permeates the entire area of all creation." It is eternal because it is "older than Adam, older than the creation of the earth," whereas the allusion to "Michael and his angels . . . in conflict with the Devil and his missionaries" invokes the eschatological vision of the apocalypse (Revelation 12:7).[63]

However, this is but a broader setting for the temporal experience of a local missionary field, a "battle, in this our planet," a "warfare" for us "to carry on." This field is nonetheless global in scope—"the whole world—the broad earth," as determined by the great co-mission between Christ and his church (Mark 16:15–16). This global field, however, can be variously divided. Campbell first divides it geographically, into concentric circles that emanate from "the first capital in the land of Judea; then . . . to Samaria, the capital of the ten tribes, and thence to the last domicile of man on earth," after the pattern of Acts 1:8. He later divides it ideologically as well, into "the four mighty realms of Pagandom, of Papaldom, of Mahometandom, and of ecclesiastic Sectariandom."[64]

Both antagonists and protagonists can be identified among the actors. These, too, exist at both the transcendent and local levels. At the transcendent level, the chief antagonist is "Satan—the enemy of God and of man." He has supernatural accomplices as well, hence the references to "the Devil and his missionaries" and "the Devil and his angels." His "battle," however, is not limited to the heavenly realms. His "assault upon our mother Eve, by an incarnation in the most subtle animal in the area of Paradise, is positive proof of the intensity of his malignity to God and man" and Christians "wrestle not against flesh and blood, but against principalities, against powers, against the rulers of the darkness of this world, against wicked spirits in the regions of the air" (Ephesians 6:12).[65]

On the more earthly plane, the antagonists also include those members of the Baptists associations for whom "theory had usurped the place of faith" and for which "consequently human institutions had been more or less substituted for the apostolic and divine." However, "the great mass of Christendom" has "almost universally" misunderstood the conjoining of the missionary cause with the commencement of the church of Jesus Christ. Hence, in this rhetorical vision, both "Papaldom" and Protestant "Sectariandom" are perceived as mission fields rather than missionary agents.[66]

God ("Jehovah") is the transcendent protagonist. As creator, He imbues his creation with the ubiquitous missionary spirit, which, though "older than the Material Universe," is yet "a rudimental and organic element of the constitution of the Universe." God both calls and sends missionaries into the world, including his angels (*"Angels* and *missionaries* are rudimentally but two names for the same officers") and his "only begotten son."[67]

Jesus Christ is, then, the ultimate human protagonist, since he was "superlatively God's own special Ambassador extraordinary, invested with all power in heaven and on earth" and "having invested in him all the rights of God and all the rights of man." He is "the Lord Messiah," "the Hero of our redemption." Predating "the Incarnate Word" in human history is Moses, "the oldest missionary whose name is inscribed on the rolls of time" and "the first Divine missionary" who, with the exception of John the Baptist, "was the second in rank and character" to Christ himself. The twelve apostles and other early evangelists are also numbered among those placed at Christ's command. Campbell's own "missionary tours" inaugurate his restoration movement, the churches and societies of which climax this succession of protagonists, for "the church . . . of right is and ought to be a great missionary society."[68]

Though many of the dramatic actions have been noted in the above, it is interesting to observe how the actions of the protagonists, in particular, apply Campbell's larger rhetorical vision to the specific exigencies of the rhetorical situation. God sends Christ his son into the world. God places "angels, apostles, and evangelists" at his command. Christ commissions these as "his ambassadors to the world" and sends "the Holy Spirit, to bear witness through his twelve missionaries—the consecrated and Heaven inspired apostles." These, in turn, "gave in solemn charge to others to sound out and to proclaim the glad tidings of great joy to all people." And, Campbell questions, "need we ask is not the Christian Church itself, in its own institution and constitution virtually and essentially a *missionary institution.*"[69]

The churches of his restoration movement, however, are uniquely constrained to "plead for the original gospel and its positive institutions, however invidious it may seem in some eyes," for "the propriety and the necessity" is "divinely imposed upon us, of preaching the same gospel which they [the apostles] preached."[70] However, their supply of missionaries is "comparatively very few" and "there is too general apathy or indifference on the subject": "The Macedonian *cry*—'come over and help us;' 'send us an evangelist'—'send us missionaries'—'the fields are large, the people are desirous, anxious, to hear the original gospel. What can you do for us?' Nothing! Nothing!! My brethren ought this so to be?—!"[71]

It is thus incumbent upon the churches of the movement, working together in cooperation through the society, to train ("schools for the prophets are wanting"), pray for, send out, and financially support the needed missionaries:

And when we gravely ponder . . . the Lord our King . . . Lord of all instrumentalities, possessing all authority in the heavens above us, under us, and around us; and in the still small voice of his claims asking our aid and cooperation with him, honoring us with a copartnery with himself . . . I ask, shall we, will we, dare we, withhold from him our cordial aid, our liberal contributions, out of the abundance of all good things which he has, in his magnificent liberality, conferred upon us? Let your response, my beloved brethren, be to him, and not to me, your humble brother.[72]

Thus, to borrow the words of Bormann, this rhetorical vision, constructed through these epideictic narratives, "contains as part of its substance the motive that will impel the people caught up in it."[73] Because the story of Campbell and the restoration movement is but a subplot in a transcendent divine drama, the symbolic reality it creates for the movement constrains its participants to interpret their support for the missionary society as consubstantial with their loyalty to God himself.

A Patriarchal *Ethos*

Campbell's address, then, presents this national assembly of the movement with a complete, coherent rhetorical vision that interprets its past, defines its present, and directs its future. However, it also constructs for its speaker an *ethos* appropriate for this mature stage of the movement whose identity is embodied in this crystallized vision—an *ethos* that, for several reasons, may be aptly termed "patriarchal."

Father of the Movement

First, Campbell emerges within this vision as the great "father" of the movement and its pioneer missionary. His testimony to the plight of deprived missionaries grows out of personal experiences that predate even his association with the Baptists—his "missionary tours" of 1812–1816.[74] His "investigation" during those years produced the conviction that formed the heart of his "Sermon on the Law": the conflict between human and divine institutions. He is credited, through the Walker and Maccalla debates, with outlining the "whole Christian institution." Here the narrative ends abruptly, saying little of subsequent decades and privileging this constitutive stage of the movement.

Consequently, the history of the *movement,* which is born in the missionary cause, is also *Campbell's personal* history. "I was then my own missionary, with the consent, however, of one church," Campbell says, constituting himself the movement's inaugural missionary. "Bethany College and Church," who were "sending out a few" missionaries, were preeminently identified with Campbell, who donated the land for the campus and served as its founding president and first professor of Bible. Mention of other missionaries, colleges, or churches by name is absent from the address. Campbell's agency thus maintains a high profile in spite of the fact that, as a whole, the address is undoubtedly characterized by what Kenneth Burke refers to as a "scene-act" ratio[75] (i.e., the nature of the scene determines which actions are appropriate).

Steward of the Heritage

The narrative elements and setting of the address also position Campbell as the movement's preeminent national storyteller. As of 1860, no attempt had been made to compose a systematic or orderly written account of the movement's history. The need for such a history was recognized as early as 1833, but Campbell responded to such overtures by insisting that such a project would be premature. He assured others, though, that he was preserving documents that would be important to such a history. In 1848, he shared some of his notes in a series of six essays in the *Millennial Harbinger.* These essays, however, focused mainly on events prior to 1830.

Garrett notes that as late as 1863 the movement "still did not have a historian."[76]

Thus, the transmission of the movement's heritage up to this time had been, for the most part, piecemeal and predominantly oral. Here, then, at this critical moment—in Campbell's last public national moment—the leadership of the movement gathers round to hear their patriarch's story —and in his story, their own as well. After four decades of unrivaled leadership, Campbell now functions as the steward of the Stone-Campbell heritage, the gatekeeper of its traditions.

Paternal Visionary

Finally, Campbell also emerges within this vision as the movement's chief executive visionary. Bruner observes that stories "have to do with how protagonists interpret things, what things mean to them."[77] Since his narratives function to constrain future action, these constraints are thus produced by Campbell's own interpretation of the past and definition of the present. *Campbell,* in effect, is thus discursively directing his movement's future, charting its course, in a manner that gazes beyond those boundaries posed by his advancing age and rapidly declining health.

It seems reasonable to assume that, as Campbell delivered this address, he was well aware that his movement would soon need to look to others for the leadership he had provided for more than four decades. He would not be at the forefront as the movement and the nation contended with ominous threats to their unity. Nonetheless, he uses the present moment to celebrate the movement's saga in such a way that the vision of the first generation is passed to the next and in the hope that it will endure.

Conclusions

The epideictic narratives in this address communicate a complete and coherent rhetorical vision that constrains its participants to act consistently with a transcendent divine drama, within which not only paganism but also Catholicism and the Protestant denominations become the target of their missionary activity. Through this rhetorical vision, Campbell is able both to construct the ACMS as a means of cooperation consistent with the inaugural spirit of the restoration movement and to compel its members to identify their support of the society with heeding God's own voice. Concomitantly, this address constructs a *patriarchal ethos* for Campbell, who emerges as the Father of the movement, the steward of its heritage, and its sagest visionary.

Yet, in the end, it must be asked whether the rhetorical vision represented in this address came to be shared by those who heard and read of it. Was Campbell's "patriarchal" *ethos* embraced by the movement? Did his larger vision for the movement "chain out" in such a way as to fashion the movement's subsequent self-understanding?

Sufficient and various evidence exists to demonstrate that the "patriarchal" *ethos* of Campbell illustrated in this address has been well fixed from his later years into the present day. One particular incident illustrates the esteem in which Campbell was held even by those who opposed him. Both Tolbert Fanning and David Lipscomb (editors of the *Gospel Advocate*), who felt that Campbell had betrayed positions published in the *Christian Baptist* by supporting the ACMS, refused to accept that Campbell had, of his own volition, taken this position. After a visit with Campbell in 1857, Fanning reported that he was shocked to find Campbell in an apparently senile condition that made it difficult for him to keep his mind on the subject of discussion. Lipscomb concluded that Campbell never recovered from (in North's terms) "an arduous trip to England [in 1847], during which he received antislavery allegations (from which he was cleared), and suffered a bad chest cold and near pneumonia. In addition, when he returned home, he learned that his ten-year-old son Wycliffe had drowned in his absence." Lipscomb subsequently popularized the view that provided a standard explanation for those who wanted to revere Campbell as a father of the movement but to reject his support of the missionary society—that after the harsh experiences of 1847, Campbell became a physically broken man controlled by others. Campbell, however, had advocated such agencies long before 1847.[78]

As mentioned, Campbell's election as president of the ACMS in 1849, is spite of his absence from the convention, illustrates the significance that other movement leaders attributed to his support of the venture. That he retained the office long after his physical and mental abilities permitted him to perform the role is further evidence of the respect other leaders had for his "patriarchal" status. Upon his death (March 4, 1866), the very first issue of the *Christian Standard* (April 7) devoted its entire front page to an obituary that celebrated his life and work. Within less than a month, Robert Richardson had been commissioned by the family to author a biography. Within less than five years, the *Millennial Harbin-*

ger, once the journalist bulwark of the movement but now without Campbell's prestige and influence, ceased publication.

In the years preceding and following Campbell's passing, competing factions often attempted to benefit from their (late) leader's *ethos* by seeking evidence to support their positions from his publications. Shifts that took place in Campbell's thought over time occasionally permitted both factions in a controversy to appeal to his discourse for precedent.[79] In 1866, for example, W. K. Pendleton used his ACMS address to demonstrate Campbell's support for the society and to chide antisociety advocates for twisting his position to their advantage.[80] Hughes observes: "With the loss of postmillennialism in the broader culture, it was inevitable that Campbell's followers would lose that vision as well and seize instead on his penultimate concerns—unity and restoration—and then divide into hostile camps around those banners. Not surprisingly, each camp claimed for its banner the place of honor in the legacy of the Sage of Bethany."[81]

Space does not permit a complete documentation of the rich body of literature that subsequent generations have devoted to Campbell's life, thought, and work, although this also testifies to his "partriarchal" *ethos.* The select bibliography included in this volume represents a mere fraction of this literature. Without exception, denominational histories have offered similar testimony both in their characterization of Campbell's contributions and the proportion of attention devoted to them. Eva Jean Wrather, restoration historian and Campbell biographer from a previous generation, in a largely epideictic essay, once described him as "a 19th-century embodiment of the renaissance conception of the 'whole man'" and compared him to Luther, Calvin, and Wesley. However, even more recent and balanced denominational histories testify to his patriarchal *ethos.* Henry Webb, a historian from the independent Christian Churches, describes him as "an Olympian figure" and notes the leadership vacuum that faced Stone-Campbell churches upon the stilling of "the voice of Bethany." According to Richard Hughes, a Church of Christ historian, "In molding the enduring character of Churches of Christ, nothing compares with Alexander Campbell's magazine the *Christian Baptist.*" Perhaps most illustrative is the standard Disciples of Christ history produced by McAllister and Tucker, which explicitly identifies the Campbells, Stone, and Scott as the "Four Founding Fathers" of the Stone-Campbell movement.[82]

But did such rhetoric as that illustrated in this address merely fashion Campbell's "patriarchal" *ethos* or did it also impart a vision that would shape his movement's self-understanding? The answer to the latter question could plausibly be, in some qualified sense, either "yes" or "no."

On one hand, a case could be made that Campbell's vision survived in various forms, as different factions within the movement appropriated it in ways that privileged elements most consistent with their own ideologies. Hughes suggests that, during the second half of the nineteenth century, the Stone-Campbell movement produced "two irreconcilable traditions—one defined by ecumenic progressivism and the other by sectarian primitivism" and consequently divided along these lines.[83]

In Hughes' words, the progressive tradition, which would eventually evolve into the Disciples of Christ denomination, "maintained their postmillennial faith in human progress but, like Alexander Campbell, increasingly defined the object of their faith as Protestant American civilization."[84] In the decades following Campbell's passing, this tradition would continue to defend and create regional and national societies to support cooperative mission work. In the years immediately after the war, the ACMS continued to struggle financially and when criticism prompted it to cease selling life memberships and directorships in 1867, it entered into severe financial crisis. At the 1869 convention in Louisville, a "Louisville Plan" was adopted to remedy the situation but it proved ill conceived. Webb observes that as of 1872, "The Disciples lagged behind as far as the missionary enterprise was concerned. While the various denominations were enthusiastically planning and promoting foreign missions, the Disciples were debating whether or not a New Testament people could utilize an organization beyond the local church to enable them to do mission work. While the discussions were being carried on in the several periodicals, giving to the program of the society was suffering a steady decline. After the adoption of the Louisville Plan, income was so low that not a single missionary was sustained."[85]

Supporters of cooperative work would reverse this trend, however. A group of leading women launched the Christian Women's Board of Missions (CWBM) in 1874; the Foreign Christian Missionary Society (FCMS) was organized in 1875; and in 1877 the ACMS, which had maintained a paper existence during the years of the Louisville Plan, was revived as a home mission society. In 1917, the ACMS would unite with the CWBM, the FCMS, the Board of Church Extension, the National Benevolence Association, and the Board of Ministerial Relief to form the United Christian Missionary Society.[86] Webb notes that by the end of the century "mission activity was vigorous and sustained" and North refers to the last quarter of the nineteenth century as "the heyday of missions for the Restoration Movement."[87]

The primitivist tradition, which, according to Hughes, would eventually evolve into the Churches of Christ, "abandoned postmillennial optimism altogether and, along with it, the original ecumenical vision. That left them with only one plank from the original Campbellian platform: the vision of the primitive church . . . These people increasingly identified the primitive church of the New Testament age with the Church of Christ movement to which they belonged, and they defended that church against all comers."[88] This tradition would privilege that aspect of Campbell's vision which arrayed not only paganism but also Catholicism and the Protestant denominations as the mission field for those who "plead for the original gospel."

The spirit of exclusivism inherent in this element of the vision had its antecedents. It was noted in chapter five that Campbell's shift in attitude toward Protestantism was, in all likelihood, at least partially prompted by the growing sectarianism he perceived within his own movement. It would only intensify in the years after his passing. Casey describes the type of discourse popular within this tradition: "In the early days of the movement Campbell and others had appealed to the 'facts' of scripture and made reasoned appeals to outsiders. Now the debaters transformed gospel 'facts' into gospel 'bullets' . . . A hard preaching style evolved out of this debating attitude of satire and ridicule. The main idea was to 'skin the sects,' implying that the religious neighbors were not only unreasonable but also subhuman or merely animals whose positions needed to be devastated, not respected."[89]

Representative of the spirit of this tradition was the *Sand Creek Declaration and Address* of 1889. Read to a mass meeting of approximately 6,000 at the Sand Creek Church of Christ in Shelby County, Illinois, on August 18, it named church fund-raisers, the use of instrumental music in worship, church choirs, the "man-made society for mission work," and "the one man, imported preacher pastor" as practices not found in the New Testament and concluded: "We are impelled from a sense of duty to say that all such as are guilty of teaching or allowing and practicing the many innovations and corruptions to which we have referred, after having had sufficient time for meditation and reflection, if they will not turn away from such abominations, that we can not and will not regard them as brethren."[90] North observes that in spite of Thomas Campbell's vision for Christian unity first expressed in his *Declaration and Address,* "By the end of the century . . . many of his followers were insisting on such a rigid application of biblical authority that they were not interested in unity with anyone who disagreed with them on the application of these principles."[91]

But if, on one hand, a case might be made that Campbell's vision—or elements of it—survived in these various manifestations, it is clear, on the other hand, that his vision for the unity of his own movement did not. Bormann suggests that "some rhetorical visions are unstable; they suffer from a continuous threat of spontaneous combustion."[92] It seems an apt description for a plea that drew upon diverse theological traditions and was consequently and consistently vexed by controversies that evolved out of a tension between its commitments to unity and restoration.[93]

If this underlying tension defined the ideological divergence within the movement, actual separation was primarily fueled by the sectional antagonisms that defined the slavery controversy and the Civil War. Considering that the annual meeting of the ACMS was the movement's only national meeting, it is little wonder that it became the focus of hostilities. Throughout the war, the ACMS continued to meet annually in Cincinnati, Ohio, but the South was cut off from access to the convention and the ACMS quickly developed a pro-Union bias. In 1863 the convention passed a series of loyalty resolutions that led to a reunion between abolitionist leaders and the ACMS before the end of the year. However, Harrell notes that this reunion "was not a surrender of Northern radical sectionalism. The reunion was simply a merging of the two Northern groups in the church which had been estranged since 1859 . . . the reunion . . . was a decidedly sectional achievement. What the reaction of the South would be to the Northern-dominated society was by no means certain in 1863."[94] North, however, describes the resolutions as "a major slap in the face to the southern Christians"[95] and Webb sums up their response to the position of the ACMS: "It was to produce a bitter reaction when published in the South, creating anti-society bias that could never be overcome and focusing Southern animosity against many who would emerge as brotherhood leaders in the decades to follow. It contributed immensely to the division that was to come."[96]

Several other issues also occasioned controversy and division within the movement. These included disagreements over whether to hire salaried ministers, whether to invite all believers to participate in communion irrespective of church membership, and whether to use musical instruments in worship services. However, as North points out, a significant pattern emerged within these controversies. Those who opposed any one of these practices generally opposed them all; those who favored one generally favored them all. The pattern was partially reflective of distinct biblical hermeneutics which variously interpreted Thomas Campbell's slogan, "Where the scriptures speak, we speak; where the scriptures are silent, we are silent"—"strict constructionists" attributing a prohibitive force to biblical "silence," "loose constructionists" considering it a realm of expediency. But a geographical pattern was manifest as well: most of the South was "strict constructionist" in its hermeneutic. The fact that two-thirds of those who eventually chose to affiliate with the Churches of Christ lived in the eleven states of the confederacy seems to justify Harrell's conclusion that "new divisive issues arose among the Disciples of Christ but the sectional alignment of factions was, at least in part, a heritage from the slavery controversy."[97]

For a movement consisting of locally autonomous churches, division was a process rather than an event. As Harrell notes, it took the remainder of the century for separation to solidify around opposing sets of institutions such as periodicals, colleges, and societies. However, by 1906, the U.S. Bureau of the Census, acting upon the advice of David Lipscomb, editor of the *Gospel Advocate,* would list the Churches of Christ and the Disciples of Christ as separate denominations.[98]

In the end, it is sufficiently clear that social forces as powerful as the slavery controversy and the Civil War proved more of a challenge to the unity of Alexander Campbell's restoration movement than its aging charismatic leader, in physical and mental decline, could discursively manage. And yet it may also be a testimony to the force of Campbell's rhetorical leadership that, in spite of its schismatic personality, it was not until the voice of the movement's patriarch fell silent and the Civil War divided the country that the movement itself actually divided.

Conclusion
Alexander Campbell
Prophet, Pastor, and Patriarch

Alexander Campbell was a significant leader within American Christianity. By the beginning of the twentieth century, the Stone-Campbell movement had grown to a membership in excess of one million and, to this day, the imprint of Campbell's "Nineteenth-Century Reformation" is on no less than three major denominations. Campbell's rhetorical leadership reached international proportions as well, for readers of the *Millennial Harbinger* in other parts of the English-speaking world acknowledged its role in the development of fraternal efforts in Great Britain, New Zealand, Australia, and Canada.[1]

Since he held no official position or office from which he derived any degree of external authority, Campbell's was a predominantly rhetorical leadership, a leadership exercised through his discursive activities. His viewpoints were circulated mostly through the *Christian Baptist* (1823–1830) and the *Millennial Harbinger* (1830–1866). However, extensive speaking tours (during which he covered great distances on horseback and by steamboat)[2] as well as his sermons, occasional debates, and regional and national addresses also played an important role in Campbell's rhetorical leadership.

McAllister and Tucker describe how the loss of Campbell's rhetorical leadership affected his restoration movement:

> Alexander Campbell's death in 1866 left Disciples unprepared for the era of transit and tension. Notwithstanding their tendency to take issue with each other, they had sensed their oneness in his commanding presence. Their acknowledged leader, he symbolized both their strength and their potential. The news of his death neither shocked nor overwhelmed them, but they never recovered from the loss of his towering influence. "Even though they grew for a while," Ronald E. Osborn has suggested, "at Campbell's death they immediately began to fall apart. No one succeeded

him, for his leadership was charismatic, not official, and the leaders who came after him had diverse spirits."[3]

This volume began by describing Campbell's "common sense" philosophy of rhetoric and acknowledging its fit with American culture during the Jacksonian era. Subsequent chapters have explored the charismatic nature of Campbell's rhetorical leadership as it was experienced, in the particular, at critical junctions of the Stone-Campbell movement's first generation. Collectively, they illustrate Campbell's sensitivity to the demands of the rhetorical situation and his ability to adapt his rhetoric to the challenges presented by dramatically shifting rhetorical situations. This adaptability generated for him an evolving leadership *ethos* that was itself progressively adapted to the shifting needs of his movement.

Specifically, his "Sermon on the Law" (1816) possessed qualities typically associated with "constitutive" rhetoric, qualities that helped to call his movement into being. For Campbell, it generated an *ethos* that was, in many ways, "protestant," even while it challenged many of the cherished practices and doctrines of the community which he addressed. Through its rhetorical action, Campbell emerged as a spokesperson whose voice and virtues were well suited for leading the kind of reforming-restoring community that his sermon called into being.

The *Christian Baptist* (1823–1830) paralleled the years of separation between the Campbellite churches and the Baptist associations in which they held membership. Both the program of this journal and the iconoclastic qualities of its rhetoric placed Campbell beyond the pale of Baptist boundaries. It served as an instrument through which Campbell articulated an alternative doctrinal and ecclesiastical self-understanding for his reforming churches. It also constructed a predominantly "prophetic" *ethos* for Campbell, an *ethos* very similar to that generated by the prophetic rhetoric of the ancient Hebrew prophets.

When Campbell published his three responses to the Lunenburg letter in the *Millennial Harbinger* (1837), he had inherited the responsibility for leading a national, independent movement of autonomous churches and begun to face the challenge of managing the tensions produced by ideological diversity. His use of dissociation, classification, and hierarchy enabled him to transcend his differences with diverse audiences and thus find common ground for identification with both the extreme conservatives within his own movement and the Protestant parties, whom he had previously vilified but whom he had more recently represented in a debate with the Roman Catholic Bishop John Purcell. Herein, a more prudent and "pastoral" *ethos* emerged for Campbell.

In 1860, Campbell, for the last time, directly addressed a national assembly of movement leaders at the general convention of the American Christian Missionary Society. In an attempt to muster support for the beleaguered society, his address ("The Missionary Cause") employed elements of epideictic narrative to praise the virtues of the missionary cause and offered the movement a complete and coherent rhetorical vision. Speaking as a "patriarch," Campbell crystallized the movement's heritage in a way that interpreted its past, defined its present, and offered direction for its future. Although subsequent developments illustrate that even important religious leaders, especially as they age and their movements grow more diverse, have their limits, Campbell's ability to hold his movement together through more than four decades of controversy and the leadership vacuum experienced by the movement upon his passing also suggest the force of his rhetorical leadership.

This, then, is how Alexander Campbell was experienced through his rhetoric—first as prophet, then as pastor, and finally as patriarch. Not all aspects of Campbell's rhetoric are praiseworthy. In the eyes of none other than his own father, Campbell's vitriolic criticism often exceeds the bounds of propriety, even in an age when the civil use of wit, satire, and ridicule were accepted within the conventions of public politeness.

Nonetheless, he demonstrated an extraordinary insight into the exigencies that gave rise to the need for persuasion and the constraints that rhetorical situations placed upon the means of persuasion available to him. What Ernest Bormann once wrote seems to apply in this case: "A viable rhetoric must also accommodate the community to the changes that accompany its unfolding history."[4] As Campbell led his movement through periods of emergence, growth, and maturity,[5] he possessed, above all else, what every rhetor needs in some measure: a keen sense of what the ancients called *kairos*,[6] the "timeliness" of having the word appropriate for the moment.

Notes

Introduction

1. Enos Dowling, *The Restoration Movement* (Cincinnati: Standard Pub., 1964) 31.

2. Lester McAllister and William Tucker, *Journey in Faith: A History of the Christian Church (Disciples of Christ)* (St. Louis: Bethany Press, 1975) 20, 31; Henry E. Webb, *In Search of Christian Unity: A History of the Restoration Movement* (Cincinnati: Standard Publishing, 1990) 243.

3. For an extended account of Stone's accomplishments and contributions, see D. Newell Williams, *Barton Stone: A Spiritual Biography* (St. Louis: Chalice Press, 2000). See also Anthony Dunnavant, ed., *Cane Ridge in Context: Perspectives on Barton W. Stone and the Revival* (Nashville: Disciples of Christ Historical Society, 1992) for a collection of lectures and essays on the significance of Stone and, in particular, the Cane Ridge Revival in the life of the Stone-Campbell movement.

4. Webb 61.

5. John Rogers, *Biography of Elder Barton W. Stone, Written by Himself with Additions and Reflections by Elder John Rogers* (Cincinnati: J. A. and U. P. James, 1843) 2, qtd. in Webb 61.

6. McAllister and Tucker 159.

7. For an extended account of Scott's accomplishments and contributions see William A. Gerrard II, *A Biographical Study of Walter Scott: American Frontier Evangelist* (Joplin, MO: College Press, 1992). Various aspects of Scott's theology and ministry are also treated extensively in Mark G. Toulouse, ed., *Walter Scott: A Nineteenth Century Evangelical* (St. Louis: Chalice Press, 1999).

8. Richard T. Hughes and Leonard C. Allen, *Illusions of Innocence: Protestant Primitivism in America, 1630–1875* (Chicago: University of Chicago Press, 1988) 123; Gerrard 35, 38–39; D. Newell Williams, "Bringing Vision to Life: Walter Scott and the Restored Church" in Toulouse 128; Richard T. Hughes, *Reviving the Ancient Faith: The Story of Churches of Christ in America* (Grand Rapids, MI: Eerdmans, 1996) 49.

9. Gerrard 28; James B. North, *Union in Truth: An Interpretive History of the Restoration Movement* (Cincinnati: Standard Publishing, 1994) 145; Amy Collier Artman, "An Implicit Creed: Walter Scott and the Golden Oracle" in Toulouse 50; Webb 138–39.

10. Brush Run did not even join the Redstone Baptist Association until 1815.

11. The most prominent example of contemporary interest is probably the attention paid to both the "rhetorical presidency" and "presidential rhetoric." The seminal work in studies of the "rhetorical presidency" has proven to be "The Rise of the Rhetorical Presidency" by James W. Ceasar, Glen E. Thurow, Jeffrey K. Tullis, and Joseph M. Bessette. This article first appeared in *Presidential Studies Quarterly* II (Spring 1981): 158–71, and was subsequently reprinted in *Essays in Presidential Rhetoric*, 2nd ed., eds. Theodore Windt and Beth Ingold (Dubuque: Kendall-Hunt Pub., 1987) 3–22. Its basic tenets were more formally explicated in Tullis' *The Rhetorical Presidency* (Princeton: Princeton University Press, 1987). More recently, Martin Medhurst has collected a series of essays, *Beyond the Rhetorical Presidency* (College Station: Texas A & M University Press, 1996), which have extended dialogue about this construct, involving scholars from both the fields of political science and speech communication. In the field of speech communication, the study of specific rhetorical acts of presidents dates as far back as 1937 when Robert D. King published "Franklin D. Roosevelt's Second Inaugural Address," *Quarterly Journal of Speech* 23 (1937): 439–44. However, as Medhurst points out (227–28), "'presidential rhetoric' did not crystallize as a specialized subfield until the early 1970's." Four analyses of Richard Nixon's November 3, 1969 address on Vietnam provided the impetus: Robert P. Newman's "Under the Veneer: Nixon's Vietnam Speech of November 3, 1969," *Quarterly Journal of Speech* 56 (1970): 113–28; Herman G. Stelzner's "The Quest Story and Nixon's November 3, 1969 Address," *Quarterly Journal of Speech* 57 (1971): 163–72; Karlyn Kohrs Campbell's "An Exercise in the Rhetoric of Mythical America," in *Critiques of Contemporary Rhetoric* (Belmont, CA: Wadsworth, 1972) 39–58; and Forbes Hill's "Conventional Wisdom—Traditional Form: The President's Message of November 3, 1969," *Quarterly Journal of Speech* 58 (1972): 373–86. Campbell later published a rejoinder to Hill's article and Hill a response to Campbell's rejoinder in *Quarterly Journal of Speech* 58 (1972): 451–60.

12. The recent interest in the study of leadership in American communication studies is not confined to a specifically rhetorical perspective. In the preface to the second edition of their book *Leadership a Communication Perspective* (Prospect Heights, IL: Waveland Press, 2000), Michael Z. Hackman and Craig E. Johnson offer evidence from the past few years that communication experts representing a variety of perspectives were "beginning to break their silence on the topic of leadership" (xi). Their work treats leadership from the perspectives of small group communication, organizational communication, cross-cultural communication and gender communication as well as from a rhetorical perspective (xiii).

13. The "rhetorical presidency" and "presidential rhetoric" are not identical constructs. Medhurst points out that scholars of the "rhetorical presidency" tend to "find their academic homes in departments of political science or government" and "have a long intellectual tradition stretching back to Aristotle's *Politics*." Their object of study is the presidency, their primary focus is institutional, and they are most concerned with "the nature, scope and function of the presidency as a constitutional office." Their fundamental stance is "essentialist." Beginning with the U.S. Constitution or early presidential inaugural messages as a normative base, this construct views

a resort to popular leadership through rhetorical discourse as debasing the presidency, transforming it in an extraconstitutional manner, and calls for a remedy. Scholars of "presidential rhetoric," on the other hand, tend to "find their academic homes in departments of speech communication" and also "have a long intellectual tradition that reaches back to Aristotle, but to his *Rhetoric*." Their object of study is rhetoric, their primary focus is the rhetorical act (specific presidential utterances) and they are most concerned "with the principles of the art and how those principles allow [a U.S. President] . . . to achieve his . . . ends by symbolic means." Their fundamental perspective is "functionalist." Beginning with the presidency as it has operated in the recent past and is operating at the present, this construct views rhetoric as an art that presidents attempt to use to their advantage as political leaders, and calls for an understanding of the power and possibilities of the means of persuasion available to presidents (xii–xiii, xx–xxii).

14. In her work *Deeds Done in Words: Presidential Rhetoric and the Genres of Government* (Chicago: University of Chicago Press, 1990), Karlyn Kohrs Campbell, a scholar whose academic home is speech communication, stresses the influence of the institution upon presidential rhetoric. Her focus, in fact, is upon "the presidency" in relation to which "presidential rhetoric is one source of institutional power" (4). And though her work is specifically "about the varying kinds of rhetoric that have come to typify the presidency over time," her "look at the presidency as an institution in which rhetoric plays a major role" assumes "that the character of presidential rhetoric has been created, sustained and altered through time by the nature of the presidency as an institution" (3). However, she also attributes to rhetoric a constitutive function in relationship to the institution. It is through rhetorical action that "presidents perform the functions essential to maintaining the presidency." The institution of the presidency and the rhetoric of the presidents thus form a constitutive dialectic: "the identity of the presidents as spokespersons for the institution . . . gives this discourse a distinctive character. In turn, that identity—the institution of the presidency—arises out of such discourse" (4). Even the instrumental functions of specific presidential utterances contribute to their constitutive impact upon the institution, for at the same time that presidents "persuade us to conceive of ourselves in ways compatible with their view of government and the world . . . presidents invite us to see them, the presidency, the country, and the country's role in specific ways" (5–6). Similarly, Jeffrey K. Tullis, whose academic home is political science and whose work has been formative in the construct of the rhetorical presidency, notes: "In an important sense, all presidents are rhetorical presidents. All presidents exercise their office through the medium of language, written and spoken . . . " ("Revising the Rhetorical Presidency," in Medhurst 3). And though he considers "the changing character of constitutional politics in America" his most important subject, it is his attention to "patterns of presidential rhetoric" that permits him access to this subject as they, on one hand, signify and reflect "an important transformation of the constitutional order" and yet, on the other hand, contribute significantly to bringing this transformation about (4). In varying degrees, this same dynamic interaction or constitutive dialectic also figures significantly in the work of other speech communication scholars. For examples see Halford Ryan's *Franklin D. Roosevelt's Rhetorical Presidency* (Greenwood Pub., 1988),

Roderick P. Hart's *The Sound of Leadership: Presidential Communication in the Modern Age* (University of Chicago Press, 1987), and Craig Allen Smith and Kathy B. Smith's *The White House Speaks: Presidential Leadership as Persuasion* (Praeger Publishers, 1994).

15. Hackman and Johnson identify three themes common to a diverse set of proposed definitions of leadership (12–13). These include the exercise of influence (to identify leadership is to identify who is influencing whom) and a group context (including social movements, state legislatures, etc.). Both apply to Campbell, the latter in that his community would evolve out of a church reform movement.

16. Michael Casey's essay, "From British Ciceronianism to American Baconianism: Alexander Campbell as a Case Study of a Shift in Rhetorical Theory," *Southern Communication Journal* 66 (Winter 2001): 151–66, presents a thorough and well-documented overview of Campbell's rhetorical theory and practice. An excellent overview, its purpose is other than the one pursued here—extended "textual" criticisms of specific rhetorical acts. Similarly, in *Saddlebags, City Streets and Cyberspace* (Abilene, TX: Abilene Christian University Press, 1995), Michael Casey's two-hundred page history of preaching in the Churches of Christ (non-instrumental), Campbell is included among several preachers treated in the first few chapters. Again, while an excellent survey text, no one preacher (even Campbell) is afforded extensive treatment and close textual analysis does not fit within the scope of his objective. Richard Hughes has devoted a chapter to the influence of Campbell's *Christian Baptist* and two chapters to his "hard style" in *Reviving*. His book, however, is a history of the Churches of Christ (non-instrumental), and, while an excellent contribution to the field of church history, neither his objectives nor his method fit within the scope of dedicated rhetorical analysis. In *The Core Gospel* (Abilene, TX: Abilene Christian University Press, 1992), Bill Love includes Campbell in a chapter that surveys the preaching of the movement's first generation. Though quite satisfactory for his purposes, Love's treatment is, to an even greater extent than Casey's, quite summative and is, moreover, fashioned to his objective of providing theological assessment of the history of preaching in the Churches of Christ. Dale A. Jorgenson's *Theological and Aesthetic Roots in the Stone-Campbell Movement* (Kirksville, MO: Thomas Jefferson University Press, 1989) is an excellent treatment of the significance of the arts and aesthetics to the ideas of the key leaders of the Stone-Campbell movement in its first two generations. However, it neither is nor claims to be either a dedicated study of Campbell or an analysis of his rhetoric. Alger Fitch's *Alexander Campbell: Preacher of Reform and Reformer of Preaching* (Joplin, MO: College Press, 1970, 118 pages) is now more than thirty years old. Though a helpful update of Granville Walker's *Preaching in the Thought of Alexander Campbell* (St. Louis: Bethany Press, 1954), Fitch's work, like its predecessor, focuses more on Campbell's thoughts *about* preaching than on Campbell's preaching. To the extent that it attempts to analyze Campbell's preaching, it much more resembles that traditional approach to criticism, which tended to study speakers more than speeches, privileging historical milieu, biography, and close paraphrase at the expense of intensive textual analysis. Archibald McLean's *Alexander Campbell as Preacher* is almost a century old (St. Louis: Christian Publica-

tions, 1908). Dwight Stevenson's *Disciple Preaching in the First Generation* (Nashville: Disciples of Christ Historical Society, 1969, 109 pages) is a brief historical survey. Writing as a historian, Stevenson's most helpful contributions pertain to backgrounds and influences and his work is more descriptive than analytical. The most thorough treatment of Scottish influences upon Campbell's rhetorical theory is Carisse Mickey Berryhill's unpublished dissertation, "Sense, Expression and Purpose: Alexander Campbell's Natural Philosophy of Rhetoric," Florida State University, 1982. For a more general survey of scholarship on the history of communication practices within the Stone-Campbell movement, see Michael W. Casey and Douglas A. Foster, "The Renaissance of Stone-Campbell Studies: An Assessment and New Directions," *The Stone-Campbell Movement: An International Religious Tradition*, eds. Casey and Foster (Knoxville: University of Tennessee Press, 2002) 25–29.

17. Aristotle, *On Rhetoric: A Theory of Civic Discourse*, trans. by George Kennedy (New York: Oxford University Press, 1991) 38 and footnote 43.

18. Stephen Lucas, "The Renaissance of American Public Address: Text and Context in Rhetorical Criticism," *Quarterly Journal of Speech* 74 (May 1988): 248–49, 253.

19. Lucas 253.

20. This is Stanley Edgar Hyman's description of Burke's critical mode (*The Armed Vision: A Study in the Method of Modern Literary Criticism*, New York: Vintage, 1955, 390).

21. The analysis in chapter three draws upon the 1816 edition of Campbell's "Sermon on the Law," published by James Wilson in Steubenville, Ohio. On its thirtieth anniversary, Campbell reprinted this sermon in the 1846 volume of the *Millennial Harbinger*. An electronic version of the 1846 edition may be consulted at: *The Restoration Movement Pages*, ed. Hans Rollman, 1995–2004, 21 Aug. 2004 <http://www.mun.ca/rels/restmov/index.html>. The Disciples of Christ Historical Society has recently acquired a copy of the 1816 edition.

22. Maurice Charland, "Constitutive Rhetoric: The Case of the Peuple Quebecois," *Quarterly Journal of Speech* 73 (1987): 133–50.

23. All citations from the *Christian Baptist* will subsequently be drawn from *The Christian Baptist*, ed. Alexander Campbell, rev. by D. S. Burnet from the second edition (1835; Joplin, MO: College Press, 1983). The reader may also consult an electronic edition, which includes the texts analyzed in chapter four, at *The Restoration Movement Pages*.

24. *Millennial Harbinger* Vol. II, No. 9 (Sept. 5, 1831): 419. All citations from the *Millennial Harbinger* will subsequently be drawn from the *Millennial Harbinger*, eds. Alexander Campbell and W. K. Pendleton (1830–1870; Joplin, MO: College Press, 1987).

25. For copies of the texts analyzed in chapter five, the reader may also consult electronic editions of selections from the *Millennial Harbinger* at *The Restoration Movement Pages*.

26. The reader may also consult an electronic copy of Campbell's 1860 address to the ACMS in his *Popular Lectures and Addresses* at *The Restoration Movement Pages*.

Chapter 1

1. Webb 67 (of Thomas Campbell).

2. At least since the publication of Benjamin Lyon Smith's *Alexander Campbell* (St. Louis: Bethany Press, 1930), it has been commonplace to identify Thomas Campbell as an "Old Light" Anti-Burgher. More recent research, however, has presented convincing evidence that Thomas Campbell was actually a "New Light." See David Thompson, "The Irish Background to Thomas Campbell's *Declaration and Address*," *Discipliana* Vol. 46, No. 2 (Summer 1986) 23–25 and Keith Brian Huey, "Alexander Campbell's Church-State Separatism as a Defining and Limiting Factor in His Anti-Catholic Activity," (diss., Marquette University, 2000) 53–58 on Thomas Campbell's activism within the Irish Anti-Burgher Synod prior to his immigration and a comparison to sentiments expressed in his *Declaration and Address* of 1809.

3. The denominational classifications of Scottish Presbyterianism are explained well by Webb. In 1733, a number of congregations seceded from the Presbyterian Church in Scotland in protest of the Patronage Act, which reaffirmed the ancient privilege of the landowners to determine the ministers of their congregations. By 1747, this Seceder Church divided over whether its members ought to take the oath required of those who would become burgesses, an oath that required them to support "the religion presently professed within the realm" (held by many to be a reference to the non-Seceder Church). Later, when disagreement arose over the proper interpretation of the twenty-third chapter of the Westminster Confession (dealing with the power of magistrates), the Anti-Burgher Seceders were again divided into Old Light and New Light factions. Thomas Campbell's theology teacher, Alexander Bruce, was a leader of the Old Light faction (Webb 69–70). As to Campbell's familiarity with Locke, McAllister and Tucker point out that Alexander read *Essay Concerning Human Understanding* under his father's direction and that Locke's *Letters Concerning Toleration* made a lasting impression upon him. As they also point out, Locke's *Essay Concerning Human Understanding* was the source of Thomas' understanding of the relationship between faith and reason and Locke's ideas on the function of the church are reflected in Thomas' *Declaration and Address*, portions of which could be almost direct quotations from Locke (98, 114). James B. North (*Union in Truth: An Interpretive History of the Restoration Movement*, Cincinnati: Standard Publishing, 1994) provides excellent examples of the parallels between these two documents (93). When Alexander was ten years old, Thomas moved his family to accept a ministry with a church in Ahorey. While there, Alexander began to keep a journal listing books that he had read (Frank Pack, "Alexander Campbell: The Scholar," *Gospel Advocate*, Sept. 1, 1988: 13). This journal provides evidence that Alexander was well acquainted with Locke's works at an early age.

4. Webb 73.

5. Robert Richardson, *Memoirs of Alexander Campbell*, Vol. I (1868, 1897; Indianapolis, IN: Religious Book Service, n.d.) 95.

6. Webb 102–4.

7. Gordon S. Wood, "Evangelical America and Early Mormonism," *New York History* 61 (1980) 362; W. R. Ward, "The Religion of the People and the Problem of

Control, 1790–1830," *Popular Belief and Practice,* ed. G. J. Cuming and Derek Baker (Cambridge, UK: Cambridge University Press, 1972) 237; both qtd. in Nathan Hatch *The Democratization of Christianity* (New Haven: Yale University Press, 1989) 220, 301.

8. Hatch 6.

9. Hatch 5, 9, 35, 222, 226. Hatch examines five mass popular movements: the Christian movement (e.g., Stone-Campbell), the Methodists, the Baptists, the black churches, and the Mormons.

10. Ernest G. Bormann, *The Force of Fantasy: Restoring the American Dream* (1985; Carbondale: Southern Illinois University Press, 2001) 104. According to Bormann, recurring forms of this rhetoric (e.g., Lincoln, Reagan) are evidence of its longevity and staying power and the extent to which it has aided in the construction of both a sacred and secular "American Dream."

11. A certain amount of religious freedom had already been realized prior to 1776 and was, at least in part, responsible for the agitation for political freedom (McAllister and Tucker 46). The nine states which had instituted state churches before the Revolutionary War abolished those establishments during or after the war—as late as 1786 in Virginia, 1817 in New Hampshire, 1818 in Connecticut, and 1833 in Massachusetts (Dowling 9).

12. Hatch 12.

13. North 17.

14. Hatch 20–21. Hatch goes on to observe that there is a significant difference between the understandings of religious liberty that characterized the First (eighteenth-century) and the Second (nineteenth-century) Great Awakenings. It was, in fact, the "respectable clergy" of the eighteenth century who helped to popularize the rhetoric of civil and religious liberty, which was, in this context, conceived as "the civil right to choose or not to choose affiliation with a church." The reformers of the Second Great Awakening, however, appropriated this same rhetoric to challenge its own inventors and to call for a transfer of power and authority out of the hands of religious elites (76–77).

15. Hatch 9–11.

16. Hatch 44.

17. Kenneth Cmiel, *Democratic Eloquence: The Fight over Popular Speech in Nineteenth-Century America* (New York: William Morrow and Company, 1990) 41.

18. Hatch 44–46.

19. William Henry Milburn, *The Pioneers, Preachers and the People of the Mississippi Valley* (New York: Derby and Jackson, 1860) 416 (qtd. in Bormann, *Force of Fantasy* 126).

20. Hatch 37–40, 59, 68–70, 73, 174.

21. Hughes and Allen 3, 24; Bormann, *Force of Fantasy* 3.

22. Hughes and Allen 4–5. For Hughes and Allen, Karlstadt typifies the quest for "primordial reform" which is distinct from the "ontological reform" sought by Luther. For a more extended discussion of these concepts of reform as well as the contributions of Christian Humanism, the Reformed tradition of the continent, and the covenant theology of William Tyndale to the development of Puritan primitivism, see Hughes and Allen 1–24.

23. Bormann, *Force of Fantasy* 3, 17, 24–25.

24. Hughes and Allen 104–5.

25. Hatch 167.

26. Hughes and Allen 3, 107. The authors draw upon Mircea Eliad's works regarding sacred and profane time in primitive religions. The distinction between sacred and profane time, they add, does not necessarily mean "that Americans were ahistorical or unhistorical" although, when "the power of the myth outweighs and even obscures the facts of the history that produce them," a "historical religion quickly may become ahistorical . . . " (3, 6).

27. Nevin, "The Sect System," in *Catholic and Reformed: Selected Theological Writings of John William Nevin*, ed. Charles Yrigoyen, Jr. and George H. Bricker, Pittsburgh, 1978, 152 (qtd. in Hatch 166).

28. Hatch 41–42.

29. Whereas Hatch tends to explain Christian primitivism as a response to a collapse of certainty within popular culture, Hughes and Allen argue against the implication that the impulse was, therefore, aberrant, suggesting that Hatch's account "obscures the power and persistence of the myth of first times in Anglo-American history" (xv–xvi).

30. Hughes and Allen 3, 103.

31. Hatch 167, 169–70.

32. Hughes and Allen 22, 13–19, xiv–xv.

33. Hughes, *Reviving* xiii.

34. Hughes and Allen 110. John B. Boles argues, however, that such millennial sentiments did not become widespread in the south until the revivals of 1801 (*The Great Revival: Beginnings of the Bible Belt*, Lexington: The University Press of Kentucky, 1996, 110).

35. Bormann, *Force of Fantasy* 133.

36. Hatch 184.

37. Thomas Campbell, *Declaration and Address* (first edition, 1809) in *The Quest for Christian Unity, Peace and Purity in Thomas Campbell's "Declaration and Address:" Text and Studies*, eds. Thomas H. Olbricht and Hans Rollman (Lanham, MD: Scarecrow Press, 2000) 16 (14). For an extended discussion of the millennialism in this document, see Hans Rollman, "The Eschatology of the *Declaration and Address*," in Olbricht and Rollman 341–63.

38. Hatch 187, 189.

39. Bormann, *Force of Fantasy* 132.

40. Bormann, *Force of Fantasy* 133, 141.

41. Premillennialism takes a more pessimistic view of the present world, holding that the intervention of Christ's second coming will be necessary to defeat the forces of evil in an increasingly degenerate world and will thus necessarily precede the millennium.

42. Hughes and Allen 121; Stevenson, *Disciple Preaching* 56. Miller's teachings, based in his interpretation of chronological symbols in Daniel, influenced both Walter Scott and Dr. John Thomas (Charles Lippy, *The Christadelphians in North America*, Lewiston, NY: The Edwin Mellen Press, 1989, 18).

43. Ruth Bloch, *Visionary Republic: Millennial Themes in American Thought, 1756–1800* (Cambridge, UK: Cambridge University Press, 1985) xvi; Hughes and Allen 112. Bloch's work provides an extended treatment of the various forms of millennialism in late eighteenth-century America, their European origins, and their role in the American Revolution.

44. Hughes and Allen 111.

45. Leonard I. Sweet, "Communication and Change in American History: A Historiographical Probe," *Communication and Change in American Religious History*, ed. Leonard I. Sweet (Grand Rapids, MI: Eerdmans, 1993) 2. Specifically, Sweet refers to the separate conclusions of Averil Cameron (*Christianity and the Rhetoric of Empire: The Development of Christian Discourse*, Berkeley: University of California Press, 1991), Roger Finke and Rodney Stark (*The Changing of America, 1776–1990: Winners and Losers in Our Religious Economy*, New Brunswick, NJ: Rutgers University Press, 1992).

46. Hatch 68; Bormann, *The Force of Fantasy* 97–98, 102–3.

47. Hatch 162; Cmiel 120.

48. Hatch 58.

49. Sweet 9, 11, 13, 16, 25, 30, 43; Hatch 24–25, 126–27, 144. Sweet also points out how George Whitfield's "print and preach" exploitation of the popular press previously helped to create a new religious intercolonial public sphere and pioneer "mass marketing" techniques in the service of revivalism (15). Similarly, he argues that religious organizations themselves played a significant role in creating and multiplying the network of print culture that continued to flourish well after 1815 (9, 11).

50. Hatch 125–26, 141; Gaylord P. Albaugh, "The Role of the Religious Press in the Development of American Christianity, 1730–1830," unpublished manuscript, 1984, 6–7 (qtd. in Hatch 142); Sweet 29–30.

51. Hatch 25, 73, 75–76, 144. In regard to the fact that evangelical propaganda was "audience" or "market driven," Sweet astutely observes, "Whether this should be called 'democratization' or 'popularization' needs further thought . . . what is clear, however, is that mastery of radical new communication forms is what made possible the spread of evangelical Christianity in America" (30).

52. Bormann, *Force of Fantasy* 130; Hatch 57, 133–34.

53. Hatch 133.

54. Cmiel argues that the "populist" rhetoric which appeared with the arrival of mass democracy in the early nineteenth century manifested itself in a variety of "middle styles" and idioms that mixed the "refined" and the "raw" (or "crude") as the evolution of a new "democratic eloquence" negotiated the relationship between political and social emancipation. The reader should consult his *Democratic Eloquence* for an extended discussion of "refined" speech as a broader cultural phenomenon during this era, the controversies surrounding the negotiation of fluid boundaries between "refined" and "vulgar" speech, and the often contradictory cultural pressures of democratic sentiment which produced a "middle culture" (17, 39, 49, 56–58, 90).

55. Bormann, *Force of Fantasy* 18–19, 104.

56. Following the maturation of the ungenteel style during the first third of the century, Bormann argues that the decade of the 1830s witnessed another stage in the

evolution of the rhetoric of romantic pragmatism with the emergence of a new "evangelical reform style" (*Force of Fantasy* 144ff). Whereas Bormann considers the Illinois circuit rider Peter Cartwright prototypical of the "ungenteel" style, he offers the preaching of Charles Grandison Finney as illustrative of the new evangelical wing of romantic pragmatism. Generally speaking, the main difference between these two styles was their respective blends of reason and faith or, in Bormann's terms, the degree to which Finney "retained the Edwardian balance between heat and light," placing a greater emphasis upon "analysis, clear descriptions of facts, and proof" and portraying "a much kinder God of love" (*Force of Fantasy* 146, 168). Similarly, Cmiel illustrates the emergence of a new "middling rhetoric" during this same decade through the example of the preaching of Henry Ward Beecher (57–66). An entry in Beecher's private journal, according to Cmiel, offers a "perfect definition of middling oratory": "He is sure of popularity," Beecher wrote, "who can come down among the people and address truth to them in their homely way and with broad humor—and at the same time has an upper current of taste and chaste expression and condensed vigor" (58).

57. Bormann, *Force of Fantasy* ix, 105, 108, 114–17, 120; Hatch 138.

58. Bormann, *Force of Fantasy* 15, 115, 129, 137–39.

59. Hatch 133, 135; Bormann, *Force of Fantasy* 140.

60. Hatch 36, 57, 73, 140; Bormann, *Force of Fantasy* 105.

61. Hatch 55.

62. Paul K. Conkin, *Cane Ridge: America's Pentecost* (Madison: University of Wisconsin Press, 1990) 91–94.

63. Boles 70ff.

64. Hatch 134–35.

65. Walter Brownlow Posey, *The Baptist Church in the Lower Mississippi Valley, 1776–1845* (Lexington, KY: University of Kentucky Press, 1957) 21–22 (qtd. in Bormann, *Force of Fantasy* 106).

66. Bormann, *Force of Fantasy* 131–32.

67. Hatch 3.

68. Others have noted the "fit" between the themes of the Stone-Campbell movement and the political atmosphere of the Jeffersonian and Jacksonian eras. In his fantasy theme analysis of the early rhetoric of the Stone-Campbell movement, Carl Wayne Hensley argues that "the Disciple's rhetorical vision contained an overarching drama that incorporated many of the features of popular American visions regarding the glory of America and her democracy," and that for "Westerners of the Jacksonian period," it "dramatized a democratic church similar to the political system of the secular drama" ("Rhetorical Vision and the Persuasion of a Historical Movement: The Disciples of Christ in Nineteenth Century American Culture," *Quarterly Journal of Speech* 61 October 1975: 250–51). Arthur Schlesinger, Jr., also points out that by operating in western Pennsylvania and western Virginia, the Campbells "were appealing to the hardy and self-reliant small farmers, shopkeepers and workers whose aspirations would help bring about the Jacksonian revolution" and further identifies five elements in Campbell's theology which such a spirit sought in theology ("The

Age of Alexander Campbell," *The Sage of Bethany: A Pioneer in Broadcloth,* ed. Perry Gresham. 1960; St. Louis: Bethany Press; Joplin, MO: College Press, 1988, 33–34). He also points out how Campbell's attack on the "obfuscations of theology" resembled "contemporary attacks of Jacksonian reformers on the obfuscations of the common law" and how his "New Testamentism would reduce the authority of ministers . . . [and] render the subject accessible to the common man and thus cut the ground from under the privileged class" (35). The matter is also discussed in W. E. Garrison, *Religion Follows the Frontier: A Diary of the Disciples of Christ* (New York: Harper and Brothers, 1931) and William Moorehouse, "The Restoration Movement: The Rhetoric of Jacksonian Restorationism in a Frontier Religion," diss., University of Indiana, 1967.

69. Casey and Foster, "The Renaissance of Stone-Campbell Studies" 35.

70. D. Newell Williams, *Barton Stone: A Spiritual Biography* (St. Louis, Chalice Press, 2000) 65–69, 79–84; North 50–53.

71. Authorship of this document has often been attributed to Stone but recent evidence favors McNemar's authorship (Webb 59; Williams 97–105).

72. Webb 70.

73. McAllister and Tucker 24, 106. Casey and Foster note Hughes's observation that the "division and discord of Scotch-Irish Presbyterianism and American frontier religion galvanized Campbell to work for Christian unity and focus on the external factors of the apostolic church" ("The Renaissance of Stone-Campbell Studies," 30; Richard T. Hughes, "A Comparison of the Restitution Motifs of the Campbells and the Anabaptists," *Mennonite Quarterly Review* 45 (October 1971): 330).

74. Webb 77–78. For definitive editions of Thomas Campbell's *Declaration and Address,* see Olbricht and Rollman, eds., *The Quest for Christian Unity, Peace and Purity in Thomas Campbell's "Declaration and Address": Text and Studies.*

75. McAllister and Tucker 112–13; Thomas Campbell, *Declaration and Address* (first edition) in Olbricht and Rollman 18–20 (16–18).

76. Lynn A. McMillon, "Alexander Campbell's Early Exposure to Scottish Restorationism, 1808–1809," *Restoration Quarterly* 30 (1988): 105–10.

77. Webb 103–4.

78. Dowling 33–61; Leroy Garrett, *The Stone-Campbell Movement: The Story of the American Restoration Movement,* revised ed. (Joplin, MO: College Press, 1994) 203.

79. Alexander Campbell, Prospectus for the *Christian Baptist,* qtd. in Robert Richardson, *Memoirs of Alexander Campbell,* Vol. II (1869, 1898; Indianapolis, IN: Religious Book Service, n.d.), 50.

80. North 21–31; 17, 54–55.

81. Thomas H. Olbricht, "Christian Connexion and Unitarian Relations, 1800–1844," *Restoration Quarterly* 9 (1966): 180–81.

82. Richardson, *Memoirs,* Vol. II, 118; Webb 157.

83. McAllister and Tucker 150–52; North 171–73.

84. McMillon, "Early Exposure," 105–9; *Alexander Campbell at Glasgow University,* transc. and ed. Lester McAllister Nashville, TN: Disciples of Christ Historicl Society, 1971) 93; Richardson, *Memoirs,* Vol. I, 384.

85. See Lynn A. McMillon, *Restoration Roots* (Dallas: Gospel Teachers Pub., 1983) and "Quest for the Apostolic Church: A Study of Scottish Origins of American Restorationism (Restoration Roots)," diss., Baylor University, 1972.

86. Hensley's fantasy theme analysis of nineteenth-century Disciples rhetoric identifies these same three phases of "the rhetoric of postmillennialism" ("Rhetorical Vision" 264).

87. As Casey and Foster point out, millennial views varied among the early leaders of the Stone-Campbell movement. Walter Scott held both postmillennial and premillennial views over the course of his career and Barton Stone held predominantly premillennial views ("The Renaissance of Stone-Campbell Studies" 19).

88. For more extended discussions of Campbell's millennial views, see Robert Frederick West, *Alexander Campbell and Natural Religion* (New Haven: Yale University Press, 1948) 163–217; Hughes and Allen 170–87; and Mont Wilson, "Campbell's Post-Protestantism and Civil Religion," *The Stone-Campbell Movement*, eds. Casey and Foster, 177–88.

89. *Millennial Harbinger* (1843) 73–74.

90. *Millennial Harbinger* (1830) 1.

91. Alexander Campbell, "The Restoration of the Ancient Order of Things, No. II—Creeds, No. I," *Christian Baptist* (March 7, 1825) 133–36.

92. *Millennial Harbinger* (1830) 55.

93. *Millennial Harbinger* (1837) 561.

94. Douglas Foster, "Hope for Christian Unity," *Gospel Advocate* (September 1, 1988): 26–27.

95. *Millennial Harbinger* (1841) (qtd. in Foster 27).

96. Alexander Campbell and Robert Owen, *The Evidences of Christianity: A Debate* (St. Louis: Christian Board of Publication, n.d.) 395 (qtd. in Hughes and Allen 174); *Millennial Harbinger* (1830) 145 (qtd. in Hughes and Allen 174).

97. First known as the "Peace Saying," this slogan was initially the product of Lutheran theologian and pastor Peter Meiderlin, who lived in Augsburg during a period of strife between Lutherans and Calvinists in the early seventeenth century. It was later used by the Puritan minister Richard Baxter, who sought reconciliation between Presbyterians, Independents, and Anglicans in Restoration England. This slogan eventually became the front-page logo of the *Christian Evangelist* (begun 1882), the heir of Barton Stone's *Christian Messenger* (begun 1826). For a complete discussion of the slogan's history and its role in the Stone-Campbell movement, see Hans Rollman, "In Essentials Unity: The Pre-History of a Restoration Movement Slogan," *Restoration Quarterly* 39 (1997): 129–39.

98. The matter of defining the "essentials" would prove problematic and a consistent source of tension within the Stone-Campbell movement. Hughes and Allen describe the challenge Campbell faced in drawing upon diverse theological traditions: "This problem became a major obstacle in Campbell's path for the simple reason that he constructed his ecclesiastical platform out of two intellectual traditions that themselves had been at odds over this very issue. Campbell derived his emphasis upon restoration from Puritanism, mediated to him through the Seceder Presbyterian church in Ireland and several secessionists from the Church of Scotland.

His emphasis on unity, he derived from the British rationalist John Locke, who sought a means to societal unity . . . the theological model in both instances was the reduction of religion to a set of self-evident essentials on which all reasonable persons could agree . . . Campbell . . . filled the rationalists' model with the Puritans' restorationist content which the rationalists had already rejected as divisive. And by predicating unity on the restoration of an institution—the primitive, apostolic church . . . he elevated the problem of essentials-nonessentials to critical significance. Campbell himself, in fact, provided thereby a fundamental source for the theological tension that would plague his movement for its duration" (177–78).

99. Hughes and Allen point out that Campbell's perspective on the relationship between restorationism and the millennium would shift over time. Specifically, they note that, in his early days, Campbell's millennial vision differed from the popular, Protestant vision in this critical respect: "The more prevalent vision hinged the millennium on the spread and influence of both the Christian religion and American social and political institutions, and generally perceived no tensions between the two. Campbell, on the other hand, did not base the millennium on the influence of America but rather on the success of his movement to unite Christendom through the restoration of the primitive church" and was "equally certain that the American nation was impotent in this regard" (173–74). However, they go on to argue that by the 1840s and 1850s, Campbell, due to the growing "sectarian conformity" within the movement, had lost faith in his hope that "a radical restoration of the primitive church" would produce the "ecclesiastical and society unity required by the millennial age" and began to view Protestantism as the common religion that American expansion would spread around the globe as "the agent through which the millennium would come." But Campbell would eventually revert to his original position: "By 1860, however, when civil war loomed on the horizon, the unity of the Republic was fragmenting and Campbell's millennial hopes were fading . . . he no longer pinned his few remaining hopes on the nation . . . he now returned to his earlier position" (171–72, 181–86).

100. *Millennial Harbinger* (1830) 58.

101. Alexander Campbell, "The Restoration of the Ancient Order of Things, No. I—Restoration-Not Reformation," *Christian Baptist* (February 7, 1825) 128.

102. Hughes and Allen 177.

Chapter 2

1. *Millennial Harbinger* (1852) 390.

2. Richardson, *Memoirs*, Vol. I, 34, 131 (as noted by Berryhill, "Sense, Expression, and Purpose" 64–65).

3. Casey, "From British Ciceronianism to American Baconianism" 154; McAllister, introduction, *Alexander Campbell at Glasgow University* 3.

4. Richardson, *Memoirs*, Vol. I, 131.

5. Winifred Horner, "Rhetoric in the Liberal Arts: Nineteenth-Century Scottish Universities," *The Rhetorical Tradition and Modern Writing*, ed. James Murphy (New York: Modern Language Association of America, 1982) 87.

6. Richardson, *Memoirs,* Vol. I, 34, 131–32.

7. Alexander Campbell, *Familiar Lectures on the Pentateuch* (St. Louis: Christian Pub. Co., 1867) 332 (qtd. in Casey, "From British Ciceronianism to American Baconianism" 154).

8. Carroll B. Ellis, "The Controversial Speaking of Alexander Campbell," diss., Louisiana State University, 1949, 78 (qtd. in Berryhill, "Sense, Expression and Purpose" 71–72).

9. McAllister, *Alexander Campbell at Glasgow University* 58.

10. Lester McAllister, *Thomas Campbell—Man of the Book* (St. Louis: Bethany Press, 1954) 26 (qtd. in Berryhill, "Sense, Expression and Purpose" 64–65).

11. Carisse Mickey Berryhill, "Scottish Rhetoric and the *Declaration and Address*" in Olbricht and Rollman 198.

12. Selina Huntington Campbell, *Home Life and Reminiscences of Alexander Campbell* (St. Louis, MO: John Burns, 1882) 451 (qtd. in Berryhill, "Sense, Expression and Purpose" 70).

13. For example, Berryhill, when describing the derivative nature of Jardine's notion of rhetoric, describes the collegial relationship between the professors of these Scottish universities: "George Jardine . . . was an important conduit of the new rhetoric in Scotland. Jardine's friend and mentor, the philosopher Thomas Reid, had laid the philosophical foundations for the new rhetoric. It had been worked out in practical terms by Reid's friend George Campbell of Aberdeen . . . " ("Alexander Campbell's Natural Rhetoric of Evangelism," *Restoration Quarterly* 30, April 1, 1988: 111).

14. Although the doctrine of "faculty psychology" is generally traced to German philosopher Christian von Wolff (1679–1754), others had already accounted for human mental operations in terms of "faculties of the mind." Among these were Francis Bacon (1561–1626) and Rene Descartes (1596–1650).

15. Karl R. Wallace, "The English Renaissance Mind and English Rhetorical Theory," *Western Speech* (Spring 1964): 71–76.

16. *De Augmentis Scientiarum,* VI, 3, in *The Works of Francis Bacon,* eds. James Spedding, Robert Leslie Ellis, and Douglas Denon Heath, Vol. 4 (London, 1879) 455.

17. Stephen Land refers to Locke's theory of ideas as "ideational atomism" because it was modeled upon the atomist theories current in both philosophy and the sciences in the latter half of the seventeenth century (*The Philosophy of Language in Britain: Major Theories from Hobbes to Reid,* New York: AMS Press, 1986, 44). According to Locke, all knowledge is reducible to the "simple" ideas generated by sensation and reflection (*An Essay Concerning Human Understanding,* ed. by Alexander Campbell Fraser, Vol. 2, 1690; Oxford, UK: Clarendon Press, 1894, 144–45).

18. Locke, *Essay,* Vol. 2, 213–14, 528.

19. Theodore Huguelet refers to David Hartley's "psycho-physical parallelism" in his introduction to Hartley's *Observations on Man,* 2 vols. in 1 (1749; Gainesville, FL: Scholars' Facsimiles & Reprints, 1966), quoting Edwin G. Boring, *Sensation and Perception in the History of Experimental Psychology* (New York: Appleton-Century-Crofts, Inc., 1942) 85.

20. Hartley, 268.

21. Locke, *Essay,* Vol. 3, 146.

22. Wilbur Samuel Howell, "John Locke and the New Rhetoric," *Quarterly Journal of Speech* 52 (December 1967): 138.

23. The inherent epistemological problem in these various psychologies is a "privacy of ideas," e.g., the problem of the subject/object split—what we "know" is not the external material object but the idea we have of it in the privacy of our minds. The implications for communication amount to a kind of incommensurability. Words serve as signs, a kind of public medium, that reflect the ideas that exist in our minds. Communication theoretically occurs when the sign given by a speaker gives rise to the same idea in the mind of the auditor. However, the only evidence the auditor has of the ideas in a speaker's mind is the words (signs) that he gives them. If ideas exist only in the privacy of the subject's mind, one cannot use *another's* ideas to recognize the signs he utters and thus it is ultimately impossible to verify the "sameness" of ideas in different minds.

24. Thomas Conley, *Rhetoric in the European Tradition* (Chicago,IL: University of Chicago Press, 1990, 1994) 196–97. The definition is taken from Buffier's *Traite des premieres veritez* [in a facsimile edition (Paris, 1971) of Buffier's *Cours de Science* (1732)] 563.

25. Conley points out the need to keep the role of philosophy in perspective, however: "From the point of view of rhetoric . . . the New Philosophy was virtually peripheral, although it is obviously necessary to keep it in the picture. Whatever effects the philosophical positions of Descartes or Locke had on rhetoric, it is clear that rhetoricians did not decide that persuasion was a matter of impression and affect and 'movements of the soul' because they had been converted to dualism and mechanistic naturalism. Rhetoricians appropriated the vocabulary of the New Philosophy because they had already become convinced . . . that such things were precisely what persuasion consisted in . . . On the one hand, therefore, we must be careful not to overestimate the importance of philosophy for this period; but at the same time we must be prepared to recognize it" (190). Similarly, when describing the influence of Bacon and Reid upon George Campbell, he notes that, "philosophy is used by Campbell in the service of rhetoric; rhetoric is not deduced from Bacon's or Reid's or anyone else's philosophy" (219).

26. James A. Berlin, "The Transformation of Invention in Nineteenth Century American Rhetoric," *The Southern Speech Communication Journal* 46 (Spring 1981): 302.

27. Conley 164.

28. Hugh Blair (1718–1800) was appointed the first Regius Professor of Rhetoric and Belles Lettres at the university in Edinburgh in the year 1762. His *Lectures on Rhetoric and Belles Lettres,* published in 1783, soon became one of the most influential books on rhetoric in the English-speaking world. Though his chief sources were Cicero and Quintilian, his use of those sources and the notion of rhetoric published in his lectures reflect the influence of both Reid's common sense realism and the post-Cartesian separation of conviction from persuasion. For further discussion, see Conley 220–23 and Harold Harding, introduction, *Lectures on Rhetoric and Belles Lettres* by Hugh Blair, Vol. 1 (Carbondale: Southern Illinois University Press, 1965) xxvi.

29. George Campbell was also an active member of the Aberdeen Philosophical Society between 1758 and 1773. Conley (218) indicates that the following were among the papers and subjects discussed at these meetings: (1) an analysis of sense perception (Thomas Reid, 1758, 1760), (2) whether eloquence is useful or pernicious (Campbell's predecessor as professor of divinity, Alexander Gerard, 1764), (3) and the relation of eloquence to logic (Campbell himself, 1761). Campbell's ideas for his *Philosophy of Rhetoric* were developed during these years.

30. See Conley 216–20; Berlin 292–304; William L. Benoit, "Campbell's *The Philosophy of Rhetoric* and the Advancement of Rhetorical Theory: The Integration of Philosophical Antecedents," *Communication Studies* 41 (Spring 1990): 89–100; Vincent M. Bevilacqua, "Philosophical Origins of George Campbell's *Philosophy of Rhetoric*," *Speech Monographs* 32 (March 1965): 1–12; Dennis R. Bormann, "Some 'Common Sense' about Campbell, Hume, and Reid: The Extrinsic Evidence," *The Quarterly Journal of Speech* 71 (November 1985): 395–421; Douglas Ehninger, "Campbell, Blair, and Whately: Old Friends in a New Light," *Western Speech* 19 (October 1955): 263–69; William A. Wallace, "Thomas Reid's Philosophy as a Basis for Rhetoric," *Scottish Rhetoric and Its Influences*, ed. Lynee Gaillet (Mahway, NJ: Hermagoras Press, 1998) 31–42.

31. George Campbell, *Philosophy of Rhetoric*, ed. Lloyd Bitzer (1776; Carbondale: Southern Illinois University Press, 1988) lxvii; lxix; lxxii–lxxiii, 1. Campbell's understanding of science, it should be noted, was one in which theology and ethics were considered "the most sublime of all sciences." As to the various species of discourse, he acknowledged that, while only one of these may serve as the "chief intent of the whole," many of these "ends" may be mixed in a discourse when they serve as means to its principal end (2–4).

32. There is no dedicated or systematic treatment of rhetorical invention in G. Campbell's *Philosophy of Rhetoric*. As Ehninger suggests, it can be fairly said that Campbell's discussion of invention lies partly here, partly there, etc. but there is no one place to which we can point and say, "Here is Campbell's discussion of invention" (267). He rejected the value of the syllogism for rhetorical invention on four grounds (62–66), which may be summarized as follows: (1) The process of descending from universals to particulars employed by the syllogism is not a method one can following in acquiring "natural knowledge" of "actual existences." Whereas the latter requires ascending from particulars to universals, the former is a proper method only for applying knowledge already acquired. (2) The syllogism has not been thought worthy of being adopted by mathematicians as a proper method of demonstration. For such, it has the disadvantage of an obscurity that has the potential to shelter fallacy. (3) Unless the universal truths from which we argue are themselves "the slow result of induction and experience" and thus self-evident, the syllogism proceeds from things less known to things better known. Thus, it is usually either superfluous or unconvincing. (4) As a consequence of the above, the syllogism is more properly an instrument for "the adjustment of our language, in expressing subjects previously known, than the acquisition of knowledge in things themselves.

33. Bitzer xxxvii–xxxix.

34. G. Campbell 35.

35. G. Campbell 35–38.

36. G. Campbell 43, 50–58.

37. G. Campbell 71–72.

38. G. Campbell 2.

39. G. Campbell 2–4.

40. " . . . passion is the mover to action, reason is the guide" (G. Campbell 77–78).

41. "But it is with the expression as with the sentiment, it is not enough to the orator that both be true" (G. Campbell 215).

42. It is in this manner that rhetoric makes use of what is provided both by logic and grammar: " . . . it is by the sense that rhetoric holds of logic, and by the expression that she holds of grammar." "Eloquence" is distinct from logic, however, in that the purpose of the latter is "the eviction of truth" whereas that of the former is "the conviction of the hearers." Campbell proceeds to identify five sorts of discourse, two of which seek conviction (one addressed to the understanding to prove some position, the other to influence the will and persuade to a certain conduct), the other three of which "address the understanding, the imagination and the passions." In the case of the latter three, "conviction, though not the end, ought ever to accompany the accomplishment of the end" (32–33).

43. G. Campbell 215. At the end of book II, chapter 4, Campbell lists five qualities of style that address "the understanding, the imagination, the passions and the ear"—"perspicuity, vivacity, elegance, animation, and music" (216). Only perspicuity and vivacity receive extensive treatment, however.

44. G. Campbell 285.

45. G. Campbell 221.

46. G. Campbell 217ff. Campbell's debt to associationism is evident in book I, chapter 5 (47–48, 50, 53); book I, chapter 7 (76–77, where he discusses Hume's principles); and book II, chapter 7 (256ff).

47. G. Campbell 285–86. "Individuation" is an especially vivid form of specialty that "enlivens the imagery" and has "an admirable effect in invigorating the sentiment" because it "tends to subject the thing spoken of to the notice of our sense, especially of our eyes" (290–91). Tropes, when used judiciously, contribute to this effect as well (293), especially those which prefer "sensible" terms over "intelligible" ones, since terms that "strike the imagination more forcibly" are those perceived by the senses rather than those perceived by the understanding (304), and those which animate things lifeless for "things animate awaken greater attention and make a stronger impression on the mind than things senseless" (306). "It is for this reason," Campbell goes on to observe, "that the quality of which I am treating hath come to be termed vivacity, or liveliness of style."

48. Horner ("Rhetoric in the Liberal Arts") provides a helpful account of how the Scottish defense of its "democratic" educational philosophy, grounded in the liberal arts, became, for many, a form of nationalistic resistance to English domination. Jardine was a leading champion of the Scottish system, his *Outlines of Philosophical Education* (1818) being his primary contribution. Lynee L. Gaillet ("George Jardine's

Outlines of Philosophical Education: Prefiguring 20th-Century Composition Theory and Practice," *Scottish Rhetoric and Its Influences,* ed. Gaillet) has chronicled Jardine's significant contributions to educational reform.

49. Carisse M. Berryhill, "Alexander Campbell: Preacher," *Gospel Advocate* 130 (Sept. 1, 1988) 14–15; Berryhill, "Sense, Expression and Purpose" 66–69.

50. Berryhill, "Alexander Campbell's Natural Rhetoric of Evangelism," *Restoration Quarterly* 30 (1988): 111.

51. "The present professor," Reid noted, begins with "a short analysis of the powers of understanding" and an "historical view of the rise and progress of the art of reasoning, and particularly of the syllogistic method, which is rendered a matter of curiosity by the universal influence which for a long time it attained." Jardine then, according to Reid, "dedicates the greater part of his time to an illustration of the various mental operations, as they are expressed by the several modifications of speech and writing." See William Howell, *Eighteenth Century British Logic and Rhetoric* (Princeton: Princeton University Press, 1971) 376, who cites *The Works of Thomas Reid,* 7th ed., ed. William Hamilton (Edinburgh, 1872).

52. George Jardine, *Synopsis of Lectures on Rhetoric and Belles Lettres* (Glasgow: The University Press, 1804) 3, 6–7.

53. Jardine, *Lectures* 7, 9. His subsequent subdivision of the "powers of understanding or of knowledge" into the following categories also evidences the influence of Locke's "ideational atomism": (1) "the simple powers or faculties by which Sensations and Ideas are directly acquired" (Perception, Attention, Reflection, Abstraction), (2) "the powers by which sensations and ideas, once received, are preserved and recalled" (Memory, Imagination), and (3) "the more complex powers by whose combined operation the Agreements, Disagreements, and Relations among our ideas are discerned" (Judging, Reasoning, Inventing, Genius) (9).

54. "Perception" serves to "open the first and wonderful communication between the mind and matter" and "the process commences with the impression which is made by an external object upon the organs of sense . . . for they are all adapted to receive certain impressions from the qualities of the material objects." The "perceiving power" then "unites the variety of impressions into one whole" and "forms a notion or idea of it." The "faculty of attention" will then "notice" the ideas ("Reflection" differs only in its degree of intensity). "Abstraction" then attends to differences between objects of thought so as to "render them separate and distinct" whereas "generalization" attends to "qualities which are in common" so as to "form classes." "Memory" will then "preserve the sensation and notions received" so that "Imagination" can "reproduce or present them again to the mind," not at random but according to "certain laws of association." "Judgment" produces knowledge of "an existing relationship betwixt two objects" according to the principles of evidence, "Reasoning" infers relationships by discovering intermediate ideas, and "Invention" performs the managerial function of forming new combinations of ideas (*Outlines of Philosophical Education Illustrated by the Method of Teaching the Logic Class in the University of Glasgow,* 2nd ed., Glasgow: The University Press, 1825, 51, 59, 99; *Lectures* 11, 15, 21, 24).

55. Jardine, *Lectures* 79. Jardine also credits Aristotle as the first "to circumscribe the more complex operations of Judging and Reasoning, by establishing rules of

comparison and inference, and by inventing a general method of arrangement" (*Lectures* 70–71).

56. Jardine, *Lectures* 79, 81–82.

57. Jardine, *Lectures* 118–20. However, in his *Outlines of Philosophical Education,* Jardine suggests that categorizing compositions according to the faculties of memory, imagination, and reason is too general and thus ill calculated for assisting young students. Instead, he suggests that, for the purpose of criticism, a more useful division of compositions would be according to (1) the end proposed by the author, (2) the nature and qualities of the material employed, (3) the form these materials assume, and (4) the style in which the materials are executed (222).

58. Berryhill notes his challenge to Robert Owen, whom he would later debate over the relative merits of Christianity and atheistic socialism (1829), to recall the religious character of the Scottish education shared by both him and Owen ("Sense, Expression and Purpose" 73; compare Alexander Campbell, *Christian Baptist,* April 2, 1827: 186).

59. Richardson, *Memoirs,* Vol. 2, 554 (qtd. in Berryhill, "Sense, Expression and Purpose" 53).

60. "Sense, Expression and Purpose" 32–51. References to George Campbell's *The Four Gospels, Dissertation on Miracles, Lectures on Ecclesiastical History,* and *Lectures on Systematic Theology and Pulpit Eloquence* are cited as well.

61. *Millennial Harbinger* (1848) 445 (qtd. in Berryhill, "Sense, Expression and Purpose" 74); Alexander Campbell, *Memoirs of the Elder Thomas Campbell Together with a Brief Memoir of Mrs. Jane Campbell* (Cincinnati: H. S. Bosworth, 1861) 117, 267 (qtd. in Berryhill, "Sense, Expression and Purpose" 68).

62. "Sense, Expression and Purpose" 69.

63. *Alexander Campbell at Glasgow University* 1, 4. Alexander's great granddaughter, Audine Adelaid Andrews, donated additional journals and notes to the Disciples of Christ Historical Society in 1965 and, in the early 1980s, the class notes with the flyleaf mentioned earlier in this chapter (Lester, "Campbell Papers Story," *Christian Standard,* May 11, 1986: 13). The resemblances between Campbell's essays and Jardine's lectures are not surprising when we remember that, as part of his pedagogical reforms, Jardine's intent in assigning the essays was not only to develop his students' skills in communication but to facilitate their command of topics corresponding to his lecture of the day (Jardine, *Outlines* 280).

64. *Alexander Campbell at Glasgow University* 10. Similarly, in his seventh essay, "On Logic," he notes that "The powers of knowledge are Perception, Attention, Reflection, Abstraction, Generalization, Memory, Imagination, Judging and Reasoning" (34). The similarities between these passages in Campbell's essays and Jardine's list of mental faculties described above in footnote 54 of this chapter are clear.

65. *Alexander Campbell at Glasgow University* 12–14, 44–45, 76–78.

66. *Alexander Campbell at Glasgow University* 36–37.

67. Berryhill, "Natural Rhetoric" 112, footnote 4; *Alexander Campbell at Glasgow University* 58–68.

68. *Alexander Campbell at Glasgow University* 68–69.

69. *Alexander Campbell at Glasgow University* 30.

70. *Alexander Campbell at Glasgow University* 32. More specifically, what Campbell describes here is a threefold classification of sentence patterns ("natural," "artificial," and "philosophical") that follow a similar threefold classification ("natural," "philosophical," and "sentimental") in Jardine's *Lectures*.

71. James N. Holm, Jr. has specifically examined the influence of Jardine's teachings upon Campbell's arguments in his 1829 debate with Robert Owen ("Alexander Campbell: A Study in the Value of Effective Rhetorical Training," *Forensic*, October 1976: 10–13, 31).

72. Burton B. Thurston, "Alexander Campbell's Principles of Hermeneutics," diss., Harvard University, 1958, 188 (qtd. in Berryhill, "Sense, Expression and Purpose" 63).

73. Casey, "From British Ciceronianism to American Baconianism" 157. Casey also observes that both Thomas and Alexander were familiar with Blair's *Lectures* prior to Alexander's enrollment at Glasgow, as evidenced by its inclusion in an 1809 catalog of their books (155). He writes, "Of all the Scottish rhetorics, Blair, incorporated more Ciceronian prescriptions than most others did" and calls attention particularly to the Ciceronian pattern of arrangement (155). As Conley points out, though, we should keep in mind that "Blair's reading of Classical rhetorics is, however, colored by the view of many of his post-Cartesian contemporaries" and that the Ciceronian arrangement followed in Lectures XXXI and XXXII subtly reflects the notion "that a speaker must first secure conviction and then, arousing desire by appealing to the passions, achieve persuasion" (222).

74. Casey, "From British Ciceronianism to American Baconianism" 158–59, 161. Berlin points out that, in many ways, the features of nineteenth-century American culture (dominated by beliefs in individualism, equality and self-government) were antithetical to the ruling conceptions and aims of George Campbell, Blair, and Whately, whose rhetorics were designed to prepare young men to enter the aristocratic ranks of polite society. Yet their works dominated American academies and colleges until about 1865. According to Berlin, Americans were able to overlook the differences because in other ways they responded to essential needs in other currents of American culture (philosophy, science, art, and religion) in which the dominant philosophy was the Scottish School of Common Sense Realism (294–95). Kenneth Cmiel's *Democratic Eloquence* includes an extended discussion of the aristocratic function of eighteenth-century Scottish rhetorics (28–40).

75. Granville T. Walker, *Preaching in the Thought of Alexander Campbell* (St. Louis: Bethany Press, 1954) 37; Alexander Campbell, *Christianity Restored* (1835; Rosemead, CA: Old Paths Book Club, 1959) 106, 114; Campbell and Robert Owen, *Debate on the Evidences of Christianity* (Bethany: pub. by Alexander Campbell, 1829) 228 and *Millennial Harbinger* (1833) 340 (qtd. in Walker 37).

76. *Christianity Restored* 113–14.

77. *Christianity Restored* 108.

78. *Christianity Restored* 108.

79. *Christianity Restored* 108–9.

80. *Christianity Restored* 109–10.

81. *Christianity Restored* 110; Campbell and Owen 68–69; *Millennial Harbinger* (1836) 166 (qtd. in Berryhill, "Natural Rhetoric" 117); *Christianity Restored* 114–15.

82. *Christianity Restored* 113.

83. Campbell, "Education," in *Popular Lectures and Addresses* (1863; Nashville: Harbinger Book Club, 1954) 243 (qtd. in Berryhill, "Natural Rhetoric" 115).

84. *Christianity Restored* 106.

85. Lee Snyder, "Alexander Campbell and the Book of Acts," *Stone-Campbell Journal* (Spring 1999): 25–37. Snyder also notes that Acts was "the only book of the Bible which he [Campbell] translated six and a half times and the only one he made the subject of a separate monograph" (23).

86. Casey, *Saddlebags* 27–29, where the influence of Bacon, Locke and Reid upon Campbell's hermeneutic is described; Casey, "From British Ciceronianism to American Baconianism" 159; Berryhill, "Preacher" 15; Hughes and Allen 117, 153–60.

87. Berryhill, "Natural Rhetoric" 113, 123. For a more complete discussion of the influence of George Campbell's doctrines of testimony upon Alexander Campbell, see "Sense, Expression and Purpose" 173–96.

88. In this model, some variation of the six-part arrangement (exordium, proposition, division, narration, argument, peroration) was typically used and as many as twenty different *topoi* were used to amplify the theme through division and subdivision. To demonstrate the influence of this medieval Ciceronian sermon arrangement upon the preaching of Thomas Campbell, Casey ("From British Ciceronianism to American Baconianism" 156) compares one of his sermons to H. Caplan's description of this model ("Classical Rhetoric and Medieval Theory of Preaching," *Classical Philology* 28, 1933: 73–96). Thomas Campbell's sermon (preached in Ahorey, Ireland, on June 22, 1800), based on James 2:24, used three main headings with three or four subdivisions under each head and employed at least three of the twenty *topoi*. As Casey also points out ("From British Ciceronianism to American Baconianism" 157), Caplan cites an eighteenth-century sermon on "malt" as an instance of this medieval Ciceronian sermon form—a version of which Alexander would incredibly cite from memory in 1825.

89. Casey, "From British Ciceronianism to American Baconianism" 158; Richardson, *Memoirs,* Vol. 1, 313–15.

90. Casey, "From British Ciceronianism to American Baconianism" 160; Stevenson, *Disciple Preaching* 23–24.

91. Casey, "From British Ciceronianism to American Baconianism" 159; Michael Casey, "Alexander Campbell's Early Sermons: An Example of Ciceronian Rhetoric and the Classical Tradition in Preaching," paper submitted to the Religious Speech Communication Association National Convention, 1984, 7, 11.

92. *Millennial Harbinger* (1860) 605.

93. Berryhill, "Natural Rhetoric" 115. For a more complete discussion of Alexander Campbell's "natural" philosophy of rhetoric, see Berryhill, "Sense, Expression, and Purpose."

94. *Christianity Restored* 303.

95. *Christian Baptist* (March 1, 1830) 632.

96. Berryhill, "Natural Rhetoric of Evangelism" 121; *Millennial Harbinger* (1835) 487; (1832) 233 (qtd. in Berryhill, "Natural Rhetoric" 120).

97. Casey, "From British Ciceronianism to American Baconianism" 162–63.

98. Conley 219.

99. *Christian Baptist* (March 7, 1825) 159.

100. *Christian Baptist* (March 7, 1825) 159.

101. *Christian Baptist* (March 7, 1825) 159.

102. *Christianity Restored* 125.

103. Berryhill, "Sense, Expression and Purpose" 244–45.

104. *Christian Baptist* (December 7, 1829) 604.

105. *Christianity Restored* 9, 11–13.

106. *Christian Baptist* (February 2, 1824) 46; G. Campbell 73.

107. While there is no dedicated treatment of memory or delivery in *The Philosophy of Rhetoric*, George Campbell's criticisms of the oratory of religious "enthusiasts" (109) are similar in sentiment to Alexander's own suspicions of emotionalism as well as his satirical descriptions of an "affected" manner of delivery. In this regard, Alexander's ridicule of the extremes of the ungenteel style, an example of which is included in chapter four of this volume, clearly suggests that while his preference for "natural" eloquence may have been consistent with the "romantic pragmatism" described by E. Bormann, it was more likely influenced by his common sense philosophy of rhetoric than by any thought of imitating frontier mannerisms. Dale A. Jorgenson also draws an interesting parallel between descriptions of Alexander's delivery found in Robert Richardson's memoirs and Puritan "plain style preaching" which rejected "ornamental rhetoric," emphasized the "power of the word" and drew a sharp line between "episcopal aesthetics" and a "utilitarian use of words" (*Theological and Aesthetic Roots in the Stone-Campbell Movement*, Kirksville, MO: The Thomas Jefferson University Press, 1989, 50–51). In this regard, Alexander's preference for a "natural" delivery is quite consistent with his overall philosophy of rhetoric.

108. Berryhill, "Sense, Expression and Purpose" 254.

109. Alger Fitch, *Alexander Campbell: Preacher of Reform and Reformer of Preaching* 73; Casey, "From British Ciceronianism to American Baconianism" 158–59. Casey's account of the September sermon and Campbell's eventual decision to give up notes is drawn from Robert Richardson's *Memoirs*, Vol. 1, 321.

110. Richardson, *Memoirs*, Vol. II, 274.

111. *Christian Baptist* (September 7, 1829) 583.

112. *Christian Baptist* (December 7, 1829) 604.

113. J. A. Williams, *Life of Elder John Smith* (1871; Nashville, TN: Gospel Advocate, 1956) 133. Both Casey ("From British Ciceronianism to American Baconianism" 160) and Fitch (71) make note of this conversation.

114. *Millennial Harbinger* (1847) 154.

115. *Familiar Lectures on the Pentateuch* 149 (qtd. in Berryhill, "Sense, Expression and Purpose" 251).

116. "The Anglo-Saxon Languages," *Popular Lectures and Addresses* (Philadelphia: James Challen and Son, 1861) 19 (qtd. in Fitch 73).

117. *Millennial Harbinger* (1845) 465.

118. Archibald McLean has preserved a similar firsthand account of Campbell's delivery: "Judge Riddle, speaking of his preaching and the effect of it, said there was no appeal to passion, no effort at pathos, no figures of rhetoric; but a warm, kindling, glowing, manly argument, silencing the will, captivating the judgment and satisfying the reason" (*Alexander Campbell as a Preacher,* St. Louis: Christian Pub. Co., 1908, 25).

119. Richardson, *Memoirs,* Vol. II, 583–84. Jorgenson cites this passage, adding that Richardson's description follows a description of one of Campbell's sermons provided by Dr. Herman Humphrey, former president of Amherst College (50–51).

120. Richardson, *Memoirs,* Vol. II, 181.

121. Aristotle 36.

Chapter 3

1. *Millennial Harbinger* (1846) 493.

2. Richardson, *Memoirs,* Vol. I, 312–17, 390; Webb 105–7; North 105, 110.

3. Richardson, *Memoirs,* Vol. I, 392.

4. Richardson, *Memoirs,* Vol. I, 469; Everett Ferguson, "Alexander Campbell's 'Sermon on the Law': A Historical and Theological Examination," *Restoration Quarterly* (April 1, 1987) 72.

5. Richard M. Tristano, *The Origins of the Restoration Movement: An Intellectual History* (Atlanta: Glenmary Research Center, 1988) 86.

6. Benjamin Lyon Smith, *The Millennial Harbinger, Abridged,* Vol. I (Rosemead, CA: Old Paths Publishing Co., 1965) 409.

7. *Millennial Harbinger* (1846) 493.

8. *Millennial Harbinger* (1848) 344–47.

9. *Millennial Harbinger* (1848) 346.

10. The Philadelphia Confession, with the exception of two articles, exactly followed the Assembly Confession of 1689, adopted by representatives of Baptist churches in Scotland and Wales. This, in turn, was merely a new edition of a 1677 Baptist revision of the Westminster Confession of 1647 (Ferguson 76).

11. North 116–17; McAllister and Tucker 121.

12. Richardson, *Memoirs,* Vol. I, 464–69; *Millennial Harbinger* (1848) 347.

13. *Millennial Harbinger* (1848) 348; Richardson, *Memoirs,* Vol. I, 470–71; Thomas E. Pletcher, "Alexander Campbell's Controversy With the Baptists," diss., University of Pittsburgh, 1955, 80–81.

14. *Millennial Harbinger* (1846) 494.

15. *Millennial Harbinger* (1848) 348; Richardson, *Memoirs,* Vol. I, 471–72.

16. *Millennial Harbinger* (1846) 494; Alexander Campbell, "Early Manuscripts Discovered in Australia" (microfilm; Nashville, TN: Disciples of Christ Historical Society, 1964), qtd. in McAllister and Tucker 122; Pletcher 81–82; Ferguson 72.

17. Richardson, *Memoirs,* Vol. I, 471–72; Pletcher 82.

18. Richardson, *Memoirs,* Vol. I, 472; *Millennial Harbinger* (1846) 494; Pletcher 82.

19. Ferguson 72; Richardson, *Memoirs,* Vol. I, 472; Pletcher 82. On the thirtieth anniversary of its delivery (1846), Campbell would reprint the sermon in the *Millennial Harbinger,* "without the change of a sentiment in it" (493).

20. Webb 110; North 120; McAllister and Tucker 131.

21. Webb 110; North 138–39; McAllister and Tucker 144–45.

22. Alexander Campbell, *The Substance of a Sermon Delivered Before the Redstone Baptist Association, met on Cross Creek, Brooke County, Virginia, On the 1st of September, 1816* (Steubenville, Ohio: James Wilson, 1816) 5.

23. Campbell, *Sermon* 5.

24. Stevenson 23–24.

25. *Christian Baptist* (July 4, 1823) 18 (qtd. in Casey, *Saddlebags* 19).

26. Alexander Campbell and Nathan L. Rice, "A Debate Between Rev. A. Campbell and Rev. N. L. Rice" [1843] (Lexington, KY: A. T. Skillman, 1844), 542 (qtd. in Casey, "From British Ciceronianism to American Baconianism" 160); *Millennial Harbinger* (1830) 138 (qtd. in Casey, "From British Ciceronianism to American Baconianism" 159).

27. Campbell, *Sermon* 5.

28. G. Campbell 217. The three principal offenses against perspicuity are obscurity, ambiguity, and unintelligibility. Confusion of thought is the first cause of the unintelligible. "Language," George Campbell notes, "is the medium through which the sentiments of the writer are perceived by the reader. And though the impurity or the grossness of the medium will render the image obscure or indistinct, yet no purity in the medium will suffice for exhibiting a distinct and unvarying image of a confused and unsteady object" (244).

29. Campbell, *Sermon* 6–7.

30. Campbell, *Sermon* 7–8.

31. Campbell, *Sermon* 8.

32. Campbell, *Sermon* 8–9.

33. Campbell, *Sermon* 5.

34. See pp. 40–41.

35. Campbell, *Sermon* 5.

36. Campbell, *Sermon* 5–6.

37. Campbell, *Sermon* 6.

38. Campbell, *Sermon* 8–9.

39. See pp. 40–41.

40. Caplan lists the *topoi* (a term used in classical Greek rhetorics in reference to the "commonplaces" of rhetorical invention) used to amplify a theme: 1) concordance of authorities, biblical, patristic, and philosophic, 2) questioning and discussion of words and terms, often with division, 3) discussion of the properties of things, 4) analogies and natural truths, 5) rationation and argument (including the use of simile, example, the topic of greater or lesser, opposites), 6) comparison (including play upon adjectives or verbs), 7) similitudes, 8) explication by hidden terminology or orating by interpretation of initials, 9) multiplication of synonyms, 10) any or all of the dialectical topics like species and genera, whole and parts, 11) explication of scriptural metaphors, 12) cause and effect in the moral realm, 13) anecdotes, 14) observation of the end or purpose of a thing, 15) setting forth the essential weight of a word, 16) interpretation of Hebrew names, 17) etymology, 18) parts of speech, 19) use of the four

senses of scriptural interpretation (historical/literal, allegorical, topological, and ana-gogical) (73–96, qtd. in Casey, "Alexander Campbell's Early Sermons" 4–5).

41. Caplan 73–96 (qtd. in Casey, "Alexander Campbell's Early Sermons" 4–5).

42. Campbell, *Sermon* 9–14.

43. Campbell, *Sermon* 11–12.

44. Campbell, *Sermon* 15.

45. Stevenson 22.

46. Casey, "Alexander Campbell's Early Sermons" 4; "From British Ciceronian-ism to American Baconianism" 156.

47. Jardine defined "reasoning" as "the discovery of these relations among things which cannot be discovered intuitively, or by immediate comparison" but "are discov-ered by intermediate ideas." "Perception, Judging, and Memory" provide reason with the notions to be compared as well as the medium of their comparison, and the "knowledge of the relationship is said to be *inferred*." Acts of reasoning may be either "simple" or "complex." An act of reasoning is simple "when the relationship is dis-covered by *one medium*." But "when the relations of things cannot be discovered by the comparison of two things with one *medium*—the same sagacity of mind leads to the discovery of a second, third, fourth, or an indefinite number of media . . . this is called a complex act of reasoning—a chain of reasoning." Complexity varies accord-ing to subject matter: "The nature of some subjects admits of a longer, others of a short chain of reasoning.—The sciences of Geometry and Arithmetic may admit of twenty or more steps.—Moral and political reasonings, seldom of more than three or four." A simple act of reasoning, Jardine noted, "has been called a Syllogism—a more complex act of reasoning is called a Sorites" (*Lectures* 26–30). According to William Duncan (*Elements of Logick* [London: R. Dodsley, 1748] 348), the propositions in a sorites are linked by using the predicate of the preceding proposition as the subject of the next (qtd. in Stephen E. Lucas, "Justifying America: The Declaration of Inde-pendence," in *American Rhetoric: Context and Criticism*, eds. Thomas W. Benson and Lewis Perry, Carbondale: Southern Illinois University Press, 1989, 89).

48. When, in his *Philosophy of Rhetoric*, George Campbell defined "logical truth" as "the conformity of our conceptions to their archetypes in the nature of things," he distinguished between "intuitive" evidence by which this conformity "is perceived by the mind, either immediately or on a bare attention to the ideas" and "deductive" evidence by which it is perceived "mediately by comparison of these with other re-lated ideas" (35). "Deductive evidence" is in turn divided into two species: the "de-monstrative" and "moral" (43). For George Campbell, however, "moral reasoning" is actually an inductive process: "In moral reasoning we proceed by analysis, and ascend from particulars to universals" (62). In contrast to both the syllogism and mathemati-cal demonstration, "wherein, from universal principles called axioms, we deduce many truths, though general in their nature, may, when compared with those first principles, be justly styled particular," moral reasoning proceeds "to general truths solely by an induction of particulars" (62–63). As an inductive process, its evidences are drawn "from consciousness and common sense, improved by experience," it ad-mits of degrees of certainty and contrary evidence, and, "is generally complicated,

being in reality a bundle of independent proofs" in which "there is often a combination of many distinct topics of argument, no way dependent on one another" (43–45). In "demonstration," on the other hand, propositions "are admitted as links in the chain." Its subject is "the unchangeable and necessary relations of ideas," its "sole object" is "essential or necessary truth," it admits of no contrary proofs and is "simple, consisting of only one coherent series, every part of which depends on the preceding" and "may be compared to an arch, no part of which can subsist independently of the rest" (43–46). It seems, then, that he uses the term "deductive" in both a generic sense (of all reasoning or evidence that depends upon a mediation or comparison of ideas, 35, 43) and a more specific sense (to distinguish the deductive, "synthetic" method of descending from universals to particulars from the inductive, "analytic" method of ascending from particulars to universals, 62–63).

49. Jardine, *Lectures* 26–27; G. Campbell 35, 44–45.

50. Campbell, *Sermon* 15–16, 19, 25–26.

51. *Millennial Harbinger* (1846) 494.

52. Whereas Charland (133, 134) goes so far as to deny to subjects "even free choice" of social identity and other matters, the radically different responses with which rhetorical acts are frequently met seems to suggest that those addressed are, at least to some extent, individually free to choose whether to participate in the social identity that the act would constitute for them. This is not to deny that social identity is a rhetorical effect; it is merely to affirm that individuals are agents who choose between the alternative identities that different rhetorical acts would constitute for them. Regardless of how one may choose to view the matter of individual freedom, Charland's analysis clearly illustrates processes through which a rhetorical act may "call its audience into being."

53. Charland 139–41.

54. As late as 1827, to a correspondent from Missouri, Campbell wrote, "I do intend to continue with this people so long as they permit me to say what I believe . . . I have no idea of adding to the catalogue of new sects . . . ," remarking of the Baptists: "In one thing they may appear, in time to come, proudly singular and pre-eminently distinguished. Mark it well. Their historian, in the year 1900, may say, 'We are the only people who would tolerate, *or who ever did tolerate,* any person to continue as a reformer or restorer among us" (*Christian Baptist* (February 6, 1826) 217; Richardson, *Memoirs,* Vol. II, 134–35). In 1837, when Campbell commented upon his relationship to the Protestant parties in general and defended himself against the charge that he aspired "to build up and head a party," he wrote, "In truth we have always been forced to occupy the ground on which we now stand" and offered his willingness to represent Protestantism in his recent debate with Roman Catholic Bishop John Purcell as proof that he "endeavored to show the Protestant public that it is with great reluctance we are compelled to stand aloof from them—that they are the cause of the great 'schism,' as they call it, and not we" (*Millennial Harbinger,* 1837, 565).

55. Campbell, *Sermon* 6–8.

56. Campbell, *Sermon* 10, 16.

57. Campbell, *Sermon* 16–17.

58. Campbell, *Sermon* 6, 16.

59. Campbell, *Sermon* 7.

60. Campbell, *Sermon* 16–17.

61. Campbell, *Sermon* 23–24.

62. Brenda Robinson Hancock, "Affirmation by Negation in the Women's Liberation Movement," *Quarterly Journal of Speech* 58 (1972): 264–71+, also in *Methods of Rhetorical Criticism*, 2nd ed., eds. Bernard L. Brock and Robert L. Scott (Detroit: Wayne State University Press, 1986), 447ff.

63. Campbell, *Sermon* 5–6, 9, 11–12, 16, 21.

64. Campbell, *Sermon* 24.

65. Campbell, *Sermon* 16, 18–19.

66. Campbell, *Sermon* 15–27.

67. McGlothlin, W. J. *Baptist Confessions of Faith* (Philadelphia: American Baptist Publication Society, 1911), 293–99 (qtd. in Ferguson 76–77). As Ferguson points out, the wording here closely resembles that in chapter XIX of the Westminster Confession.

68. Ferguson 73.

69. Campbell, *Sermon* 26.

70. Ferguson 77. Ferguson points out that a sharp distinction between old and new covenants dates to Ignatius, Justin, and Irenaeus. The Scottish independents who influenced Campbell, such as John Glas, employed this distinction. Thomas Campbell had expressed this same basic position in *The Declaration and Address* of 1809: "That although the Scriptures of the Old and New Testaments are inseparably connected, making together but one perfect and entire revelation of the Divine will, for the edification and salvation of the Church, and therefore in that respect cannot be separated; yet as to what directly and properly belongs to their immediate object, the New Testament is as perfect a constitution for worship, discipline, and government of the New Testament Church, and as perfect a rule for the particular duties of its members, as the Old Testament was for the worship, discipline, and government of the Old Testament Church, and the particular duties of its members" (qtd. in Ferguson 78).

71. Campbell, *Sermon* 10.

72. According to W. E. Garrison (qtd. in Ferguson 80).

73. As Jorgenson points out, not only did the *Declaration and Address* of 1809 express the Campbells' confidence in the sufficiency of scripture through its motto, "Where the scriptures speak, we speak, and where the scriptures are silent, we are silent," it also echoed the principle of *sola scriptura* in its confidence that "rejecting human opinions and the inventions of men as of any authority, or as having any place in the church of God" and "taking the Divine Word alone for our rule" would enable the church to transcend the controversies generated by creeds (52).

74. Hatch 179–80. Hatch further notes: "The study of the religious convictions of self-taught Americans in the early years of the republic reveals how much weight was placed on private judgment and how little on the roles of history, theology, and the collective will of the church. In a culture that mounted a frontal assault upon tradition, mediating elites, and institutions, the Bible very easily became . . . 'a book dropped from the skies for all sorts of men to use in their own way.' This shift oc-

curred gradually and without fanfare because innovators could exploit arguments as old and as trusted as Protestantism itself. Luther, Calvin, Wesley, and Backus had all argued from the principle of *sola scriptura;* unschooled Americans merely argued that they were fulfilling the same mandate. Yet, in the assertion that private judgment should be the ultimate tribunal in religious matters, common people started a revolution" (182).

75. *Millennial Harbinger* (1846) 493.

Chapter 4

1. *Millennial Harbinger* (1831) 419–20.

2. Hatch 144.

3. Richardson, *Memoirs*, Vol. I, 285 (qtd. in Gary L. Lee, "Background of the *Christian Baptist*," *Christian Baptist* [1823–1830], ed. by Alexander Campbell, rev. by D. S. Burnet, seven volumes in one, 1835; Joplin, MO: College Press, 1983, 10).

4. Lee 10–11; As Lee points out, Campbell responded to the program because it mocked virtue and morality.

5. *Declaration and Address* in Olbricht and Rollman 58 (56); Lee 11.

6. Richardson, *Memoirs*, Vol. II, 13–14. North 123, 127–28.

7. Thomas W. Grafton, *Alexander Campbell* (St. Louis: Christian Publishing Company, 1897) 23 (qtd. in Lee 1).

8. The "prophetic" tone of Campbell's rhetoric may also be considered the genesis of what Richard Hughes describes as the "hard style" in the Restoration tradition. For a more complete discussion of this matter, see Hughes, *Reviving* 21–91.

9. *Millennial Harbinger* (1839) 338 (qtd. in North 130, footnote 29). North points out that from 1838 to about 1844, the friendship between Scott and Campbell was strained due to a sharp dispute between them.

10. The selection of this date was not an accident. Campbell clearly intended to draw parallels between America's Declaration of Independence and his own declaration of religious independence (*Christian Baptist*, August 3, 1829, 569). For a fuller discussion of the matter, see West, *Alexander Campbell and Natural Religion* 3ff.

11. Lee 20–21.

12. Prospectus of the *Christian Baptist*, in Richardson's *Memoirs*, Vol. II, 50.

13. *Millennial Harbinger* (1831) 419–20.

14. McAllister and Tucker 127–28; North 155.

15. Garrett 138.

16. North identifies these as the three specific "innovations" among the churches of the 1820s which the *Christian Baptist* addressed (132), following W. E. Garrison and Alfred T. DeGroot (*The Disciples of Christ: A History*, rev. ed. St. Louis: Bethany Press, 1958, 176) and Errett Gates (*The Early History of Relation and Separation of Baptists and Disciples*, Chicago: The Century Company, 1904, 43–46).

17. Webb 115.

18. Richardson, *Memoirs*, Vol. II, 87–89, 107–18.

19. *Christian Baptist* (February 6, 1826) 217.

20. *Millennial Harbinger* (1843) 4.

21. *Millennial Harbinger* (1831) 567; *Millennial Harbinger* (1832), 574, 583.

22. Thomas Long, "Preaching in the Prophets," *Handbook of Contemporary Preaching,* ed. Michael Duduit (Nashville, TN: Broadman Press, 1992) 307.

23. James Darsey, *The Prophetic Tradition and Radical Rhetoric in America* (New York: New York University Press, 1997) 6, 16.

24. Darsey 17; also see Margaret D. Zulick, "The Agon of Jeremiah: On the Dialogic Invention of Prophetic Ethos," *Quarterly Journal of Speech* 78 (1992): 137.

25. Darsey 17–20.

26. According to Aristotle, an enthymeme is a "rhetorical syllogism," differing only from the "primary syllogism" of dialectic (or logic) in that it deduces its conclusions from fewer premises (*On Rhetoric: A Theory of Civic Discourse,* trans George Kennedy, Oxford University Press, 1991: 40–42, 1356b–1357a). Hence, an enthymeme is commonly defined as an "abbreviated syllogism," i.e., a syllogism that omits the major premise because it is already known to the audience.

27. Darsey 20–22.

28. Abraham Heschel, *The Prophets,* Colophon ed., Vol. 2 (New York: Harper and Row, 1962), xvii-86 (qtd. in Darsey 25); Bruce Vawter, *The Conscience of Israel: Pre-Exilic Prophets and Prophecy* (New York: Sheed and Ward, 1961) 128 (qtd. in Darsey 25); Darsey 25–26.

29. Darsey 16–17, 27–28; R. B. Y. Scott, *The Relevance of the Prophets,* rev. ed. (New York: Macmillan, 1968) 99 (qtd. in Darsey 28).

30. Darsey 26, 29.

31. Darsey 30–31; Vawter 20 (qtd. in Darsey 32); Weber, *Max Weber: The Interpretation of Social Reality,* ed. J. E. T. Eldbridge (New York: Charles Scribner's Sons, 1971) 229 (qtd. in Darsey 32); Darsey 32–33.

32. *Millennial Harbinger* (1837) 56; here Campbell cited phraseology he often used and applied in the *Christian Baptist.*

33. R. B. Semple, *Christian Baptist* (April 3, 1826), 227; Jeremiah Bell Jeter, *Campbellism Examined* (New York: Sheldon, Lamport and Blakeman, 1855) 23 (qtd. in Hughes, *Reviving* 24).

34. G. Campbell 3, 7, 8.

35. G. Campbell 20–21.

36. G. Campbell 20–21.

37. G. Campbell 21.

38. G. Campbell 21.

39. In his *Lectures on Logic and Belles Lettres,* Jardine's comments on ridicule resemble very much those of George Campbell. He treats ridicule among the "capacities of sensibility" that contribute to the "powers of taste" (85), defining it as "the power by which we discern, and are effected by the ridiculous, in actions and opinions" (97). "All ridiculous actions," he observes, "are palpable deviations from the standards of Reason and Common Sense—Not criminal deviations which excite horror; but slighter, though not less obvious deviations . . . Ridiculous actions are inconsistent with the exercise of reason, and cannot be supported by argument" (98). "Laughter" is the term applied to the expression of emotion which arises from this reflex sense (99). As to its purpose, ridicule "may be considered as a test of Truth" and

"effects and imperfections of this standard" (101). Though "wit and humour are allied to ridicule" (99), they differ in their objects. Subsequent treatment of each of these also resembles that in *The Philosophy of Rhetoric.*

40. Hatch 74–75.

41. Dowling 95.

42. *Christian Baptist* (July 4, 1825) 166.

43. *Christian Baptist* (July 4, 1825) 166–67.

44. *Christian Baptist* (July 4, 1825) 167.

45. *Christian Baptist* (July 4, 1825) 167.

46. *Christian Baptist* (July 4, 1825) 168.

47. Campbell's "Sermon on the Goats" is not included in the Burnet editions of the *Christian Baptist.* It can be found on pages 19–20 in Vol. 1, No. 1 (August 3, 1832) of the *Christian Baptist,* Nashville, TN: Gospel Advocate, 1955–56.

48. Five of these were published to "convert" young preachers from what Campbell called the "injurious" habits of the clergy of his day to his "natural" philosophy of preaching. *Christian Baptist* (September 7, 1829) 584–85; (December 7, 1829) 604–5; (March 1, 1830) 632–33; (April 15, 1830) 639–40, 644–46.

49. *Christian Baptist* (September 7, 1829) 585.

50. *Christian Baptist* (September 7, 1829) 585.

51. *Christian Baptist* (October 2, 1826) 275.

52. *Christian Baptist* (October 2, 1826) 275.

53. *Christian Baptist* (October 2, 1826) 275.

54. *Christian Baptist* (October 2, 1826) 275.

55. *Christian Baptist* (October 2, 1826) 275–76.

56. *Christian Baptist* (October 2, 1826) 276.

57. *Christian Baptist* (October 2, 1826) 276.

58. *Christian Baptist* (October 2, 1826) 276.

59. *Christian Baptist* (October 2, 1826) 276.

60. *Christian Baptist* (October 2, 1826) 277.

61. George Campbell refers to ridicule, alternatively, as "satire, whose end is persuasion" (213).

62. *Christian Baptist* (October 2, 1826) 277. "Abecedarian" was actually a name given to those Anabaptists of the Reformation who scorned learning and academic study. Campbell here applies it pejoratively to the papal office.

63. *Christian Baptist* (October 2, 1826) 277.

64. *Christian Baptist* (October 2, 1826) 277.

65. *Christian Baptist* (October 2, 1826) 278.

66. *Christian Baptist* (October 2, 1826) 278.

67. *Christian Baptist* (October 2, 1826) 278.

68. Parables, of various sorts, are common not only in the gospels of the New Testament but in the rhetoric of the Old Testament prophets as well (e.g., Job, Ezekiel, Habakkuk, Micah, etc.).

69. G. Campbell 20–21.

70. G. Campbell 1.

71. Prospectus of the *Christian Baptist,* in Richardson's *Memoirs,* Vol. I, 50.

72. Prospectus of the *Christian Baptist,* in Richardson's *Memoirs,* Vol. I, 50.

73. G. Campbell 20.

74. G. Campbell 22–23.

75. G. Campbell 23.

76. North 134.

77. *Christian Baptist* (February 7, 1825) 127.

78. *Christian Baptist* (February 7, 1825) 128.

79. Beginning with number two in the series, the subjects are creeds, nomenclature, the order of worship, the breaking of bread (communion), the fellowship, the washing of feet, the Bishop's office, love feasts, the spirit of ancient Christians, purity of speech, the Deacon's office, devotion, the singing of praise, the church, church discipline, and official names and titles.

80. *Christian Baptist* (August 1, 1825) 176.

81. A recurring warrant in Campbell's restorationist rhetoric is a narrative of church history that he consistently constructs in the following stages: (1) primitive purity, (2) degeneration, (3) reformation, and (4) restoration (of primitive purity). This argument from history is featured in the fourth of the articles on "the breaking of bread" (November 7, 1825) as follows: (1) "antiquity" ("the first three centuries"), (2) "In the fourth century, when all things began to be changed . . . for more than six hundred years," (3) "At the Reformation," and (4) "Since the commencement of the present century" (195).

82. *Christian Baptist* (August 1, 1825) 174.

83. *Christian Baptist* (August 1, 1825) 174–75.

84. *Christian Baptist* (August 1, 1825) 175.

85. *Christian Baptist* (August 1, 1825) 175.

86. *Christian Baptist* (August 1, 1825) 175.

87. *Christian Baptist* (August 1, 1825) 175.

88. *Christian Baptist* (August 1, 1825) 176.

89. G. Campbell 78.

90. G. Campbell 71–72.

91. G. Campbell 77–78.

92. G. Campbell 4.

93. John L. Morrison, "A Rational Voice Crying in an Emotional Wilderness," *West Virginia History* (January 1973): 115–40, *The Stone-Campbell Movement: An International Religious Tradition,* eds. Casey and Foster, 163–76.

94. McLean 25.

95. G. Campbell 285.

96. G. Campbell 340.

97. Burwick, in his essay "Associationist Rhetoric and Scottish Prose Style" (*Speech Monographs,* March 1957), notes that repetition was considered an important factor in sustaining the association of ideas through a sequence of clauses. As he puts it, "The words merely echo and chime without carrying forward the train of thought" (25). One example of this would be, according to George Campbell, the contribu-

tions to vivacity, under certain conditions, of polysyndeton: "much additional weight and distinctiveness are given to each particular by the repetition of the conjunction" (368).

98. For the purposes of analyzing style and syntax, I employ here a diagramming technique similar to that used by Richard Lanham in *Analyzing Prose* (New York: Charles Scribner's Sons, 1983). The goal is to help the reader "look *at* words and not *through* them [to the ideas beneath]" (1–2). The diagram helps the reader to "pay attention to the verbal surface" (including sound patterns; Lanham 23) and serves "to expose a style's interior logic" (28). According to Lanham, such diagrams help restore something that "we've lost when we unthinkingly accept the convention of prose typography"—the "visual coordinates" which "seem to show immediately how a style works" (89–90). What we look for in such diagramming is vertical movement, as well as the horizontal movement that we tend to take for granted in reading. In other words, it allows us "to read from top to bottom as well as left to right" (82), making repetition, subordination, parallelism, alliteration, anaphora, epistrophe, chiasmus, etc. more discernable to the eye. Lanham suggests the value of such analysis for both written and oral discourse when he notes: "Modern prose typographical conventions have made many things easier . . . see how much easier it is to read. But the ease comes at a price. If we cease to look *at* prose, we lose the visual organization so many styles depend on. And if we cease, at the same time, to read prose aloud, we lose the emphasis and tonal control the voice supplies . . . The whole weight these two powers formerly supported now falls on style's purely symbolic force" (103).

99. *Christian Baptist* (August 1, 1825) 175.

100. G. Campbell 340. Generally, George Campbell considered brevity an important maxim for vivacity: "the fewer the words are, provided neither propriety nor perspicuity be violated, the expression is always the more vivid" (333). However, he did allow that there were two occasions for exception. One is when an obscure term might be more clearly explained by a synonym. The other is "when the language of the passions is exhibited. Passion naturally dwells on its object: the impassioned speaker always attempts to rise in expression; but when that is impracticable, he recurs to repetition and synonymy, and thereby in some measure produces the same effect. The hearer perceiving him, as it were, overpowered by his subject, and at a loss to find words adequate to the strength of his feelings, is by sympathy carried along with him, and enters into all his sentiments" (340). As an example, he cites Bolingbrook: "Bolingbrook exclaims in an invective against his times, 'But all is little, and low, and mean, among us.' It must be owed that there is here a kind of amplification, or at least a stronger expression of indignation, than any one of these three epithets could have affected alone; yet there is no climax in the sentence, and in this metaphorical use of words, no sensible difference of signification" (340). Thus, Campbell concludes that, in regard to the language of the passions, "a stroke of the pencil, if I may so express myself, is almost always added to the arbitrary sign, in order the more strongly to attach the imagination" (344).

101. G. Campbell 291, 344.

102. G. Campbell 371–72. George Campbell also rejected the traditional prescription of limiting a period to no more than four members and considered periodic

sentences that contain an antithesis in their members to possess the most vivacity of all (372). Burwick's essay, which focuses on the precepts shared by the rhetorics of the "Scottish school" and thus views the periodic sentence as a violation of the principles of brevity and vivacity, does not encompass many of the particulars of George Campbell's *Philosophy of Rhetoric*, including the view he expresses about the value of the periodic sentence for the style of the writer.

103. *Christian Baptist* (August 1, 1825) 174–75.

104. *Christian Baptist* (September 5, 1825) 181.

105. *Christian Baptist* (September 5, 1825) 181.

106. Conley 164, 196, 224.

107. George Campbell himself employs such language in describing the powers of rhetoric. When discussing the mixture of the argumentative and pathetic dimensions of discourse in Book I, Chapter II, his advice to "the declaimer" for whom "argument . . . is his avowed aim" is that "the passions which he excites ought never to appear to the auditors as the effects of his intention and address . . . Although, in fact, he intends to move his auditory, he only declares his purpose to convince them. To reverse this method, and profess an intention to work upon their passions, would be in effect to tell them that he meant to impose upon their understandings . . . Nothing is better founded in the famous aphorism of rhetoricians, that the perfection of art consists in concealing art" (23).

108. Heschel, *The Prophets: An Introduction*, Vol. I (New York: Harper and Row, 1969) 16.

109. *Christian Baptist* (April 5, 1830) 640.

Chapter 5

1. *Millennial Harbinger* (December 1837) 566.

2. According to North, the terms "Stoneites" and "Campbellites" were heard, but only from opponents (161).

3. McAllister and Tucker 141.

4. *Millennial Harbinger* (1832) 138 (qtd. in North 178).

5. North 170–71, 187.

6. Garrison and DeGroot 325 (qtd. in North 187); Hughes, *Reviving* 113. Hughes's estimate, based on 1810/11 figures provided by Joseph Thomas (*The Travels and Labors of Joseph Thomas*, Winchester, VA: J. Foster, 1812, 108), may be high. North estimates the size of the Stone movement at 8,000–10,000, observing that about half of the Stone movement remained in connection with the eastern Christians and did not merge into union with Campbell's movement (187).

7. Joseph Belcher, *Religious Denominations in the United States* (Philadelphia: John K. Potter, 1857) 811 (qtd. in McAllister and Tucker 188).

8. Hatch 16, 193, 202.

9. Hatch 205–7.

10. *Christian Baptist* (July 5, 1830) 665.

11. Hensley, "Rhetorical Vision" 250–64.

12. *Millennial Harbinger* (1830) 1.

13. Webb 182–83. As Webb points out, Campbell had actually appointed Pendleton as assistant editor in 1846. The volumes for 1863–1865 were edited by Pendleton due to Campbell's poor health and the five volumes that appeared after Campbell's death were edited by Pendleton and Charles Louis Loos.

14. North 155–56.

15. McAllister and Tucker 146. McAllister and Tucker also see this contrast as evidence of Campbell's belated agreement with his father: "The tone of the magazine [the *Christian Baptist*] was extremely critical . . . The articles and essays were extremely sarcastic and iconoclastic. The elder Campbell was aroused thoroughly by his son's boldness and sought to induce Alexander to adopt a milder policy. In time the younger Campbell apparently agreed with his father, for beginning in 1830 Alexander began circulation of another, more irenic journal" (127–28).

16. See, for example, Hughes, *Reviving,* although Hughes argues that "the spirit and the outlook of the *Christian Baptist* dominated even the *Harbinger* through 1836" (22). In 1988 Richard Tristano discussed a paper presented by Hughes at that year's American Historical Association in Cincinnati, Ohio, entitled "The Two Faces of Alexander Campbell and the Singular Campbell of Myth" (168–69). Neither work explicitly examines Campbell's philosophy of rhetoric, although Hughes, at one point, alludes to the "sectarian [and] ecumenical dimensions of his rhetoric" (*Reviving* 32). Hughes considers Campbell's response to the Lunenburg letter as significant evidence of a change in Campbell's thought and his attitude toward Protestantism, citing a portion of the September editorial as evidence that "in that very year he rejected immersion as absolutely essential to one's status as a Christian" (*Reviving* 38–40). Tristano also considers these texts a "good means of examining the shift in Alexander Campbell's thought" (118) but notes that "upon reading all of the articles written by Alexander Campbell upon the subject of Christians among the sects, it seems reasonable to conclude that he was both consistent and mainstream in his contentions" (122).

17. Hughes, *Reviving* 34–35. Hughes has also pointed out that another important factor nudging Campbell toward this new alliance with Protestantism was that "many of his own followers had missed his ecumenical intent and sectarianized his vision" (37). See both *Reviving* (37–39) and Hughes and Allen (172–86) for an extended discussion of the shift that took place in Campbell's thought in the mid-1830s. Endnote 97 in chapter one of this volume summarizes their contention that the sectarianism of Campbell's followers caused Campbell to lose hope in restorationism as a means to the Christian unity required for the millennium and to view Protestantism as the common religion that would serve as the agent of the millennium.

18. This is the argument presented by Don Haymes in an unpublished paper, "A Battle of Giants: Alexander Campbell and Bishop John Purcell in Cincinnati, 1837." Hughes and Tristano both discuss its substance.

19. Hughes, *Reviving* 34–37.

20. *Millennial Harbinger* (1837) 271–73.

21. *Millennial Harbinger* (1837) 411.

22. Hughes, *Reviving* 38–40; Tristano 118.

23. *Millennial Harbinger* (1837) 413–14.

24. *Millennial Harbinger* (1837) 506.

25. *Millennial Harbinger* (1837) 564.

26. *Millennial Harbinger* (1837) 566.

27. *Millennial Harbinger* (1837) 506, 508.

28. *Millennial Harbinger* (1837) 564–67.

29. For an extended discussion of Thomas's doctrines and contributions to the history of the Christadelphians, see Lippy 27–56.

30. Lippy 35–37; Roderick Chestnut, "John Thomas and the Rebaptism Controversy (1835–1838)," *Baptism and the Remission of Sins,* ed. David W. Fletcher (Joplin, MO: College Press, 1990) 203–7.

31. *Millennial Harbinger* (1834) 478, 124 (qtd. in North 192).

32. Chestnut makes a good case that the seeds for personal animosity between Thomas and Campbell were sown during Thomas's visit to Bethany, the end of which was precipitated by Thomas's resentment of his treatment by Campbell. For an extended account of the relationship between two men and its effect on the tone of their controversy, see "John Thomas and the Rebaptism Controversy," 204–16.

33. A thorough discussion of Thomas's position on baptism and rebaptism can be found in Chestnut (216–22). Campbell's differences with Thomas both on baptism and the question of whether there are Christians among the Protestant denominations are also discussed in Chestnut (222–28), as well as in John Mark Hicks, "Alexander Campbell on Christians Among the Sects," *Baptism and the Remission of Sins,* ed. David W. Fletcher (Joplin, MO: College Press, 1990) 171–202. As both Chestnut and Hicks point out, Campbell was, in fact, defending his own baptism in 1812. Campbell himself explained that he was not explicitly baptized for the purpose of receiving the remission of sins but simply upon a confession of faith in Christ (*Millennial Harbinger,* 1832, 319). As of the Maccalla debate in 1823, Campbell still held to an essentially Reformed concept of baptism and had not yet perceived the connection between baptism and the remission of sins which he clearly demonstrated in an extra, "Remission of Sins" (*Millennial Harbinger,* Extra No. I, July 5, 1830: 1–160).

34. Chestnut 203–4.

35. Hughes, *Reviving* 38. Thomas first published these views in "The Cry of 'Anabaptism,'" *The Apostolic Advocate* (October 1834) 121–29.

36. *Millennial Harbinger* (1837) 513, 588; (1838) 226; (1862) 132.

37. Chestnut 204, 228.

38. *Millennial Harbinger* (1837) 561.

39. *Millennial Harbinger* (1837) 411.

40. Chaim Perelman, *The Realm of Rhetoric,* transl. William Kluback (Notre Dame, IN: University of Notre Dame Press, 1982) 49, 52, 81.

41. Chaim Perelman and L. Olbrechts-Tytecha, *The New Rhetoric: A Treatise on Argumentation* [1952], trans. John Wilkinson and Purcell Weaver (Notre Dame: University of Notre Dame Press, 1969) 190.

42. Kenneth Burke, *A Rhetoric of Motives* (1950; Berkeley: University of California Press, 1969) xiv, 55ff; 46; 20–21; 118, 138–41, 265; 22, 23, 25.

43. *Millennial Harbinger* (1837) 411.

44. *Millennial Harbinger* (1837) 411. Here Campbell revises his definition of a Christian from the one he supplied to a correspondent from eastern Virginia in September of 1835 (a pseudonymous "Susan," who raised questions about Thomas' practice of reimmersion): "And am I asked, *Who is a citizen of the kingdom of heaven?* I answer, Every one that believes in his heart that Jesus of Nazareth is the Messiah the Son of God, and publicly confesses faith in his death for our sins, in his burial and resurrection, by an immersion into the name of the Father, the Son and the Holy Spirit. Every such person is a constitutional citizen of Christ's kingdom" (*Millennial Harbinger*, 1835, 419). However, as Campbell explained near the end of his December article, he considered the name "Christian" capable of at least four significations: its "primitive and apostolic import," its "national and very popular sense," a "new and special or appropriated sense" resulting from the controversies that "arose about the ways and means of putting on Christ," and "the sense in which I used the term in the obnoxious phrase first quoted by the sister of Lunenburg" (i.e., of those who "make the profession wrong, but live right"). He attributed part of the controversy to confusion surrounding these distinctions: "They only misunderstood me as using the term in its strictest biblical import, while in the case before me I used it in its best modern acceptation" (*Millennial Harbinger*, 1837, 566–67). In his discussion of Campbell's responses to the Lunenburg letter, John Mark Hicks thus suggests that Campbell's answer to the question, "Are there Christians among the sects?" is thus "yes" or "no"—depending upon what is meant by the term "Christian." Hicks also points out that Campbell, at various times, not only distinguished between different significations of the term "Christian" but made a similar distinction between "the church on earth (the church militant)" from which he excluded the unimmersed and "the hope of heaven (the church triumphant)" into which the unimmersed may, in his opinion, by the grace of God enter and be saved ("Alexander Campbell on Christians Among the Sects" 186–93).

45. *Millennial Harbinger* (1837) 411.

46. *Millennial Harbinger* (1837) 412. The biblical passage alluded to here is Matthew 28:19.

47. *Millennial Harbinger* (1837) 412.

48. *Millennial Harbinger* (1837) 412.

49. *Millennial Harbinger* (1837) 412–13.

50. As Berryhill points out (*Natural Rhetoric* 118), common sense realism influenced Campbell's faith in what he called the "sovereignty of evidence to compel belief"(*Christian Baptist*, April 5, 1824, 173; *Christian Baptist*, April 4, 1825, 179). In the Owen debate, he pointed out that if a man does not believe when presented with adequate evidence, it is because he allows his prejudices to interfere with his attention to it. Unbelief is thus a willful refusal to believe.

51. It seems unlikely that the chiastic quality of this arrangement is by design given the ad hoc manner in which this rhetorical episode evolved. Though each new article clearly extends previous arguments, the conclusions suggest a degree of autonomy for each article as it responds to evolutions in the rhetorical situation. At times, in these articles, Campbell seems genuinely surprised by the scope and strength of the reaction to his position and, as the rhetorical event evolves over time, increas-

ingly frustrated over his apparent inability to put the matter to rest. It is not impossible, however, that Campbell would have purposely framed his argument at the end of the December article in order to construct an *inclusio.*

52. *Millennial Harbinger* (1837) 507.

53. *Millennial Harbinger* (1837) 507.

54. *Millennial Harbinger* (1837) 561–62.

55. *Millennial Harbinger* (1837) 563.

56. *Millennial Harbinger* (1837) 563.

57. *Millennial Harbinger* (1837) 564. Ironically, as North points out (195, 198) in these same issues of the *Millennial Harbinger,* Campbell also published a series of articles on "Opinionism," arguing that, for the sake of Christian unity, opinions, which are in the realm of human deductions (as opposed to "knowledge" which is based on our own experience and "faith" which is an assurance based in the experience of others), should not be advocated.

58. *Millennial Harbinger* (1837) 567.

59. While it is possible, within Campbell's scheme, for all imperfections (few or many) to be either voluntary or willful, his discussion mainly applies the involuntary / willful mistake dissociation to the specific question of immersion.

60. *Millennial Harbinger* (1837) 412–13.

61. *Millennial Harbinger* (1837) 507–8.

62. *Millennial Harbinger* (1837) 562, 565, 567.

63. *Millennial Harbinger* (1837) 566.

64. *Millennial Harbinger* (1837) 566.

65. Chestnut 214–15; North 194.

66. Campbell's rhetoric continued to manifest this pastoral *ethos* in the years that followed the controversy surrounding the Lunenburg letter, as his movement continued to wrestle with tensions between its commitments to restoration and Christian unity. Casey, for example, has also explored Campbell's engagement of practical questions emerging from these tensions in the 1830s, exploring the manner in which Campbell's thought shifted back and forth between democratic and monarchical metaphors depending upon the issue and the audience (*The Battle Over Hermeneutics in the Stone-Campbell Movement, 1800–1870,* Lewiston, NY: Edwin Mellen Press, 1998).

Chapter Six

1. *Millennial Harbinger* (1860) 611.

2. Hughes, *Reviving* 113; North 187; Belcher 811 (qtd. in McAllister and Tucker 188).

3. W. T. Moore, *Comprehensive History of the Disciples of Christ* (New York: Fleming H. Revell, 1909) 12.

4. *Millennial Harbinger* (1852) 391.

5. McAllister and Tucker 162–63; Webb 168. Bacon College relocated to Harrodsburg, Kentucky, in 1839 and later merged with Transylvania University in Lexington.

6. North 201; Webb 183–84.

7. *Millennial Harbinger* (1842) 523. As North points out, his five arguments were: Bible distribution, home and foreign missions, improving and elevating the Christian ministry, protecting the church from irresponsible preachers, and using the total resources of the church (206).

8. North 208–9, 214.

9. North 211–13; Webb 171.

10. *Millennial Harbinger* (1849) 691.

11. Webb 172.

12. North 215.

13. Tristano 125.

14. North 206; Webb 204–5.

15. Webb 172; Grant K. Lewis, *The American Christian Missionary Society and the Disciples of Christ* (St. Louis, MO: The Christian Board of Education, 1937) 13 (qtd. in Webb 205).

16. North 215–18.

17. *Christian Baptist* (August 3, 1823) 6 (qtd. in North 212–13).

18. *Millennial Harbinger* (1849) 270–71 (qtd. in North 212).

19. *Millennial Harbinger* (1849) 272–73 (qtd. in North 212).

20. David E. Harrell, Jr., *Quest for a Christian America: The Disciples of Christ and American Society to 1866* (Nashville, TN: Disciples of Christ Historical Society, 1966) 92.

21. Webb 191. For extended discussions of Campbell's position on slavery and the effect of the slavery controversy on the Stone-Campbell movement, see Harrell 91–138; Robert O. Fife, "Alexander Campbell and the Christian Church in the Slavery Controversy," diss., Indiana University, 1960; and Earl E. Eminhizer, "The Abolitionists Among the Disciples of Christ," diss., Southern California School of Theology, 1968).

22. *Christian Baptist* (August 3, 1823) 8.

23. *Millennial Harbinger* (1830) 1.

24. Webb 123; Harrell 103.

25. Webb 191–92. Commenting on Campbell's insight into economic realities, Webb points out, "The cost would have been only a fraction of the cost of the war and it would have spared lives, property, and the economy of the South" (192).

26. *Millennial Harbinger* (1845) 195.

27. Harrell 109; *Millennial Harbinger* (1845) 355–58.

28. On James Shannon as a leader among proslavery advocates, see Harrell 121–25.

29. Harrell 107–8, 111–12; North 230. Harrell recognizes "four significant ideological and sectional factions" within "ante-bellum Disciples history: abolitionists, antislavery moderates, proslavery moderates, and proslavery radicals" and notes, "What actually did happen between the years 1855 and 1860 was a general defection of the most radical Northern group" (136–37).

30. Harrell 115–21, 134.

31. North 236. North also points out that, by 1863, Campbell "was becoming forgetful, often rambling and confusing his daughter's letters from the Mediterranean with his experiences" (236).

32. Webb 181

33. *Millennial Harbinger* (1860) 611, 624.

34. As George Kennedy notes, Aristotle's treatment of epideictic qualities can also serve the ends of judicial and deliberative rhetoric (Aristotle, *On Rhetoric,* 1368a, 78).

35. *Millennial Harbinger* (1860) 601.

36. *Millennial Harbinger* (1860) 601.

37. Campbell borrows this language from the gospel of John. The reference to the "Incarnate Word" is derived from John 1:1, 14 and the reference to "only begotten Son" from John 3:16.

38. An allusion to Matthew 28:18–20.

39. In theology, eschatology refers to the study of "final things."

40. *Millennial Harbinger* (1860) 604.

41. When discussing the rhetorical problems of holding communities together, E. Bormann observes that one common tactic for revitalizing commitment to the vision is "celebrating the group's saga." In such cases, "these communities would have a communication episode in which speakers pronounced encomia on personae such as the founder or founders, the community itself, its geographical location, and outstanding episodes in its history. Recounting these celebration fantasies in detail served to arouse emotional responses of attachment to the community and identification with unifying personae" (*Force of Fantasy* 15–16). Campbell's use of autobiographical narrative in this address could be said to serve this function.

42. *Millennial Harbinger* (1860) 604.

43. *Millennial Harbinger* (1860) 605–6.

44. *Millennial Harbinger* (1860) 606.

45. *Millennial Harbinger* (1860) 606.

46. Ernest G. Bormann articulated the method of fantasy theme criticism in a number of writings other than the *The Force of Fantasy: Restoring the American Dream,* often cited earlier in this work: "Fantasy and Rhetorical Vision: The Rhetorical Criticism of Social Reality," *Quarterly Journal of Speech* 58 (December 1972): 396–407; "A Fantasy Theme Analysis of the Television Coverage of the Hostage Release and the Reagan Inaugural," *Quarterly Journal of Speech* 68 (1982): 133–45; and "Symbolic Convergence Theory: A Communication Formulation," *Journal of Communication* 35 (Autumn 1985): 128–38.

47. Sonja Foss, *Rhetorical Criticism: Exploration and Practice,* 2nd ed. (Prospect Heights, IL: Waveland Press, 1996), 123–25.

48. Sonja Foss, "Equal Rights Amendment Controversy: Two Worlds in Conflict," *Quarterly Journal of Speech* 65 (October 1979): 275–88+, *Rhetorical Criticism: Exploration and Practice,* 2nd ed., by Sonja Foss (Prospect Heights, IL: Waveland Press, 1996), 134.

49. Foss, *Rhetorical Criticism* 123; Bormann, *Force of Fantasy* 5.

50. Bormann, *Force of Fantasy* 5; Foss, *Rhetorical Criticism* 123.

51. Bormann in *Force of Fantasy* (8) and in "Fantasy and Rhetorical Vision" (398). In particular, Bormann defines "life-style rhetorical visions" as those which are "so all-encompassing and impelling that they permeate an individual's social reality in all aspects of living" (*Force of Fantasy* 8). Carl Hensley has authored a fantasy theme

analysis of the restoration movement as a whole that offers a more comprehensive account of the broader rhetorical vision collectively constructed by its nineteenth-century leaders ("Rhetorical Vision" 250–64).

52. Bormann ("Fantasy and Rhetorical Vision" 396) extended the work of Richard Bales (*Personality and Interpersonal Behavior*, New York: Holt, Rinehart, 1970).

53. Bormann, "Fantasy and Rhetorical Vision" 396.

54. *Millennial Harbinger* (1860) 604.

55. *Millennial Harbinger* (1860) 604.

56. *Millennial Harbinger* (1860) 606.

57. Presumably Campbell's own translation of Mark 16:15–16.

58. *Millennial Harbinger* (1860) 607–8.

59. *Millennial Harbinger* (1860) 611.

60. *Millennial Harbinger* (1860) 613.

61. James Jasinski's "Rearticulating History in Epideictic Discourse: Frederick Douglass's 'The Meaning of the Fourth of July to the Negro,'" in *Rhetoric and Political Culture in Nineteenth-Century America*, ed. Thomas W. Benson (East Lansing: Michigan State University Press, 1997, 71–89) offers a fine example of this function of epideictic narrative.

62. Aristotle, *On Rhetoric*, ed. Kennedy, 1358b, 48; Conley 61ff.

63. *Millennial Harbinger* (1860) 602–4.

64. *Millennial Harbinger* (1860) 602–8.

65. *Millennial Harbinger* (1860) 604, 609.

66. *Millennial Harbinger* (1860) 606–8.

67. *Millennial Harbinger* (1860) 601–3.

68. *Millennial Harbinger* (1860) 602–6, 611.

69. *Millennial Harbinger* (1860) 603, 608–9.

70. *Millennial Harbinger* (1860) 611.

71. *Millennial Harbinger* (1860) 604.

72. *Millennial Harbinger* (1860) 615.

73. Bormann, "Fantasy and Rhetorical Vision" 407.

74. *Millennial Harbinger* (1860) 605. Thomas Campbell authored the *Declaration and Address* and helped to organize the Christian Association of Washington in 1809. The Brush Run Church was constituted in 1811. Alexander preached the "Sermon on the Law" in 1816. Whether these travels are considered to antedate the inception of the movement depends on which event one identifies with its inception.

75. Kenneth Burke, *A Grammar of Motives* (1945; Berkeley: University of California Press, 1969) 3ff.

76. Garrett 2–4.

77. Jerome Bruner, *Acts of Meaning* (Cambridge, MA: Cambridge University Press, 1990) 51.

78. North 216–17. Garrett suggests that Fanning "either overstated what he saw or was not duly sensitive to the power of an over-solicitous wife," noting that "Selina was known to hang a sign at the gate near her husband's study, instructing any callers to see her first" (282).

79. Hughes notes: "By the dawn of the twentieth century, when the Disciples of

Christ and Churches of Christ were physically separating from one another and court battles were determining which group would retain possession of church buildings, appeals were often made to the 'earlier' or 'later' teachings of Alexander Campbell" (*Reviving* 46). Hughes identifies the Disciples of Christ with the later Campbell and the Churches of Christ with the younger Campbell.

80. McAllister and Tucker 249.

81. Hughes, *Reviving* 46.

82. Eva Jean Wrather, "Alexander Campbell and the Judgment of History," *The Sage of Bethany: A Pioneer in Broadcloth,* ed. Perry E. Gresham (1960; Joplin, MO: College Press, 1988) 166, 179; Webb 195; Hughes, *Reviving* 21; McAllister and Tucker 21–23.

83. Hughes, *Reviving* 47–48.

84. Hughes, *Reviving* 55–56.

85. Webb 229–30.

86. Webb 230–33; McAllister and Tucker 345.

87. Webb 244; North 246.

88. Hughes, *Reviving* 56.

89. Casey, *Saddlebags* 49–50.

90. *Christian Leader* (September 10, 1889) 2 (qtd. in North 250).

91. North 251–52.

92. Bormann, *Force of Fantasy* 14.

93. See note 98 in chapter 1.

94. Harrell 137.

95. Webb 203; North 235.

96. Webb 203–4.

97. Webb 209ff; North 246–47; McAllister and Tucker 33; Harrell 138.

98. Harrell 134; North 251.

Conclusion

1. McAllister and Tucker 31; Webb 192–93.

2. Webb 182. Webb also reminds us that Campbell's home was located only a few miles from a port on the Ohio River in Wellsburg, Virginia (now West Virginia) and that the railroad became an important passenger carrier only in his later years.

3. Ronald E. Osborn, "Dogmatically Absolute, Historically Relative," in *The Reformation of Tradition,* ed. Ronald E. Osborn (St. Louis: Bethany Press, 1963) 279 (qtd. in McAllister and Tucker 236).

4. Bormann, *Force of Fantasy* 16.

5. Bormann refers to "emergence, growth, maturity and decline" as successive stages that he discovers in the evolution of various "public consciousnesses related to religion and reform" during the last half of the eighteenth and first half of the nineteenth centuries (*Force of Fantasy* 22). Similarly, Anthony Wallace identifies six major tasks that must be performed by "religious revitalization movements": reformulation, communication, organization, adaptation, cultural transformation and routinization ("Revitalization Movements," *American Anthropologist* 58, 1956, 264–81; qtd. in Casey

and Foster, "The Renaissance of Stone-Campbell Studies: An Assessment and New Directions," *The Stone-Campbell Movement: An International Religious Tradition,* 13–14).

6. Of course, as Sheri L. Helsley points out, *kairos,* in both ancient and modern use, is "a concept far richer and more complex than 'saying the right thing at the right time'" ("Kairos," in *Encyclopedia of Rhetoric and Composition: From Ancient Times to the Information Age,* ed. by Theresa Enos. New York: Garland Pub., 1996, 371). For the Pythagoreans, *kairos* served as an important epistemological concept, referring to the "balance" between thesis and antithesis, doubt and belief (Helsley 371). As to the rhetorical applications derived from this concept, John Poulakis suggests that in Gorgianic rhetoric, *kairos* referred to that sense of (1) the "temporality of the situation" and (2) "the impetus for discourse, the tension in the situation" that guides the choices of the rhetor ("Toward a Sophistic Definition of Rhetoric," *Philosophy and Rhetoric* 16, 1983, 35–48; cited by Helsley 371). Jane Sutton sees three lines of thought about the relation of *kairos* to rhetoric: (1) a call for decisive action, (2) the right moment to speak, and (3) the expression of what is appropriate ("Kairos," in *Encyclopedia of Rhetoric,* ed. by Thomas Sloan. New York: Oxford University Press, 2001, 413–17). In the first, as evidenced in "the rhetorical discourse of ancient Athens" (e.g., Isocrates, Aristotle, and the Sophists), "the rhetor or orator seizes upon an opportunity that coincides with the temporal needs of the situation" (Sutton 414). In the second (also evidenced in Aristotle, Gorgias and Isocrates), *kairos* is "a window of opportunity in rhetorical deliberation" that "bears upon the practice of speaking in terms of what to say, the warp, and when to say it, the woof" (Sutton 415), stressing what Wichelns described as rhetoric's "bondage to the occasion and the audience" (Herbert A. Wichelns, "The Literary Criticism of Oratory," in *Studies in Rhetoric and Public Speaking in Honor of James Albert Winans,* New York: 1925, 212; qtd. in Sutton 415). In the third, *kairos* applies both to style—"good taste" and the "due measure" imposed by ethical considerations—and argument—a doctrine attributed to Protagoras, in which "the *rhetor* delivers the appropriate choice in the face of changing positions or relative truths," though specifically, for Aristotle, "the circumstances of time . . . give a praiseworthy character to particular actions" (Sutton 415).

Selected Bibliography

Primary Sources
Books

Campbell, Alexander, trans. *Acts of the Apostles: Translated From the Greek, On the Basis of the Common English Version, With Notes.* New York: American Bible Union, 1857.

Campbell, Alexander. *Alexander Campbell at Glasgow University, 1808–09.* Transcribed and edited with an introduction by Lester McAllister. Nashville, TN: Disciples of Christ Historical Society, 1971.

———. *The Campbell Yearbook: Choice Selections for Every Day in the Year.* Compiled by W. G. Burleigh. Biographical sketch by Peter Ainslie. Portsmouth, VA: published by the compiler, 1909.

———. *Christian Baptism: With Its Antecedents and Consequents.* Bethany, VA: Printed and published by Alexander Campbell, 1851.

———, ed. *The Christian Hymnbook: A Compilation of Psalms, Hymns and Spiritual Songs, Original and Selected, by A. Campbell and Others.* Revised and enlarged by a committee. Cincinnati: H. S. Bosworth, 1865. For first edition of this work, see *Psalms, Hymns and Spiritual Songs.*

———. *The Christian Preacher's Companion; or, the Gospel Facts Sustained by the Testimony of Unbelieving Jews and Pagans.* Bethany, VA: M'Vay and Ewing, 1836. Reprinted as *Infidelity Refuted by Infidels; or the Gospel Proved by the Testimony of Unbelieving Jews and Pagans.* Bethany, VA: Alexander Campbell, 1844.

———. *The Christian System, In Reference to the Union of Christians, and a Restoration of Primitive Christianity, as Plead in the Current Reformation.* Bethany, VA: published by A. Campbell. 3rd ed., Pittsburgh: Forrester and Campbell, 1839. For the first edition of this work see *A Connected View of the Principles.*

———. *A Compend of Alexander Campbell's Theology, With Commentary in the Form of Critical and Historical Footnotes.* Ed. Royal Humbert. St. Louis, MO: Bethany, 1961.

———. *A Connected View of the Principles and Rules by Which The Living Oracles May Be Intelligibly and Certainly Interpreted: Of the Foundation On Which All Christians May Form One Communion.* Bethany, VA: M'Vay and Ewing, 1835. Cover title, *Christianity Restored* (repudiated by Campbell as a binder's error). Rosemead, CA: Old Paths Book Club, 1959.

———. *Essays and a Dialogue on the Work of the Holy Spirit in Salvation of Men.* Broekport, NY: J. M. Yearnshaw, 1834. Reprinted from various issues of *The Christian Baptist,* Vol.2, and *Millennial Harbinger,* Vol. 2.

———. *Familiar Lectures on the Pentateuch: Delivered Before the Morning Class of Bethany College, During the Session of 1859–1860.* Ed. W. T. Moore. Cincinnati: H. S. Bosworth, 1867. Rosemead, CA: Old Paths Book Club, 1958.

———. *Lawrence Greatrake's Calumnies Repell'd.* Buffaloe, Brooke Co., VA: A. Campbell, 1825.

———. *Letters to a Skeptic.* Cincinnati: H. S. Bosworth, 1859. Reprinted from various issues of *Christian Baptist,* vol. 4. May have been reprinted as a separate by Campbell in 1826.

———. *Memoirs of Elder Thomas Campbell Together With a Brief Memoir of Mrs. Jane Campbell.* Cincinnati: H. S. Bosworth, 1861, 1871. Rosemead, CA: Old Paths Book Club, 1954.

———. "The Missionary Cause." In *Treasury of the World's Great Sermons.* Comp. Warren Wiersbe. Grand Rapids, MI: Kregel, 1977. Reprinted from *Millennial Harbinger,* 1860 and *Popular Lectures and Addresses,* 1861.

———. *Popular Lectures and Addresses.* Philadelphia: J. Challen & Son, 1863. Nashville: Harbinger Book Club, 1954.

———. *Psalms, Hymns and Spiritual Songs.* Bethany, VA: A. Campbell, 1828.

———, ed. *Psalms, Hymns and Spiritual Songs, Original and Selected, Compiled by A. Campbell, W. Scott, B. W. Stone and J. T. Johnson; Adapted to the Christian Religion.* Bethany, VA: A. Campbell, 1834. Revised and published in 1843 with the cover title, *The Christian Hymnbook.*

———, ed. *Psalms, Hymns and Spiritual Songs, Original and Selected, Compiled by A. Campbell, W. Scott, B. W. Stone and J. T. Johnson, Elders of the Christian Church, With Numerous and Various Additions and Emendations, Adapted to Personal, Family and Church Worship by Alexander Campbell.* Cover title, *The Christian Hymnbook.* Bethany, VA: A. Campbell, 1851.

———, ed. *The Sacred Writings of The Apostles and Evangelists of Jesus Christ, Commonly Styled The New Testament. Translated From The Original Greek, by Doctors George Campbell, James Macknight, And Phillip Doddridge, Doctors of the Church of Scotland, With Preface to the Historical and Epistolary Books; and an Appendix, Containing Critical Notes and Various Translations of Difficult Passages.* Buffaloe, Brooke County, VA: A. Campbell, 1826.

———, ed. *The Sacred Writings of The Apostles and Evangelists of Jesus Christ, Commonly Styled The New Testament. Translated From The Original Greek, by Doctors George Campbell, James Macknight, And Phillip Doddridge, With Prefaces, Various Emendations And An Appendix By Alexander Campbell.* Cover title, *The Living Oracles.* Bethany, VA: Alexander Campbell, 1832. Nashville, TN: Harbinger Book Club, 1951.

———. *Strictures on Three Letters Respecting the Debate at Mount Pleasant [Ohio]; Published in the Presbyterian Magazine in 1821: Signed Samuel Ralston.* Pittsburgh: Eichbaum and Johnston, 1822.

———. *The Writings of Alexander Campbell, Selections Chiefly From the Millennial Harbinger.* Ed. W. A. Morris. Austin, TX: Eugene Von Broeckman, Printer, 1896.

Campbell, Alexander, Thomas Campbell, and Barton Stone. *Discussions of the Atonement: by Thomas Campbell and Barton W. Stone, Alexander Campbell and Barton W. Stone.* Comp. Enos Dowling. Lincoln, IL: Enos Dowling, 1983.

Campbell, Alexander, and W. L. Maccalla. *A Debate on Christian Baptism, Between The Rev. W. L. Maccalla And Alexander Campbell, In Which Are Interspersed And To Which Are Added Animadversions On Different Treatises On The Same Subject Written By Dr. J. Mason, Dr. S. Ralston, Rev. A. Pond, Rev. J. P. Campbell, Rector Armstrong, And The Rev. J. Walker.* Held at Washington, KY, commencing on the 15th and terminating on the 21st day of October, 1823. Buffalo: Campbell and Sala, 1824. London: Simpkin and Marshall, 1942. Rosemead, CA: Old Paths Book Club, 1948.

Campbell, Alexander, and Robert Owen. *Debate On the Evidences of Christianity; Containing An Examination Of The "Social System," And Of All The Systems Of Scepticism of Ancient And Modern Times, Held in the City of Cincinnati, Ohio, From the 13th to the 21st of April, 1829; Between Robert Owen, Of New Lanark, Scotland, And Alexander Campbell, Of Bethany, Virginia, With An Appendix By The Parties.* 2 vols. Bethany: Alexander Campbell, 1829. Cincinnati: Robinson and Fairbank, 1829. Nashville, TN: McQuiddy Printing Co., 1946. Nashville, TN: Gospel Advocate Co., 1957.

Campbell, Alexander, and John B. Purcell. *A Debate On The Roman Catholic Religion: Held in the Sycamore Street Meeting House, Cincinnati; From the 13th to the 21st of January, 1837; Between Alexander Campbell and the Rt. Rev. John B. Purcell.* Cincinnati: J. A. James & Co., 1837. Cincinnati: Chase & Hall, 1875.

Campbell, Alexander, and Nathan Rice. *A Debate Between Rev. A. Campbell And Rev. N. L. Rice, On the Action, Subject, Design and Administration of Christian Baptism; Also On the Character of Spiritual Influence In Conversion And Sanctification, And On The Expediency And Tendency of Ecclesiastic Creeds, As Terms of Union and Communion.* Held in Lexington, KY from the 15th to the 2d of December, 1843. Lexington, KY, A. T. Skillam & Son; Cincinnati, OH, Wright and Swormstedt, J. A. James; Louisville, KY, D. S. Burnett; New York, NY, R. Carter; Pittsburgh: Thomas Carter, 1844. Rosemead, CA: Old Paths Book Club, 1956.

Campbell, Alexander, and Dolphus Skinner. *A Discussion of the Doctrines of Endless Misery and Universal Salvation: In An Epistolary Correspondence Between Alexander Campbell, of Bethany, VA, and Dophus Skinner, of Utica, NY.* Utica, NY: C. C. P. Grosh, 1840.

Campbell, Alexander, and John Walker. *A Debate on Christian Baptism, Between Mr. John Walker, A Minister Of The Secession, And Alexander Campbell, held at Mount Pleasant on the 19th and 20th June, 1820.* Second Edition, enlarged. Pittsburgh: Eichbaum and Johnston, 1822. For first edition, see *Infant Sprinkling. . . .*

———. *Infant Sprinkling Proved to be a Human Tradition; Being the Substance of a Debate on Christian Baptism Between Mr. John Walker, a Minister of the Secession and Alexander Campbell, V.D.M., a Regular Baptist Minister, Held at Mount Pleasant,*

Jefferson County, Ohio, on the 19th and 20th June 1820. Steubenville, OH: James Wilson, 1920.

Periodicals

Campbell, Alexander, ed. *The Christian Baptist.* 7 Vols. Published monthly from August, 1823, through July, 1830. Buffaloe Creek and Bethany, VA: early issues were printed by A. Campbell; reprinted, Nashville, TN: Gospel Advocate Co., 1955–56.

———, ed. *The Christian Baptist.* Revised by D. S. Burnet from the Second Edition, with Mr. Campbell's Last Corrections. Seven volumes in one. Cincinnati, OH: D. S. Burnet, 1835; reprinted with introduction by Gary Lee, Joplin, MO: College Press, 1983, 1988.

Campbell, Alexander, and Pendleton, W. K., eds. *The Millennial Harbinger.* 41 Vols. Volumes 1–34 published monthly from 1830 through 1863 with A. Campbell as editor. Volumes 35–41 published monthly through 1870 with W. K. Pendleton as editor. Bethany, VA: reprinted, Joplin, MO: College Press, 1985.

———, eds. *The Millennial Harbinger Abridged,* by Benjamin Lyon Smith. Introduction by Charles Louis Loos. 2 vols. Cincinnati: Standard Publishing Co., 1902.

Pamphlets, Tracts and Addresses

Campbell, Alexander. *Address Delivered at New Athens College to the Students of That Institution by Special Request of Students and Faculty, at Annual Commencement.* Published by the students, 1838. Printed in *The Millennial Harbinger,* 1838.

———. *An Address Delivered Before the Charlottesville [Va.] Lyceum, on the 16th of June, 1840.* Published at the request of the Lyceum, 1840. Printed in *The Millennial Harbinger,* August 1841. Reprinted in *Popular Lectures and Addresses,* 1863.

———. *An Address Delivered to the Members of the Jefferson Literary Society of Franklin College, New Athens, Ohio, September 25, 1838.* Bethany, VA: A. Campbell, 1838.

———. *An Address Delivered to the Young Men's Mercantile Library Association of Cincinnati; on the Anglo-Saxon Language, Its Origin, Character and Destiny.* December 11, 1849. Bethany, VA: 1850. Printed in *The Millennial Harbinger,* May 1850. Reprinted in *Popular Lectures and Addresses,* 1863.

———. *An Address on Capital Punishment, Delivered to the Washington Literary Institute, on the Evening of March 2d, 1846, Published by Request.* Bethany, VA: A. Campbell, 1846. Printed in *The Millennial Harbinger,* March 1846. Reprinted in *Popular Lectures and Addresses,* 1863.

———. *An Address on Demonology, Delivered Before the Popular Lecture Club, Nashville, Tenn., March 10, 1841.* No copy known of 1st ed. Printed in *The Millennial Harbinger,* October 1841. Reprinted by Charles G. Berry, 1851; in *Popular Lectures and Addresses,* 1863.

———. *An Address on the Amelioration of the Social State, Delivered . . . Louisville.* Louisville: Prentice and Weissinger, 1839. Reprinted in *The Millennial Harbinger,* July, 1840; *Popular Lectures and Addresses,* 1863.

———. *An Address on War; Delivered Before the Wheeling Lyceum, May 11th, 1848.* Bethany, VA: A. Campbell, 1848. Printed in *The Millennial Harbinger,* July 1848.

Reprinted in *Popular Lectures and Addresses*, 1863; *Congressional Record*, Nov. 22, 1937.

——. *An Address to the Members of the Union Literary Society of Miami University, Ohio*. Bethany, VA: Printed by A. Campbell, 1844. Printed in *The Millennial Harbinger*, December, 1844. Reprinted in *Popular Lectures and Addresses*, 1863.

——. *Baccalaureate Address, Delivered to Ten Graduates at Bethany College, July 4th, 1845*. Bethany, VA: A. Campbell, 1845. Printed in *The Millennial Harbinger*, July 1845.

——. *A Circular Letter Written by Mr. Alexander Campbell at the Request of the Redstone Baptist Association to the Churches in Their Connexion . . . September 4, 1817*. 1817. Reprinted as *Views of Mr. Alexander Campbell Concerning the Doctrines of Election and Reprobation*. Fulton, MO: T. L. Stephens, 1856.

——. *Facts and Documents Confirmatory of the Credibility of the Debate on Baptism Between W. L. M'Calla and Alexander Campbell, Being a Full Exposition of a "Unitarian Baptist" Created and Made by the Rev. W. L. M'Calla*. Bethany, Brooke Co., VA: A. Campbell, 1828.

——. *Lecture on Slavery, Delivered Within the Waterloo Room, Edinburgh, on Friday, August 13, 1847*. Edinburgh: R. M. Walker, 1847. Reprinted from the Edinburgh *Journal*, August 18, 1847.

——. *Life and Death*. Cincinnati: H. S. Bosworth, 1860. Reprint of an Extra of *The Millennial Harbinger*, December 1844. Reprinted in *Popular Lectures and Address*, 1863.

——. *The Lunenburg Letter, With Attendant Comments*. Nashville: Disciples of Christ Historical Society, 1966. Reprinted from the *Millennial Harbinger*, 1837.

——. *Mormonism: The Book of Mormon Reviewed, and its Devine Pretensions Exposed*. Bethany, VA: A. Campbell, 1831. Reprinted under title *Delusions*, 1832 and 1925, and *Alexander Campbell on the Book of Mormon*, 1902.

——. *On Moral Societies* New York: The International Religious Liberty Association, 1898. "The Candidus Papers," reprinted from the Washington, PA, *Reporter*, 1820.

——. *Order of Worship*. Compiled by C. M. Stubblefield. Cincinnati: F. L. Rowe, 1915. Reprinted from *The Christian Baptist*, vol. 2.

——. *The Philosophy of Memory and of Commemorative Institutions: An Address Delivered by Request to the "Union Literary Society," of Washington College, November 10th, 1841*. Bethany, VA: A. Campbell, 1841. Printed in *The Millennial Harbinger*, December, 1841. Reprinted in *Popular Lectures and Addresses*, 1863.

——. *The Rank and Dignity of Man: An Address Delivered to the Students of Florence Academy, Washington County, Pennsylvania (at their request)*. Bethany, VA: A. Campbell, 1838. Printed in *The Millennial Harbinger*, December 1838.

——. *Remission of Sins*. [Rpt. of an Extra in the *Millennial Harbinger* (July 5, 1830)] Titusville, PA: H. R. Press, 1949.

——. *Report of the Proceedings of a General Meeting of Messengers, From Thirteen Congregations, Held in Wellsburg, Va., On Saturday, the 12th of April, 1834, by J. T. M'Vay and A. Campbell*. Bethany, VA: A. Campbell, 1834. Reprinted as *Footnotes on Disciple History,* no. 5, Nashville, TN: Disciple of Christ Historical Society, 1957.

———. *Schism: Its Bane and Antidote, or the True Foundation of Christian Union.* London, Simpkin and Co.; Nottingham, R. Groombridge and T. Kirk, 1840. 2nd ed. published as *The True Foundation of Christian Union: Shewing the Practicability of the Union and Communion of All God's People,* London: 1846.

———. *The Substance of a Sermon Delivered Before the Redstone Baptist Association, Met on Cross Creek, Brooke County, Va., on the First of September 1816.* Steubenville, OH: James Wilcox, 1816. Reprinted as *The Memorable Sermon on the Law,* St. Louis: Christian Pub. Co., 1889. Reprinted in A. C. Young, ed., *Historical Documents Advocating Christian Union,* Chicago: 1904.

———. *Supernatural Facts: An Address Delivered to the Maysville Lyceum, March 25th, 1839. Published at the Request of the Institution.* Bethany, VA: A. Campbell, 1839. Reprinted from *The Millennial Harbinger,* June 1839. Reprinted in *Popular Lectures and Addresses,* 1863.

———. *A Tract for the People of Kentucky.* Louisville: Courier Office, 1849.

On-Line Resources

The Alexander Campbell Page. Ed. Hans Rollman. <http://www.mun.ca/rels/restmov/people/acampbell.html> Contains the Burnet edition of the *Christian Baptist* and many extracts from the *Millennial Harbinger,* addresses, letters and Campbell's contributions to the works of others.

Alexander Campbell's Contributions to The Christian Baptist, 1823–1830. Ed. Ernie Stefanik. <http:// www.mun.ca/rels/restmov/texts/acampbell/cb/ACINCB.HTM>

Alexander Campbell's Contributions to The Millennial Harbinger, 1830–1869. Ed. Ernie Stefanik. <http://www.mun.ca/rels/restmov/texts/acampbell/mh/ACINMH.HTM>

Secondary Sources

Books

Athearn, Clarence R. *The Religious Education of Alexander Campbell: Morning Star of the Coming Reformation.* St. Louis, MO: Bethany Press, 1928.

Boles, H. Leo. *Biographical Sketches of Gospel Preachers.* Nashville, TN: Gospel Advocate Co., n.d.

Brooks, Iverson L. *A Defense of Southern Slavery Against the Attacks of Henry Clay and Alexander Campbell.* Hamburg, SC: Robinson and Carlisle, 1851.

Campbell, Selina Huntington. *Home Life and Reminiscences of Alexander Campbell.* St. Louis, MO: J. Burns, 1882.

Casey, Michael. *Saddlebags, City Streets and Cyberspace: A History of Preaching in the Churches of Christ.* Abilene, TX: Abilene Christian University Press, 1995.

Chalmers, Thomas. *Alexander Campbell's Tour in Scotland: How He Is Remembered by Those Who Saw Him Then.* Louisville, KY: Guide Printing and Pub., 1892.

Chestnut, Roderick. "John Thomas and the Rebaptism Controversy (1835–1838)." *Baptism and The Remission of Sins.* Ed. David W. Fletcher. Joplin, MO: College Press, 1990: 203–40.

Cochran, Louis. *The Fool of God: A Novel Based on the Life of Alexander Campbell.* New York: Duell, Sloan and Pearce, 1958.

Cochran, Louis, and Leroy Garrett. *Alexander Campbell: The Man and His Message.* Dallas, TX: Wilkinson Pub., 1965.

Eames, S. Morris. *The Philosophy of Alexander Campbell.* Bethany, VA: Bethany College, 1966.

Egbert, James. *Alexander Campbell and Christian Liberty.* St. Louis, MO: Christian Publishing Co., 1909.

Fitch, Alger Morton, Jr. *Alexander Campbell, Preacher of Reform and Reformer of Preaching.* Austin, TX: Sweet Pub., 1970. Joplin, MO: College Press, 1988.

Foster, Douglas A., Paul M. Blowers, Anthony L. Dunnavant, and D. Newell Williams, eds. The Encyclopedia of the Stone-Campbell Movement. Grand Rapids, MI: Eerdmans, 2004.

Foster, R. C. *The Campbell Debates.* Compiled by Enos Dowling. Lincoln, IL: by the author, 1982. Reprinted from the *Restoration Herald* April 1943–November 1950.

Garrett, Leroy. *Alexander Campbell and Thomas Jefferson: A Comparative Study of Two Old Virginians.* Dallas: Wilkinson Pub. Co., 1963.

Garrison, W. E. *Alexander Campbell's Theology, Its Sources and Historical Setting.* St. Louis, MO: Christian Pub. Co., 1900.

Grafton, Thomas W. *Alexander Campbell: Leader of the Great Reformation of the Nineteenth Century.* St. Louis, MO: Christian Pub. Co., 1897.

Gresham, Perry E. *Campbell and the Colleges.* Nashville, TN: Disciples of Christ Historical Society, 1973.

———, compiler. *The Sage of Bethany: A Pioneer in Broadcloth.* St. Louis, MO: Bethany Press, 1960. Joplin, MO: College Press, 1988.

Groover, R. Edwin. *The Well-Ordered Home: Alexander Campbell and the Family.* Joplin, MO: College Press, 1988.

Haley, J. J. *Debates That Made History: The Story of Alexander Campbell's Debates with Rev. John Walker, Rev. W. L. McCalla, Mr. Robert Owen, Bishop Purcell and Rev. Nathan L. Rice.* St. Louis, MO: Christian Board of Pub., 1920.

Harrell, David E., Jr. *Quest for a Christian America: The Disciples of Christ and American Society to 1866.* Nashville, TN: The Disciples of Christ Historical Society, 1966.

Hatch, Nathan. *The Democratization of American Christianity.* New Haven: Yale University Press, 1989.

Hicks, John Mark. "Alexander Campbell on Christians Among the Sects." *Baptism and The Remission of Sins.* Ed. David W. Fletcher. Joplin, MO: College Press, 1990: 171–202.

———. "The Recovery of the Ancient Gospel: Alexander Campbell and the Design of Baptism." *Baptism and the Remission of Sins.* Ed. David W. Fletcher. Joplin, MO: College Press, 1990: 111–70.

Hicks, L. Edward. "Republican Religion and Republican Institutions: Alexander Campbell and the Anti-Catholic Movement." *The Stone-Campbell Movement: An International Religious Tradition.* Eds. Michael W. Casey and Douglas A. Foster. Knoxville: University of Tennessee Press, 2002: 204–18.

Hudson, John, ed. *The Pioneers on Worship: Presenting the Views of Alexander Camp-*

bell, Dr. Robert Richardson, Moses E. Lard, and a Number of Others. Kansas City, MO: Old Paths Book Club, 1947. Reprint of "Order of Worship", 57–62 (from *The Christian* vol. 4: 136–39, May 1848) and "Order of the Church As Respects Worship", 63–69 (from *Millennial Harbinger* 1835, 507).

Hughes, Richard T. *Reviving the Ancient Faith: The Story of Churches of Christ in America.* Grand Rapids: Eerdmans, 1996.

———, ed. *The American Quest for the Primitive Church.* Urbana: University of Illinois Press, 1988.

———, ed. *The Primitive Church in the Modern World.* Urbana: University of Illinois Press, 1995.

Hughes, Richard T., and C. Leonard Allen. *Illusions of Innocence: Protestant Primitivism in America, 1630–1875.* Chicago and London: University of Chicago Press, 1988.

Humble, Bill J. *Campbell and Controversy: The Story of Alexander Campbell's Great Debates with Skepticism, Catholicism and Presbyterianism.* Rosemead, CA: Old Paths Book Club, 1959, 1961. Joplin, MO: College Press, 1986.

Imbler, John M. *Beyond Buffalo: Alexander Campbell on Education for Ministry.* Nashville, TN: Disciples of Christ Historical Society, 1992.

Jennings, Obadiah. *Debate on Campbellism: Held at Nashville, Tennessee, in Which the Principles of Alexander Campbell Are Confuted and His Conduct Examined.* Pittsburgh: D. and M. Maclean, 1832.

Jeter, Jeremiah. *Campbellism Examined.* New York: Sheldon, Blakeman, and Co., 1858.

Jorgenson, Dale A. *Theological and Aesthetic Roots in the Stone-Campbell Movement.* Kirksville, MO: Thomas Jefferson University Press, 1989.

Kellems, Jesse R. *Alexander Campbell and the Disciples.* New York: R. R. Smith, 1930.

Lard, Moses E. *A Review of J. B. Jeter's Book Entitled "Campbellism Examined".* With an introduction by A. Campbell. Philadelphia: J. B. Lippincott, 1857.

Lewis, Grant K. *The American Christian Missionary Society.* St. Louis, MO: Christian Board of Publication, 1937.

Lindley, Ray. *Apostle of Freedom.* St. Louis, MO: Bethany Press, 1957.

Love, Bill. *The Core Gospel: On Restoring the Crux of the Matter.* Abilene, TX: Abilene Christian University Press, 1992.

Lunger, Harold L. *The Political Ethics of Alexander Campbell.* St. Louis, MO: Bethany Press, 1954.

Maxey, Robert Tibbs. *Alexander Campbell and the Peculiar Institution.* El Paso, TX: Spanish American Evangelism, 1986.

McLean, Archibald. *Alexander Campbell as a Preacher.* St. Louis, MO: Christian Publications, 1908. Athens, AL: CEI Store, 1955.

———. *Thomas and Alexander Campbell.* Cincinnati: Foreign Christian Missionary Society, 1910. Originally delivered as address at Missouri State Missionary Convention in St. Louis, 1909.

McMillon, Lynn A. *Restoration Roots.* Dallas: Gospel Teachers Pub., 1983.

Moore, Allen R. *Alexander Campbell and the General Convention: A History of the Rise of Organization Among the Disciples of Christ.* St. Louis, MO: Christian Board of Publication, 1914.

Richardson, Robert. *Memoirs of Alexander Campbell, Embracing a View of the Origin,*

Progress and Principles of the Religious Reformation Which He Advocated, Vol. I, Vol. II. Philadelphia: J. Lippincott, 1868, 1869. Cincinnati: Standard, 1897.

Smith, Benjamin L. *Alexander Campbell.* St. Louis, MO: Bethany Press, 1930.

Snyder, Lee. *The Book of Acts According to Alexander Campbell: An Historical and Rhetorical Commentary.* Studies in American Religion, Vol. 75A. Edwin Mellen Press, 2002.

Starkey, Armstrong. *The Diplomatic Career of Alexander Campbell.* Urbana: n.p., 1968.

Stevenson, Dwight. *Disciple Preaching in the First Generation: An Ecological Study.* Nashville, TN: Disciples of Christ Historical Society, 1969.

Thomas, Cecil K. *Alexander Campbell and His New Version.* St. Louis, MO: Bethany Press, 1958.

Today's Pictorial Story of Alexander Campbell and the Christian Churches. Pittsburgh: The R. W. Johnston Studios, Inc., 1909.

Tristano, Richard. *The Origins of the Restoratin Movement: An Intellectual History.* Atlanta, GA: Glenmary Research Center, 1988.

Tupper, Kerr. *Seven Great Lights.* Cincinnati: Cranston and Curts, n.d. New York: Hunt and Eaton; 1892.

Walker, Granville T. *Preaching in the Thought of Alexander Campbell.* St. Louis, MO: Bethany Press, 1954.

Webb, Henry E. *In Search of Christian Unity: A History of the Restoration Movement.* Cincinnati: Standard Publishing, 1990.

West, Earl Irvin. "Early Cincinnati's 'Unprecedented Spectacle.'" *The Stone-Campbell Movement: An International Religious Tradition.* Eds. Michael W. Casey and Douglas A. Foster. Knoxville: University of Tennessee Press, 2002: 189–203.

West, Robert Frederick. *Alexander Campbell and Natural Religion.* New Haven, CT: Yale University Press, 1948.

Wrather, Eva. Alexander Campbell, Adventurer in Freedom: A Literary Biography. Ed. D. Duane Cummins. Vol. 1. Fort Worth, Texas: TCU Press and the Disciples of Christ Historical Society, 2005.

———. *Alexander Campbell and His Relevance for Today.* Nashville, TN: Disciples of Christ Historical Foundation, 1955.

———. *Creative Freedom in Action: Alexander Campbell on the Structure of the Church.* St. Louis: Bethany Press, 1968.

Periodical Literature

Athearn, W. S. "Alexander Campbell Left His Mark on Glasgow University." *Christian Standard* (August 8, 1931): 779.

Berryhill, Carisse Mickey. "Alexander Campbell's Natural Rhetoric of Evangelism." *Restoration Quarterly* (April 1, 1988): 111–24. Reprinted in *Disciples Theological Digest* (1989): 5–19.

———. "Alexander Campbell: Preacher." *Gospel Advocate* (September 1, 1988): 14ff.

Blake, T. D. "The Preaching of Alexander Campbell." *Gospel Advocate* (1976): 407.

Boteler, M. M. "Alexander Campbell: 'The Sermon on the Law.'" *Christian Standard* (September 4, 1926): 863.

Brigance, L. L. "The Campbell-Purcell Debate." *Gospel Advocate* (1936): 366, 414, 466.

———. "The Campbell-Rice Debate." *Gospel Advocate* (1936): 1086.

———. "More Debates." *Gospel Advocate* (1936): 514.

———. "Studies in the Restoration (The Sermon on the Law)." *Gospel Advocate* (1940): 417, 579, 632, 706.

Casey, Michael. "From British Ciceronianism to American Baconianism: Alexander Campbell as a Case Study of a Shift in Rhetorical Theory." *Southern Communication Journal* 66 (Winter 2001): 151–66.

———. "The Origin of the Hermeneutics of the Churches of Christ: Part One—The Reformed Tradition." *Restoration Quarterly* 31 (1989): 75ff.

———. "The Origin of the Hermeneutics of the Churches of Christ: Part Two—The Philosophical Background." *Restoration Quarterly* 31 (1989): 193ff.

Cochran, Louis. "Alexander and Thomas Campbell as Preachers." *Christian Standard* (August 8, 1959): 441.

———. "Alexander Campbell as a Preacher." *Christian Standard* (August 15, 1959): 455.

Ellis, Carroll. "The Backgrounds of the Campbell-Purcell Religious Debate of 1837." *Southern Speech Journal* (November 1945): 32–41.

———. "The Preaching of Alexander Campbell." *Southern Speech Journal* (November 1948): 99–107.

———. "Master Communicator." *Gospel Advocate* (September 1, 1988): 17ff.

Ferguson, Everett. "Alexander Campbell's *Sermon on the Law*." *Restoration Quarterly* (April 1, 1987): 65ff.

Fitch, Alger. "Recent Developments in the Study of Alexander Campbell." *The Christian Standard* (May 13, 1965): n.p.

Foster, Douglas. "Hope for Christian Unity." *Gospel Advocate* (September 1, 1988): 26ff.

Heine, Ronald. "Alexander Campbell and the Old Testament." *Stone-Campbell Journal* (Fall 2002): 163–82.

Hensley, Carl Wayne. "Rhetorical Vision and the Persuasion of a Historical Movement: The Disciples of Christ in Nineteenth Century American Culture." *Quarterly Journal of Speech* (October 1975): 250–64.

Hobbs, Jeffery Dale. "Alexander Campbell: A Case Study in Metaphors of the Restoration." *Restoration Quarterly* (October 1, 1991): 225ff.

Holloway, Gary. "Alexander Campbell as a Publisher." *Restoration Quarterly* 37 (1995): 28–35.

Holm, James Noble. "Alexander Campbell: A Study in the Value of Effective Rhetorical Training." *The Forensic* (1976): 10–13, 31.

Lester, Hiram. "Campbell Papers Story." *Christian Standard* (May 11, 1986): 429ff.

———. "Old Books Loosely Wrapped in Plastic." *Mission* (March 1, 1986): 23ff.

Little, David L. "Inductive Hermeneutics and the Early Restoration Movement." *Stone-Campbell Journal* (Spring 2000): 5–18.

McCann, Forrest. "Popular Lectures of Alexander Campbell." *Restoration Quarterly* (April 1, 1988): 135ff.

McMillon, Lynn A. "Alexander Campbell's Early Exposure to Scottish Restorationism, 1808–1809." *Restoration Quarterly* 30 (1988): 105–10.

Morrison, John L. "The Centrality of the Bible in Alexander Campbell's Thought and Life." *West Virginia History* (April 1974): 185–204.

———. "A Rational Voice Crying in an Emotional Wilderness." *West Virginia History* (January 1973): 125–40+. *The Stone Campbell Movement: An International Religious Tradition.* Eds. Michael W. Casey and Douglas A. Foster. Knoxville: University of Tennessee Press, 2002: 163–76.

Neth, J. W. "Sermon on the Law." *Christian Standard* (September 3, 1966): 591.

Olbricht, Thomas H. "Alexander Campbell in Context of American Biblical Studies." *Restoration Quarterly* (January, 1 1991): 13ff.

———. "Rationalism of the Restoration." *Restoration Quarterly* 11 (1968): 77–88.

Pack, Frank. "Alexander Campbell: The Scholar." *Gospel Advocate* (September 1, 1988): 13.

Paris, Andrew. "The Immediate Influences and Results of the Campbell Debates upon the Restoration Movement of the Nineteenth Century." *Seminary Review* 28 (March 1982): 15–39.

Person, Raymond F. "The Interrelationship Between the Oral and the Written in the Work of Alexander Campbell." *Oral Tradition* Vol. 8, No. 1 (1993): 143–58.

Peters, H. H. "Alexander Campbell as a Preacher." *Christian Standard* (June 18, 1932): 587.

Platt, R. M. "More on the Lunenburg Letter." *Christian Standard* (December 7, 1957): 734.

Powell, J. M. "Campbell's Sermon Extracts." *Gospel Advocate*, (1950): 182.

Roberts, R. L. "Dissertations on Alexander Campbell." *Restoration Quarterly* 39 (1988): 169ff.

Rushford, Jerry. "Stroke of His Pen." *Gospel Advocate* (September 1, 1988): 19ff.

Sensing, Timothy R. "Baconian Method and Preaching in the Stone-Campbell Movement." *Stone-Campbell Journal* (Fall 2001): 163–86.

Snyder, Lee. "Alexander Campbell and the Book of Acts." *Stone-Campbell Journal* (Spring 1999): 23–38.

Terry, Fred. "Alexander Campbell: A Case Study in Metaphors of the Restoration." *Restoration Quarterly* (October 1, 1991): 225ff.

Thornton, E. W. "The Campbell-Owen Debate." *Gospel Advocate* (1929): 410.

Van Buren, James. "Alexander Campbell's *Popular Lectures and Addresses.*" *Christian Standard* (July 16, 1978): 652ff.

Van Rheenen, Dwayne. "Communication in the Restoration Tradition: Current Research and a Selected Bibliography." *Mission* (1987): 17–19.

Weedman, Mark. "History as Authority in Alexander Campbell's 1837 Debate with Bishop Purcell." *Fides et Historia* 28 (Summer 1996): 17–34.

West, E. "Campbell, The Debater." *Gospel Advocate* (1948): 1135.

———. "The Campbell-Walker Debate." *Gospel Advocate* (1951): 85.

Willingham, D. "Campbell-McCalla Debate." *Gospel Advocate* (1954): 214ff.

Wrather, Eva Jean. "A Nineteenth-Century Disciples-Catholic Dialogue: The Campbell-Purcell Debate of 1837." *Mid-Stream* 25 (Oct. 1986): 368–74.

Theses and Dissertations

Abernathy, Elton M. "An Evaluation of the Debating Techniques Employed by Alexander Campbell in the Campbell-Rice Religious Debate." Thesis. State University of Iowa, 1937.

Berryhill, Carisse M. "Sense, Expression and Purpose: Alexander Campbell's Natural Philosophy of Rhetoric." Diss. Florida State University, 1982.

Bever, Ron. "An Analysis of Speaking in the American Restoration Movement, 1820–1849." Diss. Northwestern University, 1968.

Bowen, Billy Doyce. "Knowledge, The Existence of God, and Faith: John Locke's Influence on Alexander Campbell's Theology." Diss. Michigan State, 1978.

Bryant, Russell. "An Analysis of Alexander Campbell's Ethos in the Debate with Robert Owen, April 13, 1829." Thesis. California State College in Long Beach, 1968.

Casey, Michael. "The Development of Necessary Inference in the Hermeneutics of the Disciples of Christ/Churches of Christ." Diss. University of Pittsburgh, 1986.

Cheeves, Lyndell. "The Rhetoric of Alexander Campbell." Thesis. La Verne College, 1967.

Duncan, Charles Finley. "Alexander Campbell as a Controversialist As Revealed in the Debate with Robert Owen." Thesis. University of Illinois, Urbana, 1952.

Ellerbrook, James Harry. "The Influence of Thomas Reid on the Thought-Life of Alexander Campbell." Thesis. Christian Theological Seminary, 1947.

Ellis, Carroll. "The Alexander Campbell and John B. Purcell Religious Debate." Thesis. Louisiana State University, 1945.

———. "The Controversial Speaking of Alexander Campbell." Diss. Louisiana State University, 1949.

Fife, Robert O. "Alexander Campbell and the Christian Church in the Slavery Controversy." Diss. Indiana University, 1960.

Gonce, Albert Anderson, Jr. "A Rhetorical Analysis and Criticism of Selected Occasional Addresses of Alexander Campbell, 1838–1858." Thesis. University of Alabama, 1950.

Hart, William Henry. "Alexander Campbell as a Speaker in Debates on Religious Subjects." Thesis. Phillips University, 1930.

Holm, James Noble. "Alexander Campbell's Debate with Robert Owen, April 1829: The Effect of a Rhetorical Event on the Speaker." Diss. University of Michigan, 1976.

Huey, Keith Brian. "Alexander Campbell's Church-State Separatism As a Defining and Limiting Factor In His Anti-Catholic Activity." Diss. Marquette University, 2000.

McMillon, Lynn A. "Quest for the Apostolic Church: A Study of Scottish Origins of American Restorationism." Diss. Baylor University, 1972.

Mercer, Bert Louis. "A Rhetorical Study of Alexander Campbell's Sermon on the Law." Thesis. Abilene Christian University, 1960.

Money, Thomas Henry. "Homiletical Theory and Practice of Alexander Campbell." Thesis. College of the Bible, 1958.

North, Ira Lutts. "The Rhetorical Method of Alexander Campbell." MA thesis. University of Illinois, 1945.

Pletcher, Thomas. "Alexander Campbell's Controversy with the Baptists." Diss. University of Pittsburgh, 1955.

Reeves, George C. "The Campbell-Owen Debate." Thesis. Cincinnati Bible Seminary, 1930.

Shields, James Leroy, Jr. "Alexander Campbell: A Synthesis of Faith and Reason (1823–1860)." Diss. Syracuse University, 1974.

Swisher, Grace Lillian. "Speech Characteristics of Alexander Campbell as Shown in the Remarks of His Contemporaries and His Successors." Thesis. Indiana State Teachers College, 1952.

Walker, David Ellis, Jr. "The Rhetoric of the Restoration Movement: The Period of Inception, 1800–1832." Diss. University of Florida, 1969.

Yeakley, Flavil. "Rhetorical Strategies Analyzed by Social Movement Theory as Applied to Conflict with the Restoration Movement." Thesis. University of Houston, 1972.

Index

Aberdeen, 29, 30, 172n29

Aberdeen Philosophical Society, 172n29

Albaugh, Gaylord: on religious journals, 12

Allen, C. Leonard, 49; on Christian primitivism, 6, 7–8, 163n22, 164n26, 164n29; on nineteenth century millennialism, 10; on Alexander Campbell's restoration plea, 25, 168–69n98, 169n99; on factions within the Stone-Campbell movement, 168–69n98; on shifts in Alexander Campbell's thought, 190n17

American Christian Bible Society, xiii, 129–30, 131

American Christian Missionary Society, xiii, xvii, 130, 131–33, 136, 146, 147, 149, 151, 155; attacks on, 131, 132; controversy surrounding, 131–33; challenges faced, 132; a and slavery controversy, 135; Louisville plan, 149

American Christian Review (Benjamin Franklin, ed.), 128

American and Foreign Bible Society, 129

American Revolution: impact upon the church, 3–4, 6, 8–9

Ames, William: and covenant theology, 72

Analogy, 31, 60, 61, 72, 95, 121

Anticlericalism, 4–5, 12, 73, 78, 84–86, 87, 94, 186n48

Apology for Renouncing the Jurisdiction of the Synod of Kentucky (Marshall, Stone and Thompson), 17

Apostolic Advocate (The) (John Thomas, ed.), 115, 116

Aristotle: on *ethos*, xiv; in rhetorical criticism, xv; and George Jardine, 34, 174–75n55; on

the syllogism, 34, 36, 174–75n55, 185n26; and Alexander Campbell, 36; definition of rhetoric, 50; influence on medieval sermon form, 61–62; on epideictic rhetoric, 141, 195n34; on the enthymeme, 185n26; and *kairos*, 198n6. See also *Politics; Rhetoric*

Asbury, Francis: and itinerant preaching, 14; on camp meetings, 15

Associationism: in Locke and Hartley, 28, 170n19; in George Campbell, 32, 43, 57–58, 98, 173n46, 187–88n97; in Alexander Campbell, 36, 43–44, 57–58, 98; and Scottish prose style, 187–88n97

Aurora (William Duane), 5

Austin, Benjamin: anticlericalism of, 5

Bacon College, xii, 129, 193n5

Bacon, Francis: and induction, xv, 36, 40, 41, 61; on psychology, 28, 170n14; on rhetoric, 28, 29, 37; and George Campbell, 30; and Scottish rhetorics, 30, 37, 171n25; and George Jardine, 33, 34; and Alexander Campbell, 36, 37, 38, 40–41, 49, 55–56, 61, 97, 177n86; Bacon College named for, 129

Baptism: in *Lunenburg letter*, xvi–xvii, 110, 114, 119, 128; the Campbells' immersionist position on, 19, 51–52, 108, 119, 121–24, 125, 138–39; subject of Campbell's debates, 76, 77, 108, 125, 127; 138–39, 191n33; John Thomas's position on, 115–16, 191n33; in *Missionary Cause*, 138

Baptists, 77, 89, 91, 138, 140, 141, 142, 145, 163n9; ministers, 4, 14, 29, 52, 53–55, 74, 78, 88, 92; populist appeal of, 11; and Cane Ridge Re-